₤8.82
N

Library of
Davidson College

MARGINALITY AND IDENTITY

ANGLO-INDIANS AS A RACIALLY-MIXED MINORITY IN INDIA

*MONOGRAPHS AND THEORETICAL STUDIES
IN SOCIOLOGY AND ANTHROPOLOGY
IN HONOUR OF NELS ANDERSON*

General Editor: K. Ishwaran

Publication 3

MARGINALITY AND IDENTITY

ANGLO-INDIANS AS A RACIALLY-MIXED MINORITY IN INDIA

BY

NOEL P. GIST

AND

ROY DEAN WRIGHT

LEIDEN
E. J. BRILL
1973

ISBN 90 04 03638 5

Copyright 1973 by E. J. Brill, Leiden, Netherlands

All rights reserved. No part of this book may be reproduced or translated in any form, by print, photoprint, microfilm, microfiche or any other means without written permission from the publisher

PRINTED IN THE NETHERLANDS

CONTENTS

I.	Introduction	1
II.	The Anglo-Indian Community in Historical Perspective	7
III.	Marginality and Identity	21
IV.	Attitudes and Images	37
V.	The Anglo-Indian World of Work	57
VI.	Social Relations and Social Structure	77
VII.	Organized Life of Anglo-Indians	95
VIII.	Education	113
IX.	Styles of Life	134
X.	Summary and Conclusion	150
Index		159

CHAPTER ONE

INTRODUCTION

DURING the past few decades cross-cultural research has become increasingly important to students of sociology and anthropology. Within the various sub-disciplines of these fields many scholars are turning to area studies in an attempt to accumulate information concerning man in world perspective.

Throughout the recorded pages of man's history one finds numerous examples of minority peoples existing as discrete entities outside of larger or more dominant groups. These groups are often visible, have categorical terms or labels applied to them, and can usually be identified by members of both the majority and minority peoples. That the members are often judged categorically, and not primarily as individuals, is indicative of their identity and position in larger society. Although the terms used to identify such groups may not have the same meaning for all persons, a generalized identification is possible. For example, the word "Negro" may not mean the same thing to all people residing within the United States, but it is nevertheless a useful identifying term.

Wherever European powers maintained colonial holdings in Asia there developed an "Eurasian" minority representing biological blending through conventional and unconventional sexual contacts. Historically, those countries maintaining colonial dominance sent representatives to the dominated areas, insuring the furtherance of their own imperial interests. In most cases this called for military forces to enter the area for the maintenance of control, thus helping insure continued dominance by the colonial power. These colonial representatives, whether for economic or military purposes, were usually males. Few women were initially allowed to venture into the frontier regions. Sexual contacts which occurred were, consequently, between European men and indigenous women. Therefore, as might be anticipated, these relationships resulted either in marriages between representatives of the two groups or in illicit sexual contacts.

Regardless of the circumstances of origin, the children of such unions had a mixed "racial" heritage. Generally their physical characteristics, which differed from those of either progenitor group, gave them a distinct appearance and had results which basically positioned these children socially between two different cultural systems. Because of a variety of social forces most of them were socialized into European culture which their fathers represented.

The Anglo-Indian Community: General Perspective[1]

In numerous societies of today's world, one can find various minority groups which exist as discrete entities in relation to one or more dominant groups. The

---

[1] The term "community" as used in this study refers to a group which is distinguished from other

INTRODUCTION

Burghers of Ceylon, the Eurasians of Singapore, the Anglo-Burmese population of Burma, the Colored minority of South Africa, the Mestizos of Latin America, and the Anglo-Indian Community of India are examples of such peoples as they exist today throughout the world. These and other groups, most of which have minority status within their respective areas, share one other important feature. Each originated as a result of colonial expansion and the subsequent biological mixture of indigenous and non-indigenous populations.

The Anglo-Indian Minority

This volume is concerned with a minority people, the Anglo-Indians of India, which owes its origin to the expansion of Europe into the sub-continent of South Asia. Various terms have been used in the past to designate this group, and those will be indicated in the chapter on the Anglo-Indian Community in historical perspective. But for clarity in this presentation the term "Anglo-Indian" will be used throughout the study.

At least four European countries were actively involved in the colonial domination of what is now India: Portugal, France, Netherlands, and Britain. The Portuguese were the first to penetrate the sub-continent and establish a colonial beach-head in the southwestern region. The influence of the Netherlands was negligible, and in the case of France it was likewise limited to a small territory on the eastern coast of the country. It was Britain that eventually established political and economic dominance of the sub-continent and left a lasting imprint on the culture of that region. Although the racial hybrids resulting from the marital and extra-marital associations generally were socialized into European culture, which could be Portuguese, French, Dutch, or British, the patrilineal progenitors were mainly British.

It is not easy to formulate a functional definition of the Anglo-Indian that will apply in all situations. The official definition accepted by the Government of India and stipulated in the new Constitution of Independent India is as follows:

> ...an Anglo-Indian means a person whose father or any of whose other male progenitors in the male line is or was of European descent but who is domiciled within the territory of India and is or was born within such territory of parents habitually resident therein and not established there for temporary purposes only...[2]

Such a definition applies, therefore, not only to persons whose patrilineal heritage is British but to other European progenitors as well. It also applies to the offspring of European parents who have been regularly and permanently domiciled in India—known in the past as Domiciled Europeans. The focus of this study, however, is on Anglo-Indians of dual heritage.

---

people by racial, religious, caste, or cultural criteria and whose members share a common identity and group consciousness that set them apart from people having different racial, religious, or cultural characteristics. As here employed, it is *not* a human settlement such as a town or city. When used in connection with the Anglo-Indian minority the term is capitalized.

[2] *The Constitution of India* (New Delhi: Government of India Press, 1963), paragraph 366.

INTRODUCTION

No precise enumeration of Anglo-Indians in India has ever been made. The last census that enumerated them as a distinct category was in 1931, but owing to conflicting definitions of the community and faulty data-gathering methods the official reports were not reliable. The published figures for the Community at that time were 138,895 for India and 19,200 for Burma (at that time a part of the Crown Colony). Contemporary demographic data for the Community are only estimates, varying from 100,000 to 300,000.

Whatever may have been the patrilineal background of contemporary Anglo-Indians, whether British, Portuguese, French, or Dutch, they now have certain attributes in common: the Christian religion, a Western style of life, and English as their "mother tongue." These cultural attributes have tended to set them apart from the vast majority of the Indian people, although some of the characteristics such as the Christian faith and the English language are shared in common with a considerable number of other Indians, although the Anglo-Indians are the only minority with English as its "mother tongue." Nevertheless, the cultural gap between the Anglo-Indians and other Indian communities — Hindu, Muslim, Sikh, tribal, Parsee — is wide. The cultural gap, however wide or narrow in specific situations, has its counterpart in the social gap characterizing interpersonal and intergroup relations.

Marginality as the Focus of this Study

It is this "gap" that will be the major thesis of the present study. In order to place it within the context of a theoretical frame of reference the concepts of marginality, marginal man, and marginal situations will be the central focus of the volume and will, hopefully, provide a meaningful perspective for an understanding of Anglo-Indian people as a human microcosm within a vast Indian macrocosm.

The emergence and development of the Community through the three hundred years of its existence will be considered in the chapter on the minority in historical perspective. Obviously, the history of the Community is interwoven with the history of India and England and can only be treated in abbreviation because of space limitations. In other chapters dealing with specific aspects of the Community limited relevant historical information will be introduced.

It must be emphasized, however, that this is not primarily a history of the Anglo-Indian Community in India. Rather, it is a descriptive analysis of the minority written from the perspective of marginality. In the third chapter the concept of marginality is discussed critically, with some comparative data added to clarify the relationship of Anglo-Indian and other Indians in the sub-continent. It was decided to place the chapter on marginality early in the volume so as to provide some theoretical preparation for the empirical materials in later chapters.

When the Anglo-Indian Community in India is viewed as a marginal minority the concept is in no sense implying an invidious distinction between them and other Indian nationals. The authors have attempted to interpret objectively the Community and its relations with other communities, to present factual information free from conscious bias. In the complex and tangled web of human

INTRODUCTION

relations this is not always easy. Empirical factual information is in itself selective, obtainable information may be only part of the multi-faceted situation, and one person's "facts" may be another person's "poison," to paraphrase an old adage. To prepare a factually complete history and analysis of the Community in its national setting would be a life-time undertaking, and even then it would undoubtedly have innumerable omissions.

This volume is not intended to be a special pleading, either for or against the Anglo-Indian Community, or any other community in India for that matter. We strive to let the facts speak for themselves. Some of the factual materials presented in the study are concerned with attitudes, of Anglo-Indians and other Indians. Whether or not these attitudes are justified is not of concern in this study; they are merely an aspect of the psycho-social environment of the peoples involved. But they are certainly an important part of the environment since they may determine the character of social behavior in interpersonal and intergroup relations.

The present study was initiated in 1963-1964 when the authors had assignments on the Fulbright program in India. During the academic year the senior author, Mr. Gist, as a visiting Professor at Calcutta University, spent a considerable portion of his professional activities on the Anglo-Indian research project, mostly in Calcutta but also in Patna, Kharagpur, Bombay, and Ootacamund. The junior author, Mr. Wright, was a graduate fellow with the U.S. Educational Foundation in India the same year. From his position in Delhi he conducted extensive interviews in the Indian capital, with some additional interview contacts in Madras, Agra, Hyderabad-Secunderabad, and Ootacamund. A fairly high proportion of the interviews by Mr. Gist were with middle-aged adults, except that a considerable body of data were obtained from university and secondary school students. About one-third of the interviews conducted by Mr. Wright were with young persons between 16 and 21, many of them students at Delhi University.

The National Library in Calcutta was explored by Mr. Gist for materials relating to the Anglo-Indian Community. In addition, the British Museum Library and the India Office Library, both in London, yielded considerable information concerning the historical development of the Community. In Delhi, Mr. Wright obtained relevant data from the National Archives of India, the University of Delhi Library, and the main offices of the All-India Anglo-Indian Association.

The University Research Council at the University of Missouri awarded a travel grant to Mr. Gist to enable him to spend the summer of 1967 in South India working on the project. The Institute of Advanced Projects at the East-West center, Honolulu, also provided an award making it possible for him to spend the first semester of 1968-69 preparing parts of the manuscript for the present volume.

Interviews were conducted with many persons, Anglo-Indians and other Indian nationals, including students, professionals, business men, manual workers, even unemployed persons. The place setting of the interviews were varied — homes of the persons interviewed and our own respective residences, offices, university campuses, and situations which brought the investigators in informal and fortuitous contacts with persons who could or would provide information or express attitudes relevant to the study. Most of the interviews were semi-structured, and in a few situations, mainly with a panel of respondents, the interviews were taped. Questionnaires were employed for certain groups, university students, students enrolled in Anglo-Indian schools and representing various communities, and employed Anglo-Indian workers in various occupations. Public and private collections of literature yielded abundant information about the historical development of the Community and its relations with other peoples, including the British in India.

The questionnaire survey did not involve a statistical sampling procedure. Such a method would have been impossible on a national or regional scale, or even on a local level in a large city, within the limits of time and money imposed by the conditions of the research. Many of the generalizations therefore must of necessity be tentative. Local situations are varied as to region and even cities; what may be true of Calcutta is not always true of Coimbatore or Lucknow. Furthermore, these situations are always undergoing change, and what may have been a reasonably valid generalization for a locality in 1940 may be invalid two or three decades later.

In the absence of a statistical sample in a city where the research was undertaken certain distortions in the distribution of the informants are likely to occur. There was probably an over-representation of middle-class persons interviewed, or from whom survey data were collected, and an under-representation of manual workers and unemployed persons. Whether a statistical sample would have yielded important different results is problematical. Our feeling is that such a sampling procedure would not have greatly altered the overall picture of the Community as it is presented in this monograph. Nevertheless, some of the generalizations cautiously arrived at do not necessarily apply to India as a whole but only to those cities in which the data were gathered, and even then for particular segments of the population.

Respondents varied considerably as to the amount of information they were able or willing to provide. Since some of them were deeply involved emotionally there could have been problems. Their information and assessments of the situation had to be critically evaluated, but even highly emotional expressions were often revealing of the attitudes they held. As in most researches of this type there were "key" respondents who were willing to share their vast store of information about the Community, historically and contemporaneously.

Both authors are indebted to many persons, Anglo-Indians and members of other Indian communities, who gave generously of their time and knowledge about the Community. To these persons the authors are deeply appreciative of their assistance and cooperation. Some of these contacts developed into personal friendships which are and will continue to be cherished by the authors.

One cannot, within the space limits of this volume, mention all who did assist us in one way or another, but among them were several whose support and cooperation should be given special recognition: The Honorable Frank Anthony, President-in-Chief of the All-India Anglo-Indian Association and member of

INTRODUCTION

Parliament; Mr. A. E. T. Barrow, director of the educational program for the Anglo-Indian community and member of Parliament; Austin D'Souza, Inspector of Anglo-Indian Schools in West Bengal; J. E. Begg, welfare worker in Calcutta; Ralph Stracey, former Indian Administrative Service official in Calcutta and presently head of a school in Bangalore; Dudley Francis, formerly a business associate in Calcutta, now living in Canada; Dr. J. Das Gupta, Department of Political Science, University of California, Berkeley; the late Norman Ferguson, member of Maharashtra Legislative Assembly, Bombay; R. J. N. Maher, associate editor, Calcutta *Statesman*; Osie P. Raymond, Kharagpur, an instructor in high school and an active worker in Anglo-Indian affairs; Joi Michael and Ena Nadir, assistants to the U. S. Educational Foundation in India, New Delhi; and the late Dr. Olive I. Reddick, former director of the U. S. Educational Foundation in India, New Delhi. The authors alone are responsible, however, for factual or interpretive statements in the book.

CHAPTER TWO

THE ANGLO-INDIAN COMMUNITY IN HISTORICAL PERSPECTIVE

ONE cannot understand and appreciate the position of any minority people without some comprehension of the historical processes that brought the body into existence and determined its status and relationships with reference to other groups. The historical record of the Anglo-Indian Community of India affords an opportunity to observe the developmental processes of a minority people with a dual racial heritage. Even though other labels have been in vogue during earlier years, the term Anglo-Indian will be used throughout this volume.

The terms designating the Community have changed at various times throughout the historical career of the group.[3] "Indo-Briton" was perhaps the first generally accepted designation of the Community. Somewhat later the term "Eurasian" was widely used. Although "East Indian" had a certain vogue at the beginning of the nineteenth century, "Eurasian" was generally accepted throughout most the century even though it acquired a derogatory meaning. It was not until after the turn of the twentieth century (1911) that the term Anglo-Indian was officially recognized and accepted by members of this Community. Even this term created some confusion, however, because it had been used earlier to refer to Britishers residing permanently in India, rather synonymous with the term Domiciled European.

In order to facilitate an analysis of the Community, the historical background of the Anglo-Indian people will be divided into four basic "periods". For the most part the dates delineating these periods are somewhat arbitrary, since the transition from one period to the next was usually gradual. Following a brief statement concerning each of the four periods a more detailed history will be presented.

The Four Periods

The first period dates from the inception of the minority (about 1500) through 1785. During this time-span the Community was favorably viewed by the controlling colonial powers, and interracial unions were often officially encouraged and sanctioned. Generally speaking, these early years constituted times of prosperity for the membership of this emerging Community because of a generous allocation of positions in both the military and civil government.

The second period begins in 1785 and continues until the Sepoy Mutiny of 1857. During this span of time the British imposed restrictions on the members,

---

[3] See: Frank Anthony, *Britain's Betrayal in India* (Bombay: Allied Publishers, 1969), pp. 1-2.

limiting their behavior in various spheres of life. The Anglo-Indian, no longer being viewed favorably by the British of India, was excluded from membership in what he considered to be his "reference" group, the overseas colonial establishment. One author has amassed evidence which indicates that during this period a form of "community consciousness" began to develop.[4] Anglo-Indians were forced to think of themselves as an ethnic community in which the connecting bond was a combination of mixed European-Indian racial heritage and a way of life derived from European culture. The final years of this period were marked by the Sepoy Mutiny (an attempted indigenous revolution) during which the Community gave military support to the East India Company of Britain. Through efforts in the military, communication, and transportation system, members of the Anglo-Indian Community were presumably instrumental in bringing about an ultimate British victory. Even before the Mutiny a mutual interdependency had developed between Anglo-Indians and British. Anglo-Indians had been especially important in the early construction and operation of the railway, telegraph, and postal system. Increasingly the British came to rely upon this minority to fill strategic occupations, and the Anglo-Indians in turn came to rely upon the British to provide employment.

The third period ranges from the Sepoy Mutiny (1857) through the development of a strong Indian independence movement, i.e., when it became obvious, as early as the 1920's, that independence would soon come to India. Following the Mutiny the British turned more and more toward the Anglo-Indian Community to fill strategic, but usually intermediary, positions in particular occupations, especially in the police and military forces. This era can generally be spoken of as representing economic prosperity for the Community.

The contemporary period begins with the Indian Independence movement in the 1920's. During the first years of this period numerous commissions were instituted by the British to investigate and make recommendations for a smooth transferral of power to an independent Indian government. During the investigations carried on by each of these commissions the Anglo-Indian Community made pleas for constitutional guarantees and protections. Competition, especially with other Indians in the job market, became increasingly important. In the pre-Independence years Anglo-Indians were still guaranteed certain jobs, but their allotted proportion of these positions steadily diminished. Except for the World War II years, when the employment situation was relatively favorable, members of the minority experienced continuous economic problems. Following Independence, in 1947, the Community was compelled to turn more and more to open competition in all spheres of life. However, constitutional provisions, enacted by the new government, provided certain occupational and political guarantees. These protective policies will be considered later in this chapter.

The Anglo-Indian Community has existed, in one form or another, for almost

---

[4] Dorris L. Goodrich, "The Making of an Ethnic Group: The Eurasian Community in India." Unpublished PhD dissertation, University of California, Berkeley, 1952.

500 years. Within the context of the above outline, the historical evolution of the Community will now be explored in greater detail.

Colonial Conquest and Reaction: 1498-1785

The colonial conquest of India can be said to have originated in 1498, when Vasco Da Gama established a Portuguese colony on the Malabar Coast, in the southwestern portion of the sub-continent. By 1510, a Portuguese governor, Alfonso d'Albuquerque, was assigned to the area. Among his many acts this governor established a policy of formally encouraging Portuguese men to marry Indian women.[5] Following an evangelical tradition the indigenous woman first had to receive the rite of baptism before the colonial authorities would approve of the marriage. Thus, the Portuguese, while providing both a furthering of the faith and a sanctioning of sexual contacts, created an atmosphere in which there would be an acceptance of the "racially-mixed" child, at least those legitimately born.

Once marriage to a European occurred, or even an illegitimate birth, the Indian woman was characteristically ostracized from her caste or community, encountering negative sanctions including rejection by her family. As a result she and her children could turn only to the Portuguese for aid or protection. When the Portuguese, either through force or design, abandoned an area, those Eurasians who did not also migrate had either to enter other non-caste groups or, whenever possible, assimilate back into the indigenous culture.

The Dutch, arriving in 1595, also attempted to make a penetration into India. Although the Dutch established a colony in the Pulicat region, north of what is today Madras City, their influence was limited and temporary. Within a few years of their arrival the United East India Company of the Netherlands was established. Most of the colonial activities of this group were, however, centered in Southeastern Asia and Ceylon. In Ceylon, another racially-mixed community, the Burghers, came into existence as a direct result of Dutch influence. But the Dutch were soon to abandon India, thus allowing the British East India Company, chartered in 1600, to establish a firm footing. Most of the children of Dutch-Indian unions seem to have rapidly disappeared, probably reassimilating with the Indian population.[6] While many contemporary Anglo-Indians have Portuguese names, and claim Portuguese ancestry, only a few by name or culture appear to be descendants of the Dutch.

The French East India Company was established in India during the 1660's, creating a rivalry with the British. Britain and France at this time could do little more than establish port cities and attempt to make economic agreements with local political leaders. The rivalry between these two colonial powers continued for some eighty years, until the French allied themselves with local rulers and actively took part in military and political conflicts. Generally victorious, the French received special favors for their services.[7] However, the rising French monopoly

---

[5] Vincent A. Smith, *The Oxford History of India* (Oxford: Clarendon Press, 1923), p. 335.
[6] F. Yeats-Brown, *Pageant of India* (Philadelphia: Macrea-Smith-Company, 1942), pp. 140-148.
[7] See W. H. Moreland and Atul Chandra Chatterjee, *A Short History of India* (New York:

was crushed when Robert Clive, historically one of the British leaders in India, formed an alliance with dissident elements against both French and French-supported rulers. Eventually the British were victorious and the French departed India, leaving only a few small territorial possessions behind.[8] Clive, however, continued the conquest for England, and the influence of the East India Company became dominant.[9]

During this period many children of European-Indian ancestry were born. With the passing of years and the general exodus of the French in about 1757 (actually the French held small possessions in India until the 1960's),[10] children of the mixed unions either united with other similar minorities assuming their identification, or assimilated into the indigenous culture.[11] Today only a few Anglo-Indians can trace their heritage back to the days of French colonialism.

During the earlier years of the operation of the British East India Company, English women were not, except in rare instances, allowed to travel to India. If a Britisher desired female companionship he could turn only to the indigenous population or already-present Anglo-Indian women.[12] The children born to these unions were generally accorded the status of their fathers, and, seemingly, there were few attempts on the part of the East India Company to officially discourage these unions. As a matter of fact, during this period the Company decided to encourage such unions by granting five rupees per month for each child born to British soldiers. The prevailing attitude concerning intermarriage during this period is summarized by an Anglo-Indian historian, Herbert A. Stark:

> The authorities of the East India Company were not slow to recognize and appreciate the advantages to the Company from the alliances formed by their servants with the Indian women. The children grew up in attachment to, and in dependence upon, the nation of their fathers. Their mothers having been cast out by their Indian relatives, the children formed the beginnings of a new race standing in detachment from the people of the soil, and separated from them by speech, religion, dress, customs and habits — by those fundamentals which go to constitute nationality. Their interests were identified with the prospects of the East India Company, and their prosperity depended upon the permanency of its footing in the country. They were reared in an atmosphere of trade; and their knowledge of the prevailing vernaculars, and local conditions, of Indian customs and modes of thinking, of natural products and manufacturers, of market place and facilities of transport, rendered them an invaluable

Longmans, Green and Company, 1945), pp. 269-272. Also see Jawaharlal Nehru, *The Discovery of India* (Garden City, New York: Doubleday and Company, Inc., 1960), pp. 179-184.

[8] S. P. Sen, *The French in India* (Calcutta: University of Calcutta, 1947), pp. 287-320.

[9] J. C. Powell-Price, *A History of India* (New York: Thomas Nelson and Sons, Ltd., 1955), pp. 425-441.

[10] R. C. Majumdar, H. C. Raychaudhuri, and Kalikinkar Datta, *An Advanced History of India* (London: MacMillan and Company, Ltd., 1948), pp. 542-669.

[11] When India gained independence in 1947, France still retained five possessions, the most important being Pondicherry (near Madras) and Chandernagore (near Calcutta). These possessions, totaling 196 square miles, were assumed in 1954 by India, although French ratification was not formalized until 1962. See: W. Norman Brown, *The United States and India and Pakistan* (Cambridge, Massachusetts: Harvard University Press, 1963), p. 327.

[12] Herbert A. Stark, *Hostages to India* (Calcutta: The Calcutta Fine Arts Cottage, 1926), pp. 30-31.

asset to those whose chief concern was with the wealth to be derived from a lucrative trade.[13]

Within England there eventually developed groups which, however, were opposed to the formal sanctioning of marriage between British men and Indian women, including those of Portuguese descent. Initially these pleas were ignored by the Company, with official policies encouraging both marriage and reproduction being continued. Thus it could be said that Company policies increased the speed with which the emerging Anglo-Indian Community developed.

The East India Company, in 1673, established a school in Madras for the education of children having British or Portuguese patrilineal heritage.[14] Here the child could be formally taught, in English, the social and cultural traditions of his father. Through this action the Company could both insure the continuation of European traditions on foreign soil, and provide trained recruits for eventual Company service.

Anglo-Indians of this early age were in an advantaged position. With the rapid expansion of British interests in India, they rapidly filled many occupational positions in both military and commercial organizations. Stark indicates that by the early 1700's there were more Anglo-Indians in India than there were overseas British.[15] Initially the British did not seem to perceive a threat from this balance, but indigenous revolts in other parts of the world eventually created a change in their attitudes and policies.

From about 1776 onward, however, both the Company and its European backers were having second thoughts concerning the increasing size and influence of the Anglo-Indian minority. An indigenous revolution had taken place in Haiti, and several mutinies within India occurred about this time.[16] Apprehension was widespread that Indian soldiers, backed by British-trained Anglo-Indians, could damage, if not destroy, the British East India Company. These fears, coupled with internal Company conflicts, led ultimately to a series of regulations restricting the activities of the Community.

The Repressive Years: 1785-1857

Prior to the severe restrictions imposed on the Anglo-Indian Community, little prejudice was directed toward its members. Some segments of the Community, especially those having Portuguese ancestry, found themselves residing in enclaves fostering a kind of symbiotic relationship to both Indian and European populations. Because of their spatial proximity and cultural heritage, they relied upon, and received, support from the Europeans. Undoubtedly the Anglo-Indians did exist as a visible entity during the early years, but they were not an organized group, nor were they as a Community the objects of discrimination and prejudice. Still they were viewed as a people apart. Overt discrimination was to come later.

[13] *Ibid.*
[14] Goodrich, *op. cit.,* p. 93.
[15] Stark, *op. cit.,* pp. 43-45.
[16] *Ibid.,* p. 53.

If their integration into the European social system had been complete, the British would probably not have reacted negatively toward them. However, integrative accommodation did not occur. Fear began to mount in many quarters that Anglo-Indians and indigenous groups were becoming too powerful, and that unless a check was made upon this power the influence and authority of the East India Company would be challenged.

Between 1785 and 1795, the East India Company introduced several resolutions designed to limit the rising influence of both the Anglo-Indian and indigenous populations. The first overt action was an order whereby Anglo-Indian children housed in the Upper Orphanage School at Calcutta would not be allowed to journey to England for the completion of their formal education.[17] A child in this institution would therefore not be eligible either for employment in the higher echelons of the civil service or a military commission. The order was generally extended to all orphans, whether of legitimate or illegitimate birth. Although some schools had been established in India, wherein the child could receive a European-style education, they were few and their level of instruction did not go beyond the lower grades.

The action that did most to change the status of the Community came in 1791, when the directors of the East India Company issued an order that no person born "the son of native India," i.e., the son of a European father and an Indian mother, would, in the future, be employed by the civil, military, or marine services of the Company. Eventually directives were issued prohibiting anyone not having European parentage on both sides from entering military services, except as "fifers, drummers, bandsmen, and farriers."[18]

With the membership of the Community dependent upon the Company for a livelihood, the result was immediate and widespread unemployment. Anglo-Indians trained to carry out the tasks of the Company generally lacked the skills needed for other employment. Shortly after the policy was announced in India, Anglo-Indians employed by the Company were dismissed. Some joined the services of princely rulers, finding employment both in their administrative organizations and their military structure. Others fell into almost immediate poverty, living on a subsistence level by whatever means were available.

By this time there had developed on the part of the British widespread dislike, distrust, and fear of the Anglo-Indian Community. The editor of *The Calcutta Chronicle* (May 15, 1792) voiced these fears:

> If forthwith drastic measures are not put into operation to keep down the East Indian (Anglo-Indian) race, they will do to the British in India what the Mulattoes have done to the Spaniards in San Domingo.[19]

---

[17] For a discussion of this and other acts of repression see Goodrich, *op. cit.*, pp. 67-177.

[18] *Ibid.*, p. 130. See also: Herbert A. Stark, *Hostages to India, op. cit.*, pp. 59-68; and *Memorandum Submitted on Behalf of the Anglo-Indian and Domiciled European Community of India for the Consideration of the Chairman and Members of the India Statutory Commission* (Calcutta: Anglo-Indian and Domiciled European Conference, 1928) p. 2.

[19] Quoted in Herbert A. Stark, *John Ricketts and His Times* (Calcutta: Wilson and Son, Printers, 1934), pp. 18-19.

Another commentary was written by Viscount Valentia, who visited the possessions of the Company and later published a diary in which his impressions were recorded. The following passage tells of his impression of the membership of the Anglo-Indian Community:

> The most rapidly accumulating evil of Bengal is the increase of half-caste children. They are forming the first step to colonization by creating a link of union between the English and the natives. In every country where this intermediate caste has been permitted to rise, it has ultimately tended to its ruin. Spanish-American and San Domingo are examples of this fact. Their increase in India is beyond calculation: and though possible there may be nothing to fear from the Hindus and the rapidly declining consequence of the Musalmans (sic), yet it may be justly apprehended that this tribe may hereafter become too powerful for control. Although they are not permitted to hold offices under the Company, yet they act as clerks in almost every mercantile house; and many of them are annually sent to England to receive the benefits of an European education. With numbers in their favor, with a close relationship to the natives, and without an equal proportion of the pusillanimity and indolence which is natural to them, what may not in the future time be dreaded from them? I have no hesitation in saying that the evil ought to be stopped; and I know of no other way of effecting this object than by obliging every father of half-caste children to send them to Europe and prohibiting their return in any capacity whatever.[20]

Opinions such as these undoubtedly had much to do with the continuation of regulations limiting certain Anglo-Indian activities. Anglo-Indians must have keenly felt alienated from their patrilineal ancestors. Through several generations they had identified with a reference group, the Europeans. Now, suddenly, this reference group rejected them. But even though rejected, the Anglo-Indian Community was destined to remain in existence. Although many of its members entered the society of their mothers, others continued to identify with the Community throughout the years of repression until the protections enjoyed during earlier times were restored.

The position of the Anglo-Indian Community continued to fluctuate. Numerous Anglo-Indians, trained in military traditions, entered the forces of Indian ruling princes. Within a few years several of these rulers revolted against the British. To build their forces, the British issued orders directing all Anglo-Indians to return to the Company's ranks or face punishment as traitors. With no other choice the membership of the Community re-entered the services of the colonial power. However, for economic and political reasons, they were again, in 1808, suddenly dismissed from the military services of the British.[21] Continued restrictions were imposed upon the members and within a decade after their dismissal they were no longer guaranteed legal protections previously afforded them. Their status was becoming more and marginal with reference to the British – the group that had long ago become their reference.

---

[20] Viscount George Valentia, *Voyages and Travels in Ceylon, The Red Sea, Abyssinia and Egypt in the Years 1802, 1804, and 1806* (London: William Hiller, 1809), Vol. I, pp. 241-242.

[21] Stark, *Hostages to India, op. cit.,* pp. 84-87.

Prior to 1833 the Company had placed limitations and restrictions on travel from England to India. With few exceptions, only men, properly appointed to service in the East India Company, could make the trip. However, when a new Company charter was announced, travel restrictions were lifted. As a result, British men and women entered the country in great numbers. The presence of European women, and the increasing number of Anglo-Indian females, seemingly reduced the number of English-Indian marriages. Herbert A. Stark writes:

> As years rolled on the practice of marrying Indian wives fell into disrepute, for the necessity for it had disappeared. The new arrival could always wed a girl of mixed parentage, and it became customary for him to do so... Nevertheless, there were still those who persisted in defying convention by finding for themselves the conveniences of married life without marrying...[22]

Several Anglo-Indians of Calcutta, feeling a need for communal solidarity and organization, formed a group for the purpose of creating educational and charitable institutions within the community.[23] Shortly thereafter this group established the Parental Academic Institution in an attempt to provide English educational facilities for Anglo-Indian youths. In doing this the membership formed the first official Anglo-Indian organization.[24] Initially the group concentrated its efforts on founding and expanding educational institutions within Calcutta. The membership of this early organization drafted a petition to be transmitted to Parliament. In the petition, carried to London in 1830 by one John Ricketts, there was an enumeration of grievances of the Community and a request that the British find solutions to the problems threatening the very existence of the Anglo-Indian people. Whether or not the petition had any effect upon official policy is debatable. However, the Charter Act of 1833, in which the East India Company was officially changed from a merchant and trade organization to an administrative body, no longer excluded Anglo-Indians from employment within the protective folds of the British.[25]

After 1833 the Anglo-Indian Community slowly achieved a relatively more prosperous life. A railway system was introduced into India, the first line commencing operation about mid-century. Shortly thereafter, an extensive railway and telegraph system was made operational, linking the major cities of India and spreading rapidly throughout the country.[26] Within a few years all parts of India were linked with relatively modern and rapid means of transportation and communication. In each of these innovations Anglo-Indians were involved. In fact, a majority of the workers participating in the construction and operation of the railway and telegraph systems were Anglo-Indians.

---

[22] *Ibid.,* p. 34.

[23] "East Indian Education and the Doveton College," *The Calcutta Review* 24 : 293-295 (January-June, 1855).

[24] For a discussion of this and other early organizations of the Anglo-Indian Community see: Goodrich, *op. cit.,* pp. 140-141.

[25] Ibid., pp. 152-158.

[26] Elmer L. Hedin, "The Anglo-Indian Community," *The American Journal of Sociology* 40 : 165-179 (September, 1934), and Stark, *Hostages to India,* pp. 139-140.

As noted earlier, the Anglo-Indian Community was forced, through British rejection, to form themselves into a cohesive unit. They reacted to this rejection by forming organizations and creating a generally self-sustaining community. Goodrich is probably correct in stating that initial stages of community consciousness evolved at this time.[27] Once this sense of community emerged it never ceased to exist.

In 1825 an Anglo-Indian club was organized in Calcutta for the purpose of creating a center for social and political activities.[28] From this beginning the Community developed a complex web of social organizations needed for the continuation of a self-sustaining minority within the larger Indian society. In Calcutta the organization which the Anglo-Indians had founded continued to broaden its base of operation. The Calcutta Apprenticing Society and the Marine School were designed to train youths in specialized skills and thus provide better economic opportunities for the Community.[29] Another program involving land development was started. In these plans land was acquired and attempts were made to place Anglo-Indians on farms.[30] All of these agricultural projects were failures and were soon abandoned. The educational institutions and training centers met with more success, however. Although the marine training program was discontinued, the apprenticing agencies continued for many years.

Community organization, however, existed primarily in Calcutta in the state of Bengal, which had the largest concentration of Anglo-Indians of any Indian city. It was many years before a complex organization was developed which could link the numerous geographic areas of India. During the years of repression, the Anglo-Indian Community was further cemented into a marginal and precarious existence. Rejecting the indigenous population, and being rejected by their own reference group, the British, they were forced to make a place for themselves within the gap between Western and Eastern cultures. Certainly there were many problems of individual and group identity. In certain circumstances they were considered to be British, while at other times they were viewed as indigenous Indians, and in still other situations they were considered neither.

Years of Prosperity and Anxiety: 1857-1920

At the time of the Mutiny, Anglo-Indians were employed throughout the various services of the Company; and whether in the military or civilian services, they generally supported the goals and policies of England. Some of the more prominent military leaders during this conflict were Anglo-Indians who had been allowed to rejoin the British military forces. The names of these early Anglo-Indian leaders are still well-known to many historically-minded members

---

[27] Goodrich, *op. cit.*, pp. 158-162.
[28] *Ibid.*, pp. 141-144.
[29] Herbert A. Stark, *John Ricketts and His Times*, pp. 53-58. For further efforts by Anglo-Indians to develop a marine school see: James Luke, "A Training-Ship Institution," *The Calcutta Review* 279: 329-333 (April, 1903).
[30] Stark, *John Ricketts and His Times*, pp. 59-66.

of the Community and are often cited to illustrate the past greatness of the group.[31]

During the Mutiny a sizable number of Anglo-Indians lost property. Their homes were sometimes destroyed by Indian nationalists in retaliation for their pro-British stance. Upon termination of the military conflict members of the Community requested compensation from England. These pleas, however, were not heard, as illustrated in a proclamation issued by the Crown stating that neither Anglo-Indians nor any other Indians who had remained loyal to England could receive any financial remuneration.[32]

Despite the refusal of Britain to reimburse Anglo-Indians for lost property, they did at least return to the policy of providing employment for members of the Community. Following the Mutiny the government attempted to form an Anglo-Indian regiment to be titled "The Eurasian Corps." The concept of such a military body failed in part because wages within the military, at least at the lower levels, did not equal what could be made by employment in the railway, telegraph, or other services.

Although the earlier years of this period were fairly prosperous, at the end of the nineteenth century nearly one-fourth of the Anglo-Indian Community in Calcutta were receiving relief payments.[33] For at least two decades economic conditions of the Community remained static resulting in the fact that numerous relief agencies were created by members of the minority in an attempt to ease the situation.[34] The main causes of these economic difficulties appear to have been: (a) increase in the cost of living throughout India, (b) job competition with Indians, and (c) inadequaecy of salaries. Undoubtedly, these factors affected other Indians as well as Anglo-Indians.

Historically, Anglo-Indians have had several stereotypes associated with them. Often, they were thought of as persons of questionable morality, that they had expensive habits (beyond what their incomes would allow), that they were lazy, and generally were a disorganized group. Perhaps some of these characteristics may be valid for specific persons, but as generalizations for the entire Community were misleading. An Anglo-Indian author's comments in the *Calcutta Review* are to the point:

> That members of this community often prefer expensive patent medicines and foods and doctors who charge heavy fees to free medicine in the dispensaries and free treatment in the hospitals and that both 'casual relief' and 'pensions' are often wasted

---

[31] Frank Anthony, *Britain's Betrayal in India, op. cit.* See especially Chapter V, "Anglo-Indians and the Mutiny." For a discussion of specific Anglo-Indian military leaders see H. G. Keens, "Indian Military Adventures of the last Century," *Calcutta Review* 71 : 55-85, (1880).

[32] For an Anglo-Indian view of these grievances see Herbert A. Stark, *The Call of the Blood* (Rangoon: British Burma Press, 1932), pp. 160-161.

[33] John MacRae, "The Problem for Charity Among the Anglo-Indian Community," *The Calcutta Review* 271 : 84-94 (January, 1913).

[34] W. H. Arden Wood, "The Domiciled Community in India and the Simla Education Conference," *The Calcutta Review* 272 : 109-132 (April 1913).

for this purpose is an instance of the craving of the Anglo-Indian for special treatment, that is worthy of notice.[35]

Economic conditions for Anglo-Indians were especially favorable during World War I, when many members of the Community were either engaged with the British in military operations, or served in positions within India which had been vacated by the British because of the European war drain. But adversity lay ahead.

Between the years of 1857 and 1920, the Community experienced both declines and rises in status. Following their return to the employment of the East India Company, they enjoyed generally improved economic conditions. Within the railroad and telegraph systems they maintained a near monopoly of employment positions. Until 1878 every branch of the telegraph department was manned almost entirely by Anglo-Indians or Domiciled Europeans.[36] Gradually other Indians obtained employment in these occupations. Shortly after the turn of the century the government made it an official policy that Anglo-Indian and Domiciled European employment within the telegraph system should not fall below two-thirds of the total, but in 1920, it had declined to approximately one-half. Customs, another service in which the Community traditionally maintained a virtual monopoly, was staffed almost entirely by Anglo-Indians or Domiciled Europeans until 1920,[37] but gradually became infiltrated with other Indians.

Thus the Community was beginning to feel the pressure of competition. Guarantees that had protected them in the labor market were being more and more relaxed. Demands for Indian independence and involvement in national development were becoming stronger with each passing year. Educated and well-trained Indians were entering the services once thought to be entirely the dominion of the Anglo-Indian and Domiciled European Communities.

Nevertheless, the Anglo-Indians continued to function as an organized community. Political organizations were formed and expanded, with numerous sub-groups being integrated into a unified whole. Yet leadership initiative and involvement of the members usually depended on the elite. There are indications that the rank and file were not seriously concerned with the political actions of the Community, or even the larger society, except as they were personally and directly affected.

Anglo-Indian education continued to be primarily within the jurisdiction of private schools. Throughout the urban centers and numerous "hill stations" (resort towns) Anglo-Indian schools were created and expanded. Their enrollments were generally small and their facilities limited. Operating on restricted budgets, few

---

[35] John MacRae, "Social Conditions in Calcutta: II. The Problem for Charity Among the Anglo-Indian Community," *The Calcutta Review* 273 : 351-371 (July, 1913).

[36] The term "Domiciled Europeans" identified those persons both of whose parents were Europeans who planned to make India their permanent domicile. In many instances they identified with Anglo-Indians.

[37] *Memorandum Submitted on behalf of the Anglo-Indian and Domiciled European Community of India for the Consideration of the Chairman and Members of the Indian Statutory Commission* (Calcutta: Anglo-Indian and Domiciled European Conference, 1928), pp. 19-21.

offered advanced training. Many were supported by religious groups, with the directors and financial sources located outside of India. The schools were expensive to attend; as a result children of lower-class Anglo-Indian families were not well represented. A few of the schools offered financial aid to exceptional children who otherwise could not afford to attend, but such aid was rare.

Continued Stresses in the Modern Era: 1920-1970

The years between 1920 and 1970 saw increased involvement on the part of Anglo-Indians. During and immediately following World War II the Community experienced an economic revival. The depression of earlier years was temporarily halted as thousands of people found employment within the services. But the mark of Indianization was being felt as demands were made by the indigenous population. The British Government, knowing that independence would eventually come, attempted to meet some of these transitional issues. Many previous guarantees given to Anglo-Indians, especially in matters of employment, were ignored.

Among the most important attempts to meet the demands were the Montagu-Chelmsford Reforms (Government of India Act of 1919). These reforms, as a reaction to the nationalist movement, provided employment for Indians in occupations previously reserved for Anglo-Indians. As a result, Anglo-Indians were forced to face the realities of open competition, often a difficult situation with which to deal.

Members of the Community, feeling themselves in an increasingly insecure political and economic position, resorted to the techniques which had been used a hundred years previously. In an attempt to make their demands known to the Crown, the Community in 1923, and again in 1925, sent a deputation to England to meet with the Secretary of State for India.[38] The chairman of the Anglo-Indian Association, Henry Gidney, served as leader of this group. Although politely received, the delegation met with little success. England, beginning to feel the demand for Indian independence, preferred to hear the demands of larger population groups, especially the Muslims.

The marginal position occupied by the Community was further accentuated when, in 1925, the Secretary of State for India officially defined the position of the Anglo-Indian Community as follows:

> For purposes of employment under Government and inclusion in schemes of Indianization, members of the Anglo-Indian and Domiciled European Community are Statutory Natives of India. For purposes of education and internal security, their status, in so far as it admits to definition, approximates that of European British subjects.[39]

With this dual definition, officially pronounced, Anglo-Indians of India were both

---

[38] J. Coatman, *India in 1925-26* (Calcutta: Government of India, Central Publication Branch, 1926), pp. 14-15, 84-86.

[39] *British Parliamentary Debates,* Vol. 189 (London: His Majesty's Stationery Office, 1929), pp. 1925-26.

legally and socially affirmed as a marginal people. Informal marginality now became formal.

Power struggles developed within the Community for leadership of an All-India association. By 1925, Henry Gidney, chairman of the Calcutta-based All-India and Burma Federation, had won the battle. There were then, as there are today, conflicts with an independent Madras-based association.[40] This Madras association, according to the Northern group, granted membership to Indian-Christians who did not have European blood ties. Members of the Madras association should therefore not be allowed to serve as the voice of the entire Community. Conflict between the North and South, still present in today's India, caused deep cleavages between the two organizations.

Many members of the Community alienated the leadership of the Indian nationalist movement and the general population in various ways, especially by keeping several of the railroads in operation, even though a national strike by Indian leaders had been called.[41] Actions such as this, still bitterly remembered, helped to keep Anglo-Indians alienated from the Indian people. Alienation of the two peoples was further manifest in discriminatory or retaliative actions by the Hindu majority.

As indicated earlier, the Community relied heavily on the railroad system for employment. In 1928, the Anglo-Indian Association estimated that approximately one-half of the Anglo-Indian and Domiciled Europeans in India were dependent upon the railroad system for jobs in the 1920's.[42] However, more Indians and fewer Anglo-Indians were accepted for employment as positions became available. The security of past years was beginning to fade.

Anglo-Indians continued to plead for constitutional protections during their replacement by Indian workers. Representatives of the Community appeared before all statutory commissions and round table conferences, attempting to make the basis for their plea widely known and understood.[43] In each of these conferences Community representatives prepared and presented reports. In the final reports of each conference recommendations were made which would allow both economic and political safeguards for the Anglo-Indians, but would not initially accept recommendations concerning separate electorates.[44]

The British government in the 1930's provided further constitutional advances for India. While the reforms did not specify any minority job guarantees, a new government act of 1935 specifically mentioned the Anglo-Indian minority with reference to employment. In addition the Community was to be provided with

---

[40] Frank Anthony, *Britain's Betrayal in India* (Bombay: Allied Publishers 1969). See especially chapter VI, "The Gidney Years." Cf. "Amalgation or Federation," *Anglo-Indian Review,* 17 : 1 (November-December, 1927). For a discussion of Gidney, see: Kenneth E. Wallace, *Life of Sir Henry Gidney* (Calcutta: A. Mukherjii and Company, 1947).

[41] *Memorandum Submitted on Behalf of the Anglo-Indian and Domiciled European Community of India, op. cit.,* pp. 10-11.

[42] *Ibid.,* p. 9.

[43] See *Report of the India Statutory Commission,* Vols. I and II (Calcutta, 1930).

[44] See Michael Brecher, *Nehru: A Political Biography* (Bombay: Oxford University Press, 1959), pp. 179-180.

legislative seats and educational grants,[45] two spheres which the Community felt to be vital. Some of the efforts of the Community were thus proving fruitful.

Between 1930 and 1945, the Anglo-Indians became increasingly concerned about their destiny in India. Independence was assured but political-economic guarantees were not as certain as the leadership of the Community had hoped. Many Anglo-Indians migrated from India in an attempt to gain political protection and economic security. Most Anglo-Indians felt that their ties were closer to Great Britain than to India and that they would have a better future in England; others, including the leadership of the Association, attempted to make alliances with the elite of the Indian nationalist movement. These alliances were to prove valuable in the early days of Independence as the Community was forced to carve a niche for itself in a newly-oriented society.

Indian Independence was achieved in 1947, intensifying the anxieties already felt by most of the Community. However, the new government provided basic political guarantees for all minority groups, including the Anglo-Indians. When, in 1949, the new Constitution of India was approved, the Anglo-Indian Community was the only minority to fight for, and receive, special guarantees in the area of education, appointments to certain services, and political representation in both state and national assemblies. If the President of India became convinced that the Anglo-Indian Community did not have adequate representation in the lower House of the People (Lok Sabha) he could nominate up to two members of the Community to serve in that body.[46] Since the enactment of the Constitution the Community has always had two members of Parliament.[47] In a similar manner, except with more latitude, if the Governor of a State decided that the Anglo-Indian Community is not adequately represented in the State Legislative Assembly, he has the authority to nominate as many members of the Community to the State Assembly as he "considers appropriate."

Since the enactment of the Constitution there have been additional problems for the Anglo-Indians. Out-migration has continued to drain the Community, especially the middle and upper classes. The anxiety associated with Independence and Indianization, as well as the fact that most Anglo-Indians have friends and relatives in other countries, provided a rationale for exodus. The precise number of out-migrants is not known; yet the number is considerable, estimated as much as fifty thousand during the post-war era. However, some of the leaders believe that the actual size of the minority has not been greatly reduced.[48] Because of the high birth rate of the Community, the number remaining may exceed the number migrating and dying.

---

[45] Goodrich, *op. cit.,* pp. 41-44.

[46] *The Constitution of India* (New Delhi: Government of India Press, 1963), paragraph 331.

[47] Frank Anthony, President of the All-India Anglo-Indian Association, and A. E. T. Barrow, Director of the Council for the Indian School Certificate Examination, have been the Anglo-Indian representatives to Parliament since the enactment of the Constitution. Barrow retired in 1971.

[48] The All-India Anglo-India Association generally asserts that the number today is between 250,000 and 300,000. A more realistic figure is probably 100,000 to 200,000. (See: Frank Anthony, *Britain's Betrayal in India, op. cit.,* pp. 9-10, and "Mr. Anthony's Presidential Address," *The Review* 60 : 37 (November/December, 1969).

CHAPTER THREE

MARGINALITY AND IDENTITY

IN this chapter we shall consider critically the concept of marginality as it has been variously applied to inter-group relations and to lay down some guidelines for research in this general area. Consequently, this presentation is not a statement of methodology, but rather a suggested conceptual approach to inter-group relations between major collectivities that differ in various ways but which are interrelated and in some respects interdependent. In addition it is intended to provide a sociological perspective of the individual's relationship to groups that restrict or prohibit social interaction between their members, that in one way or another bar them from social admission, or groups from which participants are voluntarily alienated. These relationships will be conceptualized as marginal, their social setting as marginal situations, and the actors in these situations as marginal men. Finally, this chapter is a prologue to the study of Anglo-Indians.

The present study is primarily concerned with the sociology and social psychology of marginality. For the purposes of this analysis a group may be viewed as marginal (1) when its members do not ordinarily qualify for admission into another group with which, over varying lengths of time, it is more or less closely associated; (2) when these groups differ significantly in the nature of their cultural or racial heritage; and (3) between which there is limited cultural interchange or social interaction. A group, including its individual members, may at the same time be marginal to one or more other collectivities, but in the case of multi-group situations marginality is not necessarily gauged by the same criteria for each entity. Groups may be said to exist in a marginal relationship only if they are in close enough proximity to make direct interaction between individual members possible. Any group could scarcely be considered marginal if it is so remote geographically or technologically that cultural exchange or social interaction would unlikely occur.

The concept of marginality as it has generally been used to describe inter-group relations implies some form of hierarchical ordering of groups, and consequently their members, according to differentials of prestige, privilege, or power. Such differentials may in turn reflect the evaluations of cultural properties, physical attributes of members, lineage, behavior patterns, and traditions of the people involved in some kind of inter-group relations. The notion that marginality invariably involves differentials of status and power may be questioned, however, although in most situations certain kinds of inequalities do exist. This aspect of marginality will be discussed later in this chapter.

The concept has been used in various contexts and is therefore not necessarily restricted to individuals or groups that are racially or culturally distinctive. Wittermans and Krauss employ the notion of "structural marginality," applying it particularly to youth in modern society.[49] In their view, structural marginality "may be defined as the condition of those persons whose meaningful participation in the life of their society is adversely affected by certain structural arrangements," that is, "the restriction of institutionalized roles." If there are no recognized institutionalized roles for the person to follow, he is "not a full group member. He is at most a hanger-on, a marginal person." Similarly, Wardwell interprets the concept as "an imperfectly institutionalized role, which means that there is some ambiguity in the pattern of behavior legitimately expected of a person filling the role, and that the social sanctions attending the role tend to be inconsistently applied."[50] Wardwell applies the concept to the chiropractor who, in his view, is "marginal to the well-institutionalized role of the doctor." The individual in an occupationally marginal situation of relationship may be less involved emotionally with his status than the person who is marginal, say, to a racial group because the latter relationship may profoundly affect every facet of his life.

Marginality and Social Barriers

Marginality presupposes some kind of "barrier" limiting or obstructing social interaction and cultural interchange between members of groups that are in some form of relationship with each other.[51] If these groups should happen to have the same cultural heritage and if no obstructions to social interaction are imposed by either group, they could hardly be considered marginal. There are innumerable groups, such as voluntary associations, that are not marginal when a "barrier" definition is applied. We prefer, however, to restrict the concept to relations between groups that have a relatively large membership and are more or less permanent. The term "community" in the sociological, not geographic, sense seems to describe best the form of grouping to which the concept of marginality most appropriately applies.

The functions of the barrier may be varied: to maintain social distances between individuals and collectivities, to keep individuals and groups spatially apart, to retain separateness of identity, to restrict or prevent the interchange of cultural possessions, and perhaps other similar functions. These barriers may vary in rigidity or flexibility according to the specific situation or conditions governing social interaction or cultural exchange. In the final analysis they reflect the attitudes and values relative to restrictions on interaction, whether manifest in overt behavior or in the maintenance of traditions upholding exclusionist arrangements. They may rigidly have the force of legal sanctions, may simply be a matter of custom, or in some circumstances be both. In most inter-group interaction these barriers seldom have unanimous approval of all members of that

[49] Tamme Wittermans and Irving Krauss, "Structural Marginality and Social Worth," *Sociology and Social Research*, 48 : 348-350 (April, 1964).

[50] Walter I. Wardwell, "A Marginal Professional Role: "The Chiropractor," *Social Forces*, 30 : 339-340 (March, 1952).

[51] The term "barrier" seems to have been first used by Kurt Lewin in his *Resolving Social Conflicts*, (New York: Harper and Brothers, 1948).

group overtly imposing the restrictions. Indeed, there may well be a wide range of opinions among the members as to the desirability of an intergroup barrier or, if one in fact exists, the form it should take.

Marginal Groups and Community Formation

Barriers tend to be divisive rather than integrative in inter-group relations, but the same barriers may be integrative rather than divisive for intra-group relations. They may narrow social distances within each group by intensifying a consciousness of identity. This awareness of identity may be sufficiently intense to generate a sense of community, and the emergence of a community solidarity and awareness may occur if it experiences deprivation over a considerable length of time as a result of discrimination, exploitation, or physical attack. In the opinion of Goodrich, a sense of community among the Anglo-Indians in India emerged as a result of deprivation and hardship imposed by the British in the eighteenth century.[52]

Marginality may, however, have the effect of shattering intra-group relations and delaying the growth of community consensus and organization. If a spirit of optimism concerning the future is shared by the members of a marginal group, at least the psychological climate is favorable to the emergence of a community; but if the prevailing climate is one of despair, a feeling of helplessness and hopelessness, the appearance of genuine community feelings may be delayed. Even in situations generally favorable to the development of community life, it does not always follow that a community in the sociological sense will result. Members of the marginal group may lack the consensus necessary for such a development, or may be prevented from taking the necessary organizational steps, even if the will to do so is there.

Types of Barriers

In modern society there are many specific types of barriers that delimit the boundaries of groups and prevent or restrict the interaction of their members across these boundary lines. There are barriers based on race or ethnicity, including not only visible physical attributes, such as color, but also racial "lineage," whatever may be the physical characteristics of individuals who make up the marginal groups. A case in point is the "white Negro" who is rejected by the members of a racially dominant group, not because of physical traits but because of "lineage," real or imagined.

There are numerous legal and political barriers which may prevent or restrict the individual from enjoying the rights accorded others. There are barriers based on religious affiliations or values in which individuals are denied admission into either sacred or secular groups, or even prevented from participating in activities because the exclusionist group seeks to maintain its own religious preserve

---

[52] Dorris L. Goodrich, "The Making of an Ethnic Group: The Eurasian Community in India," Unpublished Ph.D. dissertation, University of California, Berkeley, 1953, p. 7.

undiluted by outside influences. There are barriers of caste and class creating situations in which members may be judged by such matters as lineage, power, wealth, or style of life, and therefore accepted or rejected by others in a variety of social situations. There are other social barriers assuming the form of taboos, enforced by the prospect of punitive measures, that prohibit or restrict inter-marriage, inter-dining, and other forms of intimate social intercourse between groups. Any of these barriers may limit the individual's right to gainful employment, the right of full citizenship, the right to follow certain occupations. Probably the barriers that are most rigid and emotionally charged are those of race, religion, nationality, and caste.

By-passing the Barriers

Barriers separating groups may be bent, broken, or penetrated, even when the penalties for so doing are severe. Penalties may, in some instances, apply to violators of the laws or customs of either group, as in the case of laws or moral sanctions prohibiting sexual cohabitation or inter-marriage of Africans and whites in South Africa or Negroes and whites in the United States. Most barriers, however, are penetrable, at least to the degree of partial acceptance or admission by one or both groups, provided the individual seeking acceptance or admission exhibits appropriate social credentials, such as manners, appearance, skills, stability or reliability, cultural or intellectual sophistication, piety, loyalty, and the like. Generally the rules for such penetration are created and sanctioned by the dominant group, and such behavior must follow these rules.

The penetration of barriers may involve an acculturative or assimilative process in which the individual may acquire certain aspects of the out-group culture that make for acceptability. Members of immigrant groups in the United States have exhibited this kind of behavior when on acquiring appropriate social credentials they have been admitted, at least on probation, to groups representing the dominant culture, or to groups which are at least prestigious or powerful. Some achieve a sort of hyphenated membership; others hurdle the barriers completely and identify with the new group. This is a familiar story in the upward mobility process in American society — or any other open-class society, for that matter.

But penetration of the barrier separating peoples depends largely on the motivation and interests of the individual, his qualifications for membership in the out-group, as well as ultimately his general acceptability. Until recently most Anglo-Indians did not seek acceptance in Indian society, but even if they had desired admission they probably would have been denied it for reasons that will be discussed in another chapter.

If the barriers are rigid and the disadvantage of one's own group identity burdensome, the personal problem may be resolved by clandestine and perhaps illegal penetration of the barrier. This is commonly known as "passing," a process which may either be temporary or permanent, partial passing into a work situation during the daytime, or total passing involving a permanent change of identity.

Since passing obviously involves concealment of the individual's previous group identity it is difficult for individuals with visible racial attributes to penetrate the barriers, but those who are only culturally distinctive may successfully make the transition to another group. Anglo-Indians whose physical characteristics are not necessarily a distinguishing mark of identity may "pass" as an Indian-Christian or Hindu for real or imagined advantages. Members of a subordinate Indian caste may, in an anonymous situation as in a large city, successfully pose as members of a higher caste, at least in the job market. Such passing may be difficult or impossible in informal situations.

Cultural Marginality

Marginality with reference to the relationships of two or more groups may be either cultural or social.[53] These two component elements are interrelated and interdependent and can only be separated for analytical or methodological purposes. Cultural marginality, as the concept is used in this analysis, has reference to the belief and value systems, established behavior patterns, forms of social organization, skills and bodies of knowledge, and symbols representing the cultural possessions or status of a group which exists more or less permanently in some kind of functional relationship to another group.

Perhaps most "visible" of all cultural possessions are language and other forms of symbolic behavior, but others such as "manners," diet, rituals, attire, and family behavior are likewise perceptible and often furnish the yardstick by which the worthiness or unworthiness of individuals and groups is gauged. Marginality may imply, though not necessarily, an invidious cultural distinction expressing the values of one or both groups. The cultural possessions of one of the groups may be admired, respected, or despised by members of the other related group. It is these culture-directed attitudes and values that determine, to some extent, the relations of the groups and their respective members. These relations are commonly defined, although not always, in terms of subordinate and superordinate status and power.

The rejection of the culture of another people, especially a minority group, is not at all unusual in many societies, but it sometimes happens that individuals reject or abandon part or all of the culture heritage of their own natal community. An individual may cling tenaciously to one or more of his cultural possessions, say language, but discard such aspects of culture as diet or attire in favor of the other-group culture. It is not at all unusual in a stratified, multi-ethnic society for children, say, of immigrant parents, to be socialized into the culture of the other-group more than into their own parental community. The marginal position

---

[53] *Cultural* as distinguished from *social* marginality was formulated by the senior author and presented in a paper at the 1965 meeting, in Chicago, of the American Sociological Association under the title, "Cultural vs. Social Marginality: The Anglo-Indian Case." It was subsequently published, in revised form, in *Phylon* 28 : 361-75 (Winter, 1967) under the same title. The work of Dickie-Clark was not available to him until after the paper was presented at the Chicago meeting. See his *The Marginal Situation* (London: Routledge and Kegan Paul, 1966).

of parents may thus be reduced or abolished altogether in the case of their children.

It may be that members of one of the groups are *culturally* similar or identical to the other related group or groups, but different in other respects. The cultural heritage of both the Anglo-Indians and the British was essentially the same. One would hardly be justified in saying that they were culturally marginal to the British, either in India or in England. Correspondingly, the Coloured community in South Africa is culturally identical to the Europeans of British descent in that region, and is therefore not marginal in this respect, although they are by other criteria. But both Anglo-Indians and the Coloured community remained *socially* marginal to the British in those respective regions.

A particular group may be culturally distinct from another related group, and may, or may not, wish to perpetuate this distinction. If, in the members' judgment, it is to their advantage to reject the culture of the other group and to identify exclusively with their own traditional heritage, this they will likely do; but if, on the other hand, they are willing or eager to embrace the other-group culture, for whatever reason, or are required to do so, their consequent acculturation may tend to reduce their cultural marginality. Their children may undergo a process of socialization into the other culture and come to have limited familiarity with the heritage of their parents; or they may, on the other hand, be socialized exclusively into the traditional culture of their indigenous community. The stance of either group may variously be one of indifference or opposition to the acculturative process. If one of the groups is politically or militarily dominant, it may even require that acculturation take place. The imposition of English by the British as a medium of instruction in the schools of India was a form of mandatory acculturation.

It is the thesis of this analysis that the Anglo-Indians are (and were) culturally marginal to the other Indians in India. This is because their mother tongue, religion, family organization, and general style of life distinguishes them from Indians who are relatively distinctive in these respects. Yet it should be noted that the culture of India is by no means homogeneous. It is a society of numerous ethnic groups, each of whose cultural heritage, including the Anglo-Indian Community, distinguishes them from the others. The cultural differences between the various groups, or between the Anglo-Indians and the others, are not of the same dimension. This group may possess a greater cultural similarity to Indian-Christians than to other groups because of the religious component. In terms of cultural similarities or dissimilarities the numerous communities of India might possibly be arranged on some type of cultural distance scale.

The cultural distances between ethnic groups may remain more or less constant, become narrower, or even become wider. On the cultural level the distances between the Anglo-Indian group and other communities is being reduced through the medium of the school system. Anglo-Indian students now receive instruction in the history, philosophy, literature, art, and languages of India. Stated differently, their cultural marginality is being reduced through institutional mechanisms. This acculturative process, or Indianization, operates so as not to change drastically the cultural identity of Anglo-Indians but rather to reduce the barriers that have traditionally separated this Community from other communities of India. Through this process the Anglo-Indian Community will acquire cultural attributes it did not initially possess.

Social Marginality

Social marginality, as the concept is here employed, has reference to inter-group and inter-personal relations that exist between two or more groups. If an individual representing a particular group is not socially acceptable by members of another related group, or if he is acceptable only within specified limits, or in specified ways, he may be said to occupy a socially marginal position and be in a marginal relation to members of that group. This is a marginal situation. The relationships that govern marginality may, therefore, be patterned and formalized, involving a protocol specifying the appropriate mode of interaction in particular situations, or a set of taboos prohibiting designated forms of interaction. The protocol may specify who shall or shall not interact with whom across boundary lines or barriers, under what circumstances, in what form, and for what purpose. Inter-group or inter-personal relations may, on the other hand, be informal, non-patterned, fortuitous. They may be harmonious and cooperative, or hostile and conflicting.

Within this rather broad spectrum of relationships there are many specific ways in which interaction between the groups may be manifest: In inter-group courtship and marriage, inter-dining, common membership and participation in organizations, joint recreational activities, sharing in political and civic undertakings, neighborhood and family visitation, and so on. The criteria of marginality on the social level, then, would be the degree of acceptability or unacceptability of members of a particular group by another group for designated relationships or roles. A group acceptable in all respects by the other-group could hardly be considered socially marginal; and logically it would follow that persons who are completely rejected in every respect are likewise non-marginal. In almost every conceivable real-life situation individuals are acceptable by the other-group in varying degrees and by different criteria. An individual who would be totally unacceptable in an inter-group marital relationship might be readily approved as a colleague in a work role. Stating this situation differently, a barrier may exist so far as intermarriage is concerned, but not in admission to an occupational situation.

These differentials of social acceptability and non-acceptability were observed by Myrdal in his classic study of race relations in the United States wherein he formulated them as the "rank order of discrimination". This formulation indicated that, among whites, the barrier against racial intermarriage was the most rigid of all, with other barriers ranked in order of their effectiveness in preventing or reducing social interaction.[54] The same general idea was formulated by Bogardus

---

[54] Gunnar Myrdal, *An American Dilemma* (New York: Harper and Brothers, 1944). Chap. 3.

in his well known social distance scale. The criteria of social acceptability will likely vary from one group situation to another, depending on the values attached to particular cultural, behavioral, physical, or psychological characteristics of the person involved. There is certainly no universal rank order of social acceptability.

Marginal relationships are always complex. As Kolaja and Kaplan have observed, "Multiple marginality denotes not only marginality in regard to several dimensions as far as two cultures are concerned, but the term also denotes marginality in regard to more than two cultures".[55] Not only are there different levels of acceptability within a particular group or community, as social distance scales clearly indicate, but there may also be three or more cultures to which an individual is marginal. Actually, this seems to be true of the Anglo-Indian situation; marginality is not limited to relations with a "homogeneous Indian community" but with several distinctive communities, including Hindus, Muslims, Sikhs, Parsees, and still others. A further complicating factor is social change. With the passage of time the relationship of the individual, or his group, to the other-group almost invariably undergoes a change which may increase or reduce the dimension of marginality; and likewise, with the passing of time, the involved individuals may define the situation differently.

What we have designated as cultural and social marginality are conceptualized as separate but interrelated phenomena. In a sense, however, they are merely different facets of the same or similar processes of inter-group and inter-personal relations. The cultural properties or behavior of any group almost always have some status significance and are evaluated in terms of their symbolic relevance to prestige or power or both. There are barriers erected against particular cultural properties and against individuals having these cultural assets. There are, on the other hand, cultural properties against which no barriers have been erected. At the same time there may be no barriers specifically against the human carriers of these properties. An individual may thus be *socially* marginal or non-marginal because of his *cultural* possessions, beliefs, patterned behavior, or other characteristics.

The two-dimensional aspect of marginality does not imply equal fitness in all marginal situations. As here noted, individuals, or groups, may be culturally marginal but not socially marginal, or the reverse. Or, on the other hand, they may be marginal in both dimensions. Dickie-Clark has stated the same general idea in somewhat different terminology:

> ... At one theoretical extreme would be the case of complete cultural similarity accompanied by absolute social rejection. At the other extreme would be the opposite or the total absence of acculturation along with complete social acceptance. In between these unlikely cases would fall those marginal situations of various degrees of social status and participation. These are the situations actually found in concrete societies and dealt with in the literature on marginality... One other theoretical possibility should be mentioned to complete the picture. That is where the degree of acculturation or socialization is precisely matched with the appropriate degree of social acceptance. This would not be a marginal situation in the sense used here.[56]

[55] J. Kolaja and S. J. Kaplan, "Case Study in Multiple Marginality," *Phylon* 21 : 338 (Winter, 1960).
[56] H. F. Dickie-Clark, *The Marginal Situation, op. cit.,* p. 44.

The Social Psychological Dimension of Marginality

Virtually every aspect of marginality is social-psychological in the sense that the concept itself implies a set of attitudes and values concerning the inter-relationships of groups, their cultural possessions, their position in the social order, and the nature of the barriers that separate them. Marginality implies not only an awareness of differences between groups, but also assumes an assessment of these differences, sometimes amounting to a moral judgment of the strengths or weaknessess, virtues or vices, of the other-group. It invariably involves the notion of *ethnocentrism* which, after all, is a judgment of one's own group as well as an implied, if not explicit, judgment of other groups.

Whether we consider marginality in its cultural or its social aspects we invariably invoke, by implication at least, value-judgments as they may be directed toward others. It is not so much culture *per se* that constitutes either a barrier or a passport of admission, but the values attached to specific objects or patterns of culture and the attitudes toward the human carriers of that culture. Dietary habits and behavior, for example, as an aspect of a group's cultural heritage, may be offensive to those who follow different food practices, and therefore become a barrier to social interaction and social acceptance.

Marginality, whether cultural or social, is undoubtedly influenced by other-directed attitudes of hostility or friendliness, of prejudice or preference, of the need or desire to identify with another group and be accepted by it, or the desire to avoid such an identity. The individual may not only be excluded from membership or participation because of lack of acceptance for one or more reasons; he may simply not *wish* to be so identified or to be accepted in another group.

Other-directed attitudes that exist in a marginal situation may be friendly or unfriendly, but alone they do not necessarily govern the nature of all social interaction that may occur. There are situations in which even friendly attitudes do not result in intimate social interaction. In South Africa, as Dickie-Clark observes, white persons and Coloureds are often friendly and kindly disposed toward each other, but the South African mores, reinforced by legal sanctions traditionally imposed by those in positions of power, severely limit the number of contacts and the nature of social interaction between the two groups.[57] Such writers as Charles S. Johnson have dealt extensively with the nature and function of "racial etiquette" in defining the character of social interaction between Negroes and whites in the American South.[58] On the other hand, attitudes of hostility do not necessarily lead either to overt conflict or to social isolation. The exigencies of a situation may demand that mutually-hostile groups cooperate in certain affairs of life, and in so doing come in frequent contact with each other. The doors of a white labor union may be opened to Negroes by government order, for example, in spite of mutually hostile inter-group or inter-personal attitudes. Even

---

[57] *Ibid.*, Chap. 7.

[58] Charles S. Johnson, *Growing Up in the Black Belt* (New York: Schocken, 1941). See also: *Patterns of Negro Segregation* (1943) Cf. Bertram W. Doyle, *The Etiquette of Race Relations* (Kennikat, 1968).

when account is taken of these inconsistencies between attitudes and behavior, attitudinal dispositions are central in shaping inter-group and inter-personal relations.

Marginality, Social Organizations, and Mobility

Marginality may be sustained, reduced, or increased through organizational or institutional structures. The basic reason for this is that social interaction commonly occurs within the framework of institutions or organizations. Thus an organization may provide a setting for intimate interaction between individuals representing subordinate and superordinate groups; or it may, on the contrary, erect barriers that are insurmountable. The public school is a case in point. The free public school, according to egalitarian ideology, is an institution affording an interplay of ideas and a source of knowledge for children and youth regardless of the status and culture of their parents. But it may also raise impenetrable barriers to such interaction by excluding students whose racial or cultural characteristics are unacceptable to persons in positions of power. Even when no legal barriers exist, economic barriers may limit the attendance of students to those having parents in a favorable financial situation.

Some schools, although not explicitly excluding designated categories of people, nevertheless function to that end if their institutions are designed especially for a certain group. The Anglo-Indian schools in India initially admitted only children of Anglo-Indian or European parentage, thus restricting or barring interaction with children of indigenous Indian families. These barriers have been altered in recent years, as we shall note in a subsequent chapter, but what at one time was a quasi-legal policy of exclusion has been replaced by other kinds of barriers.

If status and power differentials exist between peoples that are inter-related, or if members of one or more of these groups are disadvantaged in one or more ways, or if there are social stigmas created by labels that symbolize social inferiority, the subordinates may change the labels of identification by acquiring some of the cultural possessions of the superordinates; or they may become upwardly mobile and identify with a higher group. Acculturation and upward mobility are thus generally associated as aspects of social change. The process is more likely to occur in groups that are only culturally distinct, not racially different, and its occurrence generally increases with oncoming generations. Illustrative is the familiar picture of immigrant minority peoples in the United States whose distinctions were mainly cultural and social rather than physical.

On the American scene this twin process of acculturation and social mobility occurred over a span of generations as individuals hurdled the cultural and social barriers, ceasing to be marginal as they acquired some of the culture of the dominant sector of American society and moved upward into more advantageous social and economic positions. If the first, or even the second, generation of these peoples were culturally and socially marginal, this marginality has tended to recede with later generations. The change of their self-identity from foreign nationals to

Americans was a definite step toward integration and a significant change in their marginal status. But the process could have been terminated, or even reversed, at any stage.

The process just described does not necessarily occur, and if it does take place it may be slow and uneven. The French-Canadians have for generations lived in an interdependent relationship with Canadians having an English background, but mutual acculturation has been limited, social barriers have been relatively rigid, and social mobility between the subordinate and the superordinate community has been slow. Marginal situations created by cultural and social distinctions have persisted.

The situation in India, so far as the Anglo-Indians are concerned, has never paralleled the scene in the United States or Canada. The dominance of a colonial power and intense national loyalties, as well as cultural differences, complicated the process of acculturation and the integration of Anglo-Indians into Indian society. Whenever social differences are also complicated by visible racial features the barriers to interaction create persistent problems of marginality.

Marginal Situations and Status Differentials

If one interprets marginality in terms of inter-personal or inter-group relations it follows that the marginal situation must be defined in terms of these relationships. A few researches offer some clues in this respect. Kerckhoff and McCormick interpret a marginal group in terms of reference group theory, concluding that an individual is marginal when he "uses a nonmembership group as a reference group" if he himself represents a collectivity of lower status.[59] In this instance the marginal group was composed of American Indian children who had taken whites as their reference group, although they were not members nor were they generally acceptable socially by the whites. This, in the view of the authors, constituted a marginal situation. If this concept of marginality is applied to the Indian situation it would mean that the British, at least until Independence, was the reference group of the Anglo-Indians. The central focus of the Kerckhoff-McCormick research, however, was not so much on the sociological aspects of marginality as on the psychological effects of marginal relationships.

Dickie-Clark, on the other hand, interprets a marginal situation as a special aspect of social hierarchy between groups that are either subordinate or superordinate to each other in power or prestige. "What makes an hierarchical situation marginal in character is any inconsistency in the ranking of individual or collectivity in any matter regulated by the hierarchical structure." He goes on to say that this inconsistency is "almost always" between the cultural and social rankings as they are determined by the stratum or group which is dominant in power or prestige, but this is qualified with the statement that "it need not be so

---

[59] A. C. Kerckhoff and Thomas C. McCormick, "Marginal Status and Marginal Personality," *Social Forces,* 34 : 48-55 (1955). Cf. Kerckhoff, "An Investigation of Factors Operating in the Development of the Personality Characteristics of Marginality," Unpublished Ph.D. dissertation, University of Wisconsin, Madison, 1953.

and the inconsistent rankings may be entirely in one or the other of the two dimensions."[60]

It might reasonably be asked what justification is there for defining the subordinate group as marginal, but not the superordinate group. In case there is uncertainty about which is subordinate and which dominant, what group would be defined as marginal? The question could be even more complicated if a group were clearly subordinate in one respect and dominant in another. An equally relevant question would be the criterion, or criteria, of subordination and dominance in each marginal situation.

While some kind of differential in terms of power or prestige, or both, may be involved in most marginal situations, to make this the *sine qua non* of marginality appears to be too restricted an interpretation. Particular communities or collectivities may wilfully reject or accept the cultural traits or patterns of another group without any necessary reference to subordinate - superordinate positions in power or prestige of the groups involved; they may likewise reject or accept individuals or groups socially, for reasons unrelated to the matter of status or power. Furthermore, members of a particular group may have no desire to become socially acceptable in another specified group, or for that matter even to be identified with it, for any of a variety of reasons.

If we view the Anglo-Indians in India from this perspective it appears that they have little or no desire to be culturally or socially identified with, say, the Muslim community, nor do the Muslims appear to desire intimate identification with Anglo-Indians. The reasons for these reactions probably have little or no direct relevance to differentials of status or power because the two communities do not generally "appear" to be associated in a subordinate - superordinate relationship. Yet as distinctive religious or ethnic communities they are associated in common undertakings and responsibilities as citizens of India. It is possible, however, that Anglo-Indians may desire cultural and social acceptance by the Muslims, all the while being unacceptable to that community. In either of these situations, then, are the Anglo-Indians a marginal group? If they are accepted culturally or socially in part but not entirely, are they still a marginal group? It is our own view that they are marginal, even though, in theory, there may be no observable difference in status or power, or no categorical acceptance or rejection of them.

The phrase, "observable difference," itself creates a problem of analysis because differentials of status or power, of dominance and subordination, may or may not be easily determined, at least by any objective measure. Probably the most relevant criterion of status relations between the groups would be the subjective definitions of persons who are themselves involved. The status and power differentials between the South African communities (Whites, Coloureds, Indians, Africans) included in Dickie-Clark's research were fairly clear. But in some localities the differentials would not be so easily discerned.

It must be conceded, however, that among groups separated by barriers of race,

---

[60] F. H. Dickie-Clark, *op. cit.*, p. 185.

religion, nationality, language, or cultural heritage there are often differentials of status or power. This is so because these components are commonly loaded with sentiment and charged with emotion so that by their very nature they are generally evaluated as desirable or undesirable, good or bad, superior or inferior, subordinate or dominant, prestigious or otherwise. Those distinctions, sometimes invidious, are subjective and often irrational, but for the groups involved they are important in defining inter-group and inter-personal relationships.

Marginality and Ambiguities of Status and Role

The individual may find a marginal situation conducive to internal strains and tensions because of the ambiguity concerning his status and expected role. There are two facets to ambiguity: One, the uncertainty in the individual's mind as to who he is or where he belongs; second, the uncertainty concerning his proper or expected role performance. He may ask, Who am I? How shall I behave? Or, With whom can I interact, in what way, and in what kinds of situations? The ambiguity internalized in the individual may reflect the nebulous character of the situation, especially if there are conflicting definitions concerning the status and role of the individuals, or even of their actual identity. If the person's identity is unclear, or his expected role confusing, such a situation is likely to be disturbing, especially if he is emotionally involved in an uncertain relationship with one or more groups. The individual in such a situation we shall consider a marginal person.

Two illustrations may suffice: In the early days of the Anglo-Indian people in India there was no unanimity among others as to their actual identity. Were they Europeans living in India? Or Indians with a European cultural and racial heritage? What their own reactions were to this ambivalent situation we do not know, but it seems probable that many may have been confused as to their own social identity.

Whatever ambiguities that occur or problems of self-identity that arise may depend, in considerable measure, on the way the marginal individual defines the situation and the existing relationships. It is proverbial that individuals often view situations from different perspectives and read into them different meanings. What for one person is an ambiguous set of status-role expectations or confused self-identity may be quite clear to others of the same group. It is also true that the same individual may experience changes in perspective and definitions, resulting either in increasing or diminishing ambiguities of status, role, or self-identity. By the same reasoning, the situations may change, thus contributing to the uncertainties or ambiguities.

The Problem of Dual or Multiple Identity

Those ambiguities frequently associated with marginal situations may take the form of perplexing problems of self-identity. This problem may be intensified if there is no general consensus in reference to the group or community identification of particular individuals. The answer to the question, Who am I? may be unclear, and if it is unclear it can be disturbing. It is likely to be disturbing to the individual, however, only if he is emotionally involved in his relationship with persons in one or more groups.

Clarification of the individual's conception of his own identity may be enhanced by the transformation of his own group into a "community" that will afford him an anchorage in what may otherwise be an unstable and confusing social situation. It may provide an answer to the question, Who am I? The certainty provided by the answer may help to ease the internal strains that so often are associated with ambiguity. But there are other identities, some of which are important for the individual. That the Anglo-Indians in India have also developed a strong sense of community there can be no doubt. This has helped to sustain them in difficult situations when they were regarded as *persona non grata* by other peoples related to them by blood or culture.

The individual of dual racial parentage may have difficulty in developing a clear self-image partly because he is related by heredity to two (or more) peoples, one or both of which may reject him. If he identifies with one racial group and not the other he may alienate the group which he himself rejects and at the same time be unacceptable to the people of his choice. Throughout much of their history as a minority group this was the dilemma faced by many Anglo-Indians.

One of the difficulties that the person of dual racial heritage may encounter is the shifting of identity under political or social pressure. It can scarcely be doubted that most Anglo-Indians identified with the British while the Empire was firmly established in India. But when it came apparent that the days of the Empire in India were numbered, that an independent India was destined to emerge, Anglo-Indians were faced with the prospect of identifying with the indigenous population as Indian nationals or being labeled as aliens in their own country. Such a shift of identity has involved considerable soul-searching. It should not be concluded, however, that a dual or multiple racial ancestry automatically creates problems of identity for the individual. This problem arises only when one or both kin groups judge him unworthy and unacceptable, provided he strongly desires acceptance by such groups.

Dual or multiple identity with reference to racial or cultural communities often becomes the basis for charges of divided loyalties and allegations that individuals having separate identities represent a threat to the dominant society or to particular communities. During a period of American history when public sentiment toward immigrants was negative and suffused with considerable hostility, the term "hyphenated Americans," applied opprobriously to them, inferred that they were divided in their loyalties and were therefore not desirable citizens. Such a climate of opinion directed to minorities whose cultural or racial heritage set them apart from the majority was the basis for increasing their cultural and social marginality and consequently intensifying their feelings of insecurity. Under social and political pressures some renounced their own cultural heritage or endeavored in various ways to demonstrate their loyalty as Americans. Others solved the dilemma by returning to their original homeland. Anglo-Indians in India have likewise been suspected of divided national loyalties. Most of them have declared or otherwise attempted to demonstrate their loyalty to Mother

India, but many have sought a solution to the ambiguities of marginality by migrating to another country. The "divided loyalty" charge has also been directed, at times, to the Jewish community in various countries.

Marginality and Personality Syndromes

A marginal situation or relationship may be described objectively in terms of social interaction, patterns of social relations, or cultural difference, but the way that a situation is defined by the individual, the meanings he reads into it, and the significance it has for him personally, or for his group in general, are also important. Not only do the situations vary, but the reactions to these situations are also variable. The nature of these reactions and their consequences to the structure of personality are central to psychological studies of the individual. If it can be established that certain kinds of situations tend to produce certain personality syndromes, a giant stride will have been made toward an understanding of the nexus between personality and the social order. In the following section a brief discussion will be presented concerning the nature of this problem only because it is relevant to any analysis of marginality. The principal focus of this book, however, is not psychological but sociological in terms of situations and relationships that may be defined as marginal.

The issue concerning the effect of marginality on personality and behavior is still unresolved. The pioneers of "marginal man" theory, Park[61] and Stonequist,[62] viewed the marginal man as one who, because of his marginal position in one or more groups, is beset with inner conflicts and strains often manifest in psycho-neurotic syndromes or in aberrant behavior. They arrived at these judgements not from the findings of disciplined investigation but from general observations or from personal documents such as biographical or autobiographical accounts by persons in marginal situations. The marginal man was seen as essentially a product of cultural or racial conflict, covert or overt, which induces internal stresses and tensions. They conceded, however, that the marginal man might be more intellectually sophisticated or culturally emancipated than others because of stimulating experiences in a marginal situation between two or more groups.

That certain psychological syndromes do appear in individuals occupying a marginal position seems certain, but it does not necessarily follow that they are any more prevalent in marginal individuals than in others, or that their nature is predictable from known facts. Indeed, the ideal-construct of a universal marginal man exhibiting particular attributes is not supported by convincing empirical evidence. The problems of psychological marginality are important, however, but they have not been the focus of much solid empirical research.

[61] Robert E. Park, "Human Migration and the Marginal Man," *American Journal of Sociology* 33 : 881-893 (May, 1928). Cf. Park's collected papers in *Race and Culture,* (Glencoe, Illinois: The Free Press, 1950).

[62] Everett V. Stonequist, "The Problem of the Marginal Man," *American Journal of Sociology,* 41 : 1-12 (July 1935). Cf. Stonequist, *The Marginal Man* (New York: Scribners, 1937).

From various studies and observations, the tentative proposition might be proposed that a crucial component in the appearance of marginality syndromes involves both the felt need of an individual to identify with a particular group, or to be accepted by it, and the rejection of the individual by that group. One who has no such needs or aspirations would not likely experience internal strains as a result of rejection.

Marginal situations and relationships do not always create ambiguity as to status and role, nor are conceptions of self-identity necessarily blurred. Much depends on the cultural or social differences that exist between groups, how these differences are defined, and the attitudes of members of the in-group toward the other-group.

The group that represents the subject of this research, the Anglo-Indian minority community of India and Britain, is viewed from the perspective of cultural and social marginality in its varied aspects. As we have already noted, the group is culturally similar to the British in India or in England, but socially marginal to them in that they have not been accorded full social acceptance in many aspects of social life. On the other hand, they are both culturally and socially marginal to the indigenous Indian "communities'" whether Hindu, Muslim, Parsee, Sikh, Jewish, or any other. In subsequent chapters we shall explore the various facets of Anglo-Indian marginality in India.

CHAPTER FOUR

ATTITUDES AND IMAGES

THE purpose of this chapter is to examine the attitudes others hold toward the Anglo-Indians, the attitudes that they hold toward other peoples and toward themselves. These attitudes are commonly associated with stereotypes — images that others, mainly Indians or British, carry in their minds about the Anglo-Indians, perceptions the Anglo-Indians have of others, and the images they have of themselves and of their own Community.[63] These attitudes and images determine, in considerable measure, the nature of inter-group and inter-personal relations.

Throughout most of the recorded history of the Anglo-Indian Community the subjective aspect of their relations with other Indians must, by necessity, be inferred from overt acts of one kind or another. It seems reasonable that acts of discrimination, for example, generally reflect negative attitudes of the discriminator toward the objects of discrimination. There is considerable historical evidence concerning overt behavior, especially of the British, directed toward the Anglo-Indians. Most of the data in this chapter, however, are direct expressions of attitudes and images that bear upon contemporary inter-personal and inter-group relations.

Attitudes and Actions in Historical Perspective

The position of the Anglo-Indian people in the colonial empire was influenced by various factors or situations, one of the most important being color. Color prejudice was widespread among the British in India and England, apparently more so than among the Portuguese, Dutch, or French, who also attempted an empire-building enterprise in the sub-continent. Goodrich, in her social-historical analysis, presents the opinion that color prejudice among the British was mainly on an individual basis before the end of the eighteenth century, and the Anglo-Indians were so judged.[64] One type of evidence to support this conclusion

---

[63] Data on attitudes relating to the Anglo-Indian Community, as presented herein, were obtained from a variety of sources: interviews with Anglo-Indians and other Indians, historical documents, letters, personal opinions in books and periodical literature, and questionnaires filled out by Anglo-Indians and Indian college students.

There are numerous methodological problems involved in such a study. One is the problem of validity. Another is the representativeness of the sample. There was no way, within the limits of the methodology here employed, that the validity of statements could be systematically checked, nor was it possible to obtain a statistically representative sample of Anglo-Indians either in the country as a whole or in particular communities.

[64] Dorris Goodrich, "The Making of an Ethnic Community: The Eurasian Minority in India," Unpublished Ph. D. dissertation, University of California, Berkeley, 1952, p. 236.

was the policy followed by the East India Company of sending *fair* Anglo-Indian children to England for an education, at the same time excluding *dark* children. After the eighteenth century color prejudice was directed against the Anglo-Indians *as a class*. This psychological climate gave rise to numerous stereotypes, mostly negative, which purported to describe the character and behavior of the Anglo-Indian minority.

The negative attitudes of the British toward the Anglo-Indian people persisted, with varying degrees of intensity, throughout most of the span of the Empire in India. This is evidenced by various acts of discrimination directed against Anglo-Indians or by indifference to their economic or political plight. In the courts of India members of the Community did not have the same protection that other peoples enjoyed. "Hindus were subject to Hindu law, Muslims to Muslim law, and British subjects (those born in Britain) to British law."[65] But the Anglo-Indians, however, were legally in a marginal situation. Their position was defined according to what provided the British with the greatest benefit. The discrimination exercised against them in military service and general employment likewise reflected attitudes of distrust or hostility on the part of the European overlords. Even when, in the latter years of the Empire in India, they were favored in occupations strategic to the Empire's operations they were nevertheless rejected in the arena of European social life. The British "looked down" on their kinsmen as hapless creatures who lacked the moral fiber of the Englishman but who could nevertheless be used to further the interests of the East India Company or the Empire, or for that matter even of individual Britishers. The fact that marriages between Anglo-Indians and the British in India were generally opposed, at times prohibited, could be regarded as efforts by the British to maintain wide social distance between themselves and the Anglo-Indian Community.

Although there is limited historical evidence of Anglo-Indian reactions to this discrimination, and to the negative attitudes of the British, their awareness undoubtedly affected their own attitude both toward the British and toward themselves. Goodrich argues that the rise of anti-Anglo-Indian sentiment and the varied forms of discrimination against the Anglo-Indian people helped to create a community-consciousness among them.[66] Numerous meetings involving action-oriented members of this minority were held during which the problems of the group were considered and the prospects of the future discussed. It was the beginning of an organized community life.

Although they must have resented British snobbery and the discrimination against them, they were nevertheless cultural and biological kinsmen of Britons (or sometimes Portuguese, French, or Dutch) and were largely dependent upon their colonial masters for their very existence.

Throughout the colonial period of India's history the Anglo-Indians, in spite of their disadvantaged position, tended to identify with the British and to admire much in British character and culture. But this was not merely blind admiration

---

[65] *Ibid.* p. 230-237.
[66] *Ibid.,* p. 7.

or servile acceptance of the position and power of the British overlords. Anglo-Indians were resentful of the arrogance of many Britishers and chafed under the discrimination to which they were often subjected.[67] Young Anglo-Indians especially resented the intrusions of the British soldiers who often sought to exploit sexually Anglo-Indian women or to "crash the gates" as uninvited guests at social functions. Sometimes these situations resulted in physical assaults. The "gate-crashing" behavior, still exhibited by young Indians, is resented by members of the Community.

If the British generally viewed the Anglo-Indians with contempt and disdain, while often exploiting them for their own advantage, Anglo-Indians in turn reflected British snobbery in their relations with other Indians. Their cultural and biological kinship to the British, and in the latter decades of the Empire in India their occupationally advantaged position, undoubtedly gave them a feeling of superiority over other Indians, whom they regarded, stereotypically, as an inferior order of humanity. Like the British, they sometimes employed the opprobrious term "nigger" with reference to other Indians.

Most of them manifest little regard for indigenous Indian culture, had little knowledge of Indian philosophy, literature, religion, or art, and seldom made a serious effort to learn an Indian language. European civilization, in their judgment, was superior to Indian civilization, and Europeans had certainly demonstrated their military superiority over Indians. Anglo-Indian parents commonly indoctrinated their children with these attitudes and endeavored to isolate them from intimate association with Indian children. If the other Indians were dominated or exploited, like themselves, by the British they received little sympathy from the Anglo-Indians, who felt a close cultural kinship to the Europeans even though they realized they were not socially acceptable to them.

Under these circumstances it was virtually inevitable that the other Indians would resent the Anglo-Indians, whom they tended to regard as British lackeys. It was not so much that the Anglo-Indians were oriented to European rather than Indian culture—many other Indians were also Europeanized—it was because their motives were suspect and their character questionable. At best they were regarded as persons with divided loyalties; at worst, as outright or potential enemies. From the Indian viewpoint they were arrogant interlopers who could not rightfully claim the protection of Mother India. Indians and Anglo-Indians went their own respective cultural and social ways, although tolerating each other's existence and cooperating in some of the main affairs of life.

As Contemporary Indian Students View the Anglo-Indians

A limited survey of attitudes of students toward Anglo-Indians was conducted in Calcutta and Jadavpur universities and St. Xavier's College, all in Calcutta, in 1964, with 67 students, mostly Bengali Hindus, participating. Using a modified

[67] Frank Anthony, *Britain's Betrayal in India* (New Delhi: Allied Publishers, 1969), pp. 375-77.

version of a well-known social distance type of test, a questionnaire was administered to the sample, with the request that they indicate the rank order of acceptance or non-acceptance in specified relationships for six designated categories of people: Egyptians, Parsees, British, Jews, Anglo-Indians, and African Negroes. These relationships were as follows: inter-marriage, inter-dining, close personal friendship, residence in the same flat or house, and membership in the same club. Thus a question: "I would − −, or would not − − be willing to marry a person from this group, or approve a member of my community or family marrying such a person; or have no opinion," may be viewed as a willingness or unwillingness to accept an individual from another group in one of the most intimate of relationships. The six ethnic peoples are here ranked preferentially as follows, the digits indicating the number, out of a total of 67, who approved inter-marriage with each group:

Rank order
1. British   56
2. Parsees   44
3. Egyptian   35
4. Anglo-Indian   26
5. Jew   25
6. African Negro   12

A similar rank order of acceptability was found for other kinds of relationships. For example, rank order of acceptability for Anglo-Indians in each of these relationships was as follows: inter-dining, 2 (tied with Parsees); close friendship, 5; membership in same club, 3; neighbor in the same house or flat, 5.

The rank order of acceptability for each of the relationships does not alone give a complete picture of preferences. But in each stated relationship, or situation, the British were by far the most acceptable. As indicated above in two of the situations the Anglo-Indians ranked next to the least acceptable group, but in one they were just below the British, along with the Parsees. A longer list of ethnic groupings might have provided a more accurate calibration of preferences among students, but by limiting the list to six groups, carefully chosen, the respondents were able to complete the questionnaire in one class period.

To supplement the foregoing data obtained from the questionnaire, the students were asked to take an overall or categorical view of these six ethnic groups and rank them in order of personal preference, assigning a rank value of 1 to the most preferred group and so on to the least preferred group with a value of 6. A score was obtained by recording the number of expressed selections on each preferential level from 1 to 6, multiplying the number of preferences by the value of that level, adding the results to obtain the gross sum, then dividing by the total number of preferences designated.[68] By arranging the scores on a scale the

---

[68] Egyptians and African Negroes were selected because the students had limited personal knowledge of these people. Hence their evaluations were mainly stereotypical images − or possibly no image at all. The evaluative ranking of Egyptians and African Negroes was compared with the ranking of the four people about whom the students had considerable first hand knowledge.

rank order of ethnic preferences was obtained. The rank order and scores are as follows:

    1. British[69]   1.7
    2. Parsees   3.5
    3. Egyptians   3.5
    4. African Negroes 4.2
    5. Jews   4.2
    6. Anglo-Indians 4.5

Finally, the students were requested to designate the terms that, in their judgment, (1) most nearly described the members of the Anglo-Indian community (and also the five other communities) and (2) the characteristics or attributes, if any, of the Anglo-Indians that they especially liked or disliked. Of the seventy descriptive terms proposed, most of them appeared to be stereotypical images of the Community and its members. Some were negative; others positive.

One stereotype frequently appearing in this study was that they are fickle, shallow, and concerned primarily with frivolous matters and having fun. Another was that they are good workers on routine or mechanical tasks but lack the intellectual depth or seriousness of purpose in efforts that require much mental effort. Still another was that they are lacking in moral character, especially the girls. Some of them believe that Anglo-Indians are industrious, but spend their earnings recklessly in the pursuit of pleasure.

In designating the qualities or attributes which the Indian students especially liked or disliked about the Anglo-Indians, 34 "likeable" qualities were mentioned as compared with 68 "unlikeable" characteristics. As in the case of the descriptive terms mentioned above, many of the expressions although worded differently, referred to essentially similar attributes. Furthermore, there was considerable overlapping of descriptive terms — the stereotypes — and the terminology of "like" and "dislike". Among the reputed qualities of the Anglo-Indians which were admired were their industriousness, their capacity to enjoy life, and their friendliness. On the negative side were their uncertain loyalty, questionable morals, snobbishness, and general style of life, the latter a vague characterization which could include several things and therefore have a variety of meanings. Said one student, whose viewpoint seems to be widely held:

> They (Anglo-Indians) possess a superiority complex toward us Indians. They have exceptionally loose morals, and pretend to be Westernized. The fairer ones proudly proclaim themselves to be of British origin, whereas the darker ones reluctantly admit that they are Indians.

The following are representative of the "desirable" and "undesirable" qualities applied to the Anglo-Indians by the Indian College students in their own terminology:

---

[69] Obviously, if *all* the students had preferred the British, the score for that ethnic category would have been 1. Similarly, if all of them had ranked the Anglo-Indians in sixth place, their score would have been 6. But there was no unanimity as to the preferential rankings.

"Desirable"	"Undesirable"
Cleanliness	Imitation of the British
Ability to work hard	Fickleness
Friendliness	Anti-Indian attitude
Bravery	Easy virtue
Perseverance	No taste for culture or civilization
Cleverness	Lack of love for the country
Capacity to make the best of life	Do not regard themselves as Indians
Good Natured	Feelings of superiority toward Indians
Energetic	Their bias toward Western culture
Sportsmanship	Snobbery

One would not be justified in making broad generalizations concerning attitudes held by Indians toward Anglo-Indians on the basis of statements made by a limited number of University students in Calcutta. But what is generally known about the attitudes of Indians in various stations of life and regions of India, it seems reasonable that the student reactions are fairly representative of attitudes and stereotypes of middle-class urban people in Calcutta and perhaps even in other cities. It certainly would be misleading to assume that *all* Indians are unfavorable in their attitudes toward Anglo-Indians; even among students there are persons who feel warmly toward the Community, admire some of the qualities of its members, and attempt to understand their disabilities as well as their abilities. Most of the students listed terms that were both positive and negative, and some suggested neutral or merely descriptive characteristics. In ranking Anglo-Indians sixth in order of preference, one of the students explained the rationale for placing them last in his rank order:

> The Anglo-Indians, much though I like and know many of them individually, have never done anything spectacular — nor do they show any such promise. As a result, I have to place them last in order of preference. This does not, however, imply that I'm in any way prejudiced against them or am unwilling to mix with them.

It is instructive to compare Indian student attitudes toward the Anglo-Indians with their assessment of the British. In every hypothetical situation, and on all counts, the British ranked highest in the esteem of the Indian students. Although the British were neither culturally nor biologically akin to the Indians, and were for many decades their colonial masters, the students were generally more favorably disposed toward them than toward the Anglo-Indians who have all along been citizens of India and are "half brothers" to the Indians themselves. Even though the Indians were often socially rejected by the British, their stereotypes of Englishmen tended to be more favorable than unfavorable. In fact, the number of expressed "likes" exceeded the number of "dislikes" by two to one, just the reverse of student evaluations of the Anglo-Indians. Even the Parsees, whose cultural kinship to most Indians is rather limited, ranked well ahead of the Anglo-Indians in the acceptability score. The expression of adulation by one of the students may offer a clue to the high preferential ranking accorded the British: "I prefer the Britisher most. For, despite many characteristic flaws, they are one of the greatest people on earth, shrewd, efficient, and well-meaning. Their greatness is emphasized by their world leadership till the end of the last war." The same student also stated, however, that he disliked British "snobbery and hypocrisy."

The unfavorable attitudes of Indians toward Anglo-Indians, wherever and whenever they may exist today, reflect an accumulation of experiences, over the decades, that have characterized relations between the Anglo-Indian Community, on the one hand, and the British and Indian peoples, on the other. The Indians remember, or know about, the support that the Anglo-Indians gave the British in the Sepoy Mutiny in 1857, as well as the many other forms of assistance that helped to strengthen the Empire in India. They remember the preferential treatment accorded Anglo-Indians by the British in the allocation of jobs in such fields as transportation, communications, and the police forces, commonly to the exclusion of other Indian workers. They remember the arrogance toward Indians so often exhibited by Anglo-Indians and the transmission of these attitudes of superiority to their children, who in turn expressed the same attitude in their relations with other Indian children. They may have observed the obsequious behavior of Anglo-Indians in the presence of the British, who reciprocated with behavior expressive of contempt for their own kith and kin. It is not surprising, then, that the Anglo-Indians are suspect by many other Indians, that their genuine sincerity was doubted when they asked to be considered as *bona fide* Indian nationals with all the rights and prerogatives of Indian citizenship.

If the voices of criticism of Anglo-Indians are more strident than the voices of friendly understanding it is not necessarily because there are no admirers or supporters of the Anglo-Indian Community. Quite the contrary. Some feel that the Anglo-Indians were victims of historic forces and circumstances and that their present behavior should be viewed, and therefore understood, in light of this historic past. A knowledgeable Anglican church official in Calcutta remarked that the protection provided by the British gave Anglo-Indians a false sense of security and that some of their present economic difficulties stem from the long years of dependency; hence when Independence came they were unable to bridge the gap to self-sufficiency as the Parsees and other minority groups have done. In his view, the Community is in need of sympathetic understanding by the Indian people, who should "let bygones be bygones."

A similar point of view was expressed by a well-known nun in charge of Catholic welfare services for the City of Calcutta. In the distribution of food, clothing, and medical supplies to the indigent she reported that the cultural distinctions between Anglo-Indians and others were recognized. Anglo-Indian children were generally furnished shoes because wearing shoes is a cultural practice of their Community, whereas indigent children of other Indians had less cultural need for shoes. Yet the sympathetic attitudes of numerous religious leaders have not been sufficient to avoid criticism that the churches, Catholic and Protestant, have not measured up to their moral responsibilities for the Anglo-Indian Community. The British principal of a school in Bangalore asserted, for example, that such church-related organizations as the YMCA and YWCA were primarily concerned with providing a place to live and certain physical amenities, but were not much interested in the protection and rehabilitation of Anglo-Indian children and youth in serious need of assistance.

How Others View the Anglo-Indians

A few novelists have dealt with the Anglo-Indian, commonly in an unfavorable way. In a well-known fictional work, *Bhovani Junction,* by John Masters, the principal character is a young Anglo-Indian woman of high intelligence, rare beauty, and exceptional courage and resourcefulness whose bedroom activities with British Officers were described in considerable detail. Anglo-Indians generally resent the Masters portrayal of the young woman, saying that it is a slanderous and unwarranted attack on Anglo-Indian womanhood. Earlier, such writers as Katherine Mayo, Somerset Maugham, and Rudyard Kipling depicted the Anglo-Indian in an unfavorable light. The central character of Bruce's novel, *The Eurasian,* was pictured as a weak, drug-addicted, illegitimate son of a British officer and an Indian prostitute. So far as we are aware, fictional literature rarely depicts either the Anglo-Indian man or woman as admirable persons of unblemished moral character or outstanding intellectual competence.

Some Indians are outspokenly hostile toward members of the Anglo-Indian Community, charging them with all the sins of apostasy and moral dereliction. They are, in the eyes of these harsh critics, unworthy of Indian citizenship. This extremist view is exemplified in the following statement by one who is clearly contemptuous of the entire Anglo-Indian Community:

> The "products of British adultery" are once again in the news. The worm that was content to sidle behind the rears of burra sahibs and lick the boots of uncouth British tommies has not turned, and it appears it is no longer in the mood to do the "dirty work" of an "ungrateful administration."
>
> ... A leopard can never change its spots — it can only change its masters, and this sudden transformation on the part of Anglo-India must be considered more of a case of rats leaving a sinking ship than a sudden love for Mother India.
>
> ... Let them go back to where they have always wanted to be: in the arms of white soldiers and licking the jack boots of Imperialism.
>
> ... No, we do not want them. We never did and we never shall. India has fought alone and India shall continue to fight alone. Their high sounding platitudes now must not deceive us. The very fact that they are now willing to change allegiance and come over to the other camp should be enough to betray them for what they really are — a freak section of humanity, opportunists of the first water and traitors to the very core of their halfcaste hearts.
>
> "Give them the boot," therefore should be the reply of Mother India to Mr. Frank Anthony.[70]

One rarely encounters such vitriolic hostility toward the Anglo-Indians as in this verbal attack. Such a statement must, however, be placed in the proper time perspective: the pre-Independence period when Anglo-Indians were suspect, when

---

[70] Mohammed Nazir, pamphlet printed by Wagh Process Studio and Press, Bombay, July 1946.

anti-British hostilities were strong, when even Western attire was symbolic of imperialism. Here several stereotypes stand out: stooges of the British; lax morality of Anglo-Indian women; traitors to India; opportunists. The entire Anglo-Indian Community is attacked, without reference to the characteristics of individuals within that minority. Other writers, more restrained, may nevertheless deal with the Community in stereotypical fashion. The following excerpt from the recent work of a well-known Bengali writer is an example:

> Young Eurasians (Anglo-Indians), both boys and girls, showed a weak and degenerate form of exuberant animal spirits of the English schoolboy and girl ... To young Eurasian girls, more especially, the instability gave a deceptive beauty, like that of a rime-covered, but canker-eaten, moss rose. ... Even before age and married life had congealed the Eurasian wives into their natural commonplaceness, they showed themselves as women with whom it was impossible to live. They were either wax dolls without a mind but capable, nevertheless, of looking frighteningly unhappy, or demons driven by a heady but very volatile essence of sensuality with no body.[71]

The author seems particularly preoccupied with the purported sexual habits of Anglo-Indian women, commenting on the abundance of prostitutes and their snob appeal to Indian men, and also on the "amateur practitioners in the community" who, with the professionals, have jeopardized the reputation of morally upright Anglo-Indian women. There is a tendency, he says, "among the Hindus who are on the sensual quest to look upon all Eurasian girls, irrespective of their conduct, as fair prey."[72] We are not here concerned with the accuracy of these observations but with the fact that they are stereotypical images of Anglo-Indian womanhood. This image appears to be widespread among Indians who are negatively disposed to the Anglo-Indian Community. It is presumably what they *want* to believe.

Social scientists have generally subjected prevailing stereotypes to critical examination, usually rejecting them as invalid evidence of the character of a people, but even recognized scholars have sometimes accepted the stereotypical images of racial or ethnic groups without serious examination of the evidence. Thus E. B. Reuter, a sociologist with special interests in race relations, repeats uncritically, in a book published in 1918, some of the stereotypes of Anglo-Indians as presented in popular literature. To quote from him:

> Physically the Eurasians (Anglo-Indians) are slight and weak. Their personal appearance is subject to the greatest variations. ... They are naturally indolent and will enter into no employment requiring exertion or labor. This lack of energy is correlated with an incapacity for organization. They will not assume burdensome responsibilities, but they make passable clerks where only routine labor is required... The native woman is inordinately proud of her half-caste offspring. In infancy he is nursed, and in youth pampered by his native servants upon whom he is dependent... In manhood he is wily, untrustworthy, and untruthful. He is lacking in independence and is forever begging for special favors.... The girls in some cases are sold into prostitution. The

---

[71] Nirad C. Chaudhuri, *The Continent of Circe: An Essay on the Peoples of India,* (London: Chatto and Windus, Ltd., 1965), 260-261.
[72] *Ibid.,* p. 264.

men are employed for the most part by the government in subordinate clerical positions... They (the Eurasians) are miserable, helpless, despised, and neglected.[73]

It would be difficult indeed to find in social science literature an array of stereotypical images as grossly distorted and misleading as the ones presented by Reuter in the guise of sociological scholarship.[74] That these and other images of the Anglo-Indians have been widely disseminated and uncritically accepted there can be no doubt. They persist because they are reinforced by the prejudices of individuals who have a psychological need for such stereotypes and a mental aversion to objective assessment of the culture and behavior of people.

Expressions of unfavorable attitudes tend to be focused, however, on other allegedly questionable character traits of the Anglo-Indian, notably their claims to the rights and privileges of citizenship, which many Indians regard as spurious and deceptive. "Go into any Anglo-Indian home," an educated Hindu woman in Bombay remarked to the senior author, "and there you will see on the wall, conspicuously displayed, a picture of the British queen. This reveals how they feel about their own nationality." In the authors' experience this is a gross exaggeration, but the fact that such stereotypes do exist is revealing of anti-Anglo-Indian attitudes. A young Indian-Christian man in Bangalore remarked that he had no sympathy for the Anglo-Indians who are now experiencing unusual hardships because, he said, they were contemptuous of the Indians as long as they were sheltered by the British in India. "They deserve what they are now getting." An educated Bombay Hindu, holding a minor clerical position, was critical of Anglo-Indians on the grounds that they do not identify with India. He was especially harsh in his criticism of Anglo-Indians who held British passports and hope to leave India.

Even Indians who are not especially unfavorable to Anglo-Indians generally feel that the matter of national identity is the principal obstruction to social acceptance by non-Anglo-Indians. The director of a social science institute in Bombay, himself a Hindu, said that much of the hostility toward Anglo-Indians was based on the widespread assumption that they do not consider themselves Indians, or at least did not in the past. A more favorable attitude toward Anglo-Indians was held by an Indian-Christian woman in Bombay, a librarian, who remarked that while the Anglo-Indians did consider themselves superior to Indians, at least during the British period, this feeling of superiority was also true of other Indian communities, especially in inter-caste relations.

In the world of work Anglo-Indian girls are generally considered good secretaries and nurses. However, a Parsee business woman in Calcutta agreed that Anglo-Indian girls, while technically competent and efficient, are often unreliable,

---

[73] E. B. Reuter, *The Mulatto in the United States: Including a Study of the Role of Mixed-Blood Races Throughout the World* (Boston: Gorham Press, 1918), pp. 29-31. Reuter cites some of the sources of his information.

[74] Even earlier, H. N. Ridley, a well-known scientist, stated in a paper presented at the meeting of the Straits Philosophical Society in 1895: "Taking the race (Eurasians) as a whole, they are weak in body, short-lived, deficient in energy, and feeble in morals." Quoted in Cedric Dover, *Cimmerii? or The Eurasians and Their Future* (Calcutta: The Modern Art Press, 1929), p. 16.

prone to neglecting their work, leaving early, or arriving late, unless closely supervised. A young Calcutta Hindu woman, a clerical administrative assistant, made the assessment that Anglo-Indian secretaries are usually so impersonally involved in office matters that they could be depended upon not to reveal office confidential information — their major interests were in pretty dresses, dances, movies, and having a "good time." Most Indians, however, see the Anglo-Indian girl in a quite different light — as a skillful and responsible worker whose services are in considerable demand.

How Anglo-Indians Imagine Others See Them

Anglo-Indians may infer from the statements or acts of others the attitudes toward them or the images held of them. If, for example, they conclude that they have been the objects of discrimination, the logical inference is that the discriminatory acts reflect unfavorable or hostile attitudes. In a questionnaire submitted to 52 employed Anglo-Indians in Bangalore, the question was asked: "Have you at any time ever felt rejected or discriminated against by members of other communities? Explain." Nearly three-fourths answered in the negative, and one did not respond. A comment by one who indicated that he had never felt rejected was, "Being a long-time resident family in Bangalore, we are treated with great respect by all we come in contact with." Another said, "No, because I move amicably in all communities." Most of the fifteen who stated that they felt rejected offered some explanation. Representative comments from those who answered "Yes" to this question follow:

> Yes, but I don't know exactly why for I don't have much to do with other communities, except in the factory. It's only during the lunch hour that I know they reject us eating meat and eggs because they consider the cow sacred. (Male manual worker)

> I have felt very discriminated against especially by Brahmins. They have called me "khaki," "eight anna," and "legacy of the British." (Male teacher)

> Other communities "accept" us formally, but "hate our guts" for various reasons. Not obviously, of course, but one has to admit it exists. (Male service officer)

> As an Anglo-Indian with a British way of life and English for a mother tongue, I have felt that I symbolize an age and regime that is odious to present Indian sentiment. I have felt myself rejected because my values, in the realms of language, religion, food, music, entertainment, and fair play are different from those of my contemporaries. My complexion has also contributed to a certain degree of discrimination. (Male service officer)

> The discriminatory attitude of the Indian toward the Anglo-Indian community is always present as we are constant reminders to them of the qualities of English gentlemanliness and decency which in spite of their education and travel abroad will never be able to emulate as these qualities are not ingrained in them. (Male accountant)

About half of the respondents stated that they had received special advantages from another community, which would suggest that some of them regarded these actions as expressions of friendliness. Others interpreted such actions as a *quid pro quo.* These positive responses to the query, "Have you ever been given any special advantages or favorable treatment by members of other communities?" do not, however, rule out the possibility that they may also have been favorably treated by one community and rejected by another. A considerable variety of "explanations" were offered, among which the following were representative of those who answered "Yes" in the questionnaire:

> Their behavior toward me has always been friendly and respectful. (Male electrician in Navy)

> In India if you do anyone a favor you expect one back yourself. (Male physical director)

> To begin with I am able to converse freely in two Indian languages, and being an Anglo-Indian it always gives due importance. (Female office manager)

> Muslims accept us more readily, firstly because they are a minority like us, and secondly because of religious reasons. (Male service officer)

> I have been respected by other communities, perhaps because of my good behavior, training, and discipline taught me at an Anglo-Indian school. (Male secretary)

> We Anglo-Indians are treated by other communities as one of their own, and they have a lot of respect especially for a well-behaved Anglo-Indian. (Male Mechanic)

Anglo-Indians are generally aware of the attitudes that other Indians hold toward them and of the popular images which are held concerning Anglo-Indian behavior and character. The awareness that these attitudes and images are often unfavorable tends to intensify feelings of insecurity and to elicit reciprocal responses of a similar nature. Because they are exceedingly preoccupied with their status, present and future, as a small Western-oriented minority in a vast Asian society they are sensitive to real or imagined discrimination, especially in the labor market. They know full well that many Indians regard them as interlopers unworthy of Indian nationality. Hence they are confronted with the dilemma of working out a satisfactory *modus vivendi* that might reduce their social and cultural marginality, or ultimately with leaving the country altogether. Because of their tenuous position as a marginal minority they tend to be discreet or restrained about criticisms of Indians or the Indian system, although some are more articulate in this respect than others.

Because he occupies a position of power and influence, not only in the Anglo-Indian Community but in wider circles as well, Frank Anthony, member of the *Lok Sabha* (Parliament) and president of the All-India Anglo-Indian Association, is sometimes publicly outspoken in his criticisms of treatment accorded minority peoples in India. In a widely publicized speech in the *Lok Sabha* in 1964, Anthony asserted that "the minority peoples of India walk in the shadow of death," apparently implying that none of the minority groups was secure because of the attitudes of other Indians and discrimination exercised against them. It was an attack on the evils of "communalism," on bigotry and against mistreatment of minority peoples. The speech elicited such a violent reaction among other members of Parliament present that it was not possible even for him to complete his prepared manuscript. Later, in an explanatory statement concerning the speech, Anthony stated that the rude interruption prevented him from communicating the purpose of the charge, namely, that he was deeply concerned about the rise of communalism in India and wished to warn the public of this danger.

Judging from the tone of letters published in the press, the Anthony speech elicited considerable disagreement, mainly from other Indians. Even among Anglo-Indians there was some disagreement, although most of the letters supported his position. One Anglo-Indian wrote, "The statement made by Frank Anthony is baseless and malicious... Statements like these are bound to create unrest." A letter to the editor, written by a Hindu, stated that Anthony "has done great harm to the Anglo-Indian community, which he represents." On the other hand, a Muslim wrote that "Mr. Frank Anthony deserves a vote of thanks for his outspoken speech in the *Lok Sabha*," and a prominent Anglo-Indian community leader stated that Anthony's accusations squared with the facts as he knew them. "The truth of these observations cannot be denied by any impartial observer," he said.[75] The reactions to Anthony's speech seem to indicate a rather wide "understanding gap" between minority communities and the larger body politic consisting mainly of Hindus. Of several Anglo-Indians with whom this matter was personally discussed, only one disagreed with Anthony's "shadow of death" speech. But we would expect the majority of Hindus to refute it.

As Anglo-Indians See Other Indians

Like other Indians, Anglo-Indians have long memories. They remember, with some feeling of resentment, the difficulties they have experienced in the job situation as a result, some aver, of discrimination against them. They are resentful of what they consider to be an unjust assessment of their moral character, especially the character of Anglo-Indian womanhood. They are deeply concerned about the political maneuvers of certain Indian politicians to terminate the use of English as a medium of instruction in Anglo-Indian schools, saying that this is an indirect attack on the Community itself. They smart under the insinuations that they are not loyal citizens and feel resentful that they are regarded as unwanted guests in the land of their birth. Admitting that their past attitudes and behavior toward the Indian people were often regrettable, that they enjoyed preferential treatment by the British, they now insist that times have changed, and with the passing of time have come changes in their own attitudes. Above all, they want to be judged on their merit as loyal citizens willing and eager to work with other Indians for the welfare of their country.

Anglo-Indians are by no means unanimous in their attitudes toward other Indians. Probably this variance reflects the kinds of experience that individuals or families have had concerning their relationships with Indian people. Those who have experienced discrimination, or some form of social rejection, by other Indians

---

[75] The foregoing quotations from letters printed in *The Statesman* (Calcutta), April 15, 16, and 17, 1964.

are probably more prone to criticism than those who are secure in their jobs and are socially accepted. This interpretation suggests a simplistic version of the frustration-agression hypothesis, but such a version would scarcely be adequate unless it takes into account the complex web of social interaction among Anglo-Indians and between Anglo-Indians and other Indian people.

A member of the legislative assembly in West Bengal was strongly assertive of occupational discrimination because no Anglo-Indian has the right kind of power or influence to obtain desirable jobs. A retired army officer, preparing to migrate to a Western country, expressed harsh criticism of the Indian system, of the alleged corruption in the form of bribery and black marketing which he had encountered, of the probable imminence of a Hindu *raj* in which all minorities would be at a diasadvantage, and of discrimination against Anglo-Indians in the military services. Despite all the talk about freedom of speech, he said, one quickly realized that it was mostly a myth that had little relation to reality.

The attitudes both of Anglo-Indians and other Indians may be the result (1) of socialization into the value system of family, community, or peer group or (2) the consequence of pleasant or unpleasant relations with members of another community. These attitudes may be slow to change, especially if they stem from some emotional involvement. The principal of a Calcutta school, himself an Anglo-Indian, stated that many Anglo-Indians had been taught to believe, as children, that they were superior to other Indian children, and that these attitudes are resistant to change. Yet, he said, the present generation of children are seldom indoctrinated with such invidious distinctions.

Many Anglo-Indians, with reference to their relations with other Indians, attempt to view the situations objectively. This seems to be more true of Anglo-Indians who enjoy economic security and status than of those who are unsuccessful. A prominent educational administrator in West Bengal expressed the view that the traditional distrust between Anglo-Indians and other Indians is fading and is being replaced by attitudes of mutual respect and confidence. A young Anglo-Indian manager of a small industrial enterprise in Calcutta expressed satisfaction with his own occupational success, saying that he could not have risen to this position in the days of the Empire in India. Criticisms of government and public officials are common, but they tend to be directed more toward state and local governments, or even private business, than against the Center at New Delhi. Numerous Anglo-Indians in interviews have expressed their appreciation of the generous treatment that the Community received from the newly-formed central government when it assumed power. Even as early as the 1920's a prominent Anglo-Indian historian stated, "Painful as is the position of my Community, I must frankly say that I have no complaint against the government or our fellow-Indians."[76]

Down-and-out persons who are disillusioned often express their frustrations in hostile terms directed toward individuals or groups regarded as responsible for the situation, whether they are other Indians, the British, or even leaders of the

---

[76] Herbert A. Stark, in a letter to *The Statesman,* Calcutta, June 4, 1922.

Community. If they are unable to get a job, it is probably somebody else's fault; if they live in slums, it is because they are exploited by unscrupulous persons; if they do have a job, they are not paid what they deserve or have not been rewarded by promotion to a better position. Frustration arising from penury and joblessness may also be manifest in defeatist attitudes — "what's the use, the cards are stacked against me." Individuals who have experienced better days but who are mired in poverty are often expressive of bitterness and apathy.

The Anglo-Indian View of the British

As much as the Anglo-Indians admire the British and their culture, there is a considerable residue of anti-British hostility among the middle-aged and older members of the Community who feel that they were betrayed at the time of Indian Independence. They assert that Anglo-Indians worked, fought, and died for the British, that they supported the Empire in many ways, yet when the crisis of Independence came they were ruthlessly abandoned by the British government. This alleged ingratitude has deeply troubled many Anglo-Indians ever since. A school principal in Bangalore referred bitterly to the "perfidy" of the British in their refusal to provide a national home in England for Anglo-Indians at the time of Independence. An official in the Anglo-Indian Association expressed deep resentment of the British: "When the British were in power," he said, "I could not get a job at a decent salary, and when they withdrew from India they callously deserted the Community." A clerk in a British organization in Calcutta was equally vituperative in his remarks about the British. "I hate their guts, but I have to keep my job because others are very difficult to get," he said. He berated himself for not obtaining a British passport and migrating to England when this could easily have been done. His outlook was that of a trapped individual whose future, as he sees it, is uncertain.

Many Anglo-Indians have ambivalent feelings about the British, resenting them because of alleged mistreatment in the past, but respecting them for their admirable qualities of character. Anti-British hostilities engendered by colonial domination and exploitation on the political and economic level have tended to diminish as memories of the imperial past have faded and been replaced by positive attitudes toward Britain as a friendly partner in the concert of nations. With Independence has come an effort by many thoughtful Anglo-Indians toward re-evaluation of their own attitudes. A prominent member of the Anglo-Indian Community has stated the matter as follows:

> There is a mature and knowledgeable segment of the Community whose reaction is of a positive nature. Although aware of the deliberate policy of discrimination practiced against them in the past, despite sincere and loyal service, they began to appreciate that, with Independence, they were given the opportunity to exercise responsibility and attain a level of achievement hitherto denied them. Their feelings against the British ceased to be a negative attitude of resentment. Self-pride replaced self-pity, and a sense of admiration gave way to critical appraisement.[77]

---

[77] From correspondence by Dudley Francis, March 26, 1971.

Self-Images and Self-Criticism

In a questionnaire submitted to 52 Anglo-Indians in Bangalore, the respondents were asked to indicate the terms which, in their judgment, best described members of the Anglo-Indian Community. As one might expect, the favorable terms outnumbered by far the unfavorable or merely descriptive words or phrases: about three-fourths of 107 words or phrases submitted were favorable, around one-fifth were unfavorable and the remainder neutral or merely descriptive. The term "hardworking" was mentioned most frequently, and similar terms such as "efficient," "diligent," "industrious," "ambitious," and "disciplined" were likewise offered, apparently approvingly, of Anglo-Indian character. Others mentioned two or more times were "courageous," "dependable," "trustworthy," "loyal," "self-sacrificing," "helpful," "disciplined," "carefree," and "sincere." Among the expressions that appeared to be unfavorable or negative were such terms as "extravagant," "spendthriftiness," and "unambitious," with one person referring to his own group as a "gimme community, continually wanting charity, self-centered, and inclined to be deceitful." There were also several expressions that appeared to be descriptive, or at least non-evaluative, such as "poor," "good dancers," "downtrodden," "pro-British," and "born soldiers."

Anglo-Indian writers are inclined to present a favorable image of the Community. An example is a book by Reginald Maher, a competent journalist, in which the author describes what he considers the essential elements of Anglo-Indian character. Among the qualities he discusses are loyalty, devotion to duty, sportsmanship, generosity, physical courage, discipline, obedience to constituted authority, hospitality, a love for orderliness, and a sense of responsibility concerning work tasks.[78] He argues that it is unfair to charge the Anglo-Indians with disloyalty to India. Rather, he says, they have historically been loyal to whatever constituted authority existed at any particular time or place: When the British were in power they were loyal to the Empire; before the Empire was consolidated in India they were loyal to the native princes who were in power; now they are loyal to the government of India as the established authority. He refutes the charge of immorality and profligacy among Anglo-Indians, saying that behavior which is regarded as proper and conventional in the Anglo-Indian Community may be viewed in a quite different light by orthodox Indians.

Maher challenges the notion that Anglo-Indians are lacking in physical courage or discipline, mentioning persons, civil and military, who have heroically risked or sacrificed their lives for others or for a cause to which they were devoted. He rejects the criticism that Anglo-Indians are preoccupied with hedonistic pleasures, observing that they built and operated the railways and telegraphic facilities, often experiencing severe hardships in these undertakings. In his defense of the Community, however, Maher does not recognize some of the problems of behavior and personality which are of concern to many Anglo-Indians and other Indians alike.

Even before Independence some Anglo-Indian writers were taking an

---

[78] Reginald Maher, *These Are the Anglo-Indians* (Calcutta: Swallow Press, 1962), pp. 75-83.

optimistic view of the situation by recording important changes that had occurred in Anglo-Indian attitudes and behavior. Writing in the 1930's, C. N. Weston, a Bangalore educator, noted that the attitudes of Anglo-Indians toward other Indians and British had changed in the course of his own lifetime. He writes:

> "There has been in the past a cringing attitude toward the Englishman because he had it in his power to bestow favors. Today the influence of patronage is rapidly on the wane in India... Their attitude toward the Indian has also changed for the better. It was common in my boyhood days to hear Anglo-Indians talk of Indians as 'niggers.' This attitude has changed completely, and Anglo-Indians are realizing that Indians are their equals and brothers in the family of peoples of India."[79]

There are self-evaluations on other grounds. A school principal in Calcutta was harshly critical of the behavior of other Anglo-Indians, past and present. The stereotype of the "kept women" during the British regime had a considerable element of truth in it, he said. "Often," he commented, "the Britishers took Anglo-Indian women as mistresses, and as 'kept women' they were paid a high salary. Because these women had a high income and could live in style, and partly because they were so closely associated with the British, they developed a condescending attitude toward other Indians, and even toward Anglo-Indian men who could not measure up to the British in some respects. This 'poison' came to spread widely in the Community."

The respondent emphasized that this situation no longer exists. However, he stated that a good many Anglo-Indians have false values with respect to color and that these values are at the root of some of their difficulties today. "A white man, regardless of his qualities," he said, "is likely to rank above other Indians, especially in the preferences of Anglo-Indian women." In his view, however, color differences are less important for members of this minority than they have been in the past. The respondent himself is unusually fair in complexion.

The unfavorable images that certain other Indians have of Anglo-Indian women are not generally appreciated by Anglo-Indians, who are nevertheless aware of some of the behavior problems of the Community. An Anglo-Indian principal of a Calcutta school for girls expressed awareness that there were many "cheap" girls in the Community, but insisted that the unfavorable stereotype held by others mainly resulted from conflicting value systems. She said:

> "Anglo-Indian boys and girls, like Europeans, mingle freely, have dates, dance together, go out together without an escort, and kiss. Hence a tendency for other Indians, whose daughters usually have much less freedom, to jump to the conclusion that Anglo-Indian girls are immoral."

Anglo-Indians are sometimes forthright about the shortcomings and limitations of individual members of the Community. A school supervisor in Calcutta was especially critical of Anglo-Indians who are in difficult financial circumstances. "If they are in a sad plight," she said, "it is largely their own fault

---

[79] C. N. Weston, *Anglo-Indian Revolutionaries* (Bangalore: Scripture Literature Press, 1938), p. 137.

because they did not save anything when they did have good jobs. They are spendthrifts. They want good things, but now their incomes are not sufficient to provide these things, or if they do obtain them there is not money enough left over for their basic needs." The gap between a Western standard of living, which they idealize, and an Eastern income, which they receive, presents a serious psychological problem for many.

A number of members of the Community commented in interviews that the extravagance of many Anglo-Indians, their hedonistic philosophy of "live today and let tomorrow take care of itself," has been the source of much difficulty, especially among those who have been forced down into the mire of slum life. An Anglo-Indian high school teacher in Calcutta attributed part of the difficulties of Anglo-India today to the profligacy of many members of the Community. During a Christmas season one year he spent considerable time and effort taking up a collection of articles and money for indigent Anglo-Indians and their children, but he said that the money was squandered and that the adults looked upon the gifts as handouts to which they were entitled. The same respondent criticized many members of the Community for their political and civic apathy. "The typical Anglo-Indian is not a political animal," he said.

Teachers and school administrators develop stereotypes, like others, but they do have the advantage of being in close contact with students of varying ages and may be able, therefore, to form a fairly realistic conception of them. As we have observed in another chapter, Anglo-Indian students *as a group* are less successful in academic competition than most other communities in India. An Anglo-Indian teacher in Bangalore stated that many Anglo-Indian boys "are not turning out well," that they are unstable, lacking in ambition, and irresponsible. She attributed this to their frustrations because of the job situation and to their alienation from Indian society.

A teaching nun in a convent school and home in Bangalore said that she had more trouble with Anglo-Indian girls than with other girls. "One Anglo-Indian girl may be more of a problem than ten girls of other communities," she said. She and the mother superior (neither Anglo-Indians) agreed that many of their Anglo students lacked the character and motivation necessary to make them stable and responsible adults, but they attributed this instability to home conditions, particularly the lack of proper supervision and support by the parents. Most of the children or youth in this institution, it should be noted, were from indigent families.

Most knowledgeable Anglo-Indians, like the nuns mentioned above, are fully aware of the adjustment problems of younger members of the Community, attributing their difficulties to past and present social situations. A retired civil service officer in Bangalore expressed the opinion that the behavior of young Anglo-Indians was the consequence, in the main, of economic and political circumstances. He said:

> "The habit of frugality and planning has never been a part of the Anglo-Indian way of life. This was the result of British protection afforded the Community, which stifled

ambitions to get ahead. So, there developed a pattern of spendthriftiness, of having a good time. Now the Community is paying a dear price for this style of life. When it is coupled with unemployment and low incomes, the effect on the Community is not good."

The Dilemma of Identity

The matter of identity appears to have always been of concern to Anglo-Indians. Throughout much of the 18th century they were variously defined by Europeans and Indians. Under these circumstances it was not easy for Anglo-Indians to develop a clear conception of their own identity. Europeans tended to think of them as Indians with some European blood; Indians thought of them as Europeans with some Indian blood. They were *persona non grata* with Europeans and Indians alike. On both the cultural and social level they were alien to many other Indians, though kin to them on the biological level.

If members of this minority are self-identified as Anglo-Indians they are also a part of other collectivities. If they were born in India they may be expected to identify as Indian nationals. This is not always easy, for at least two reasons: one, a feeling that they are unwelcome in India and are not authentic Indian nationals; and second, they cannot easily identify culturally with particular ethnic, religious, or caste groups, except "domiciled Europeans" or Indian-Christians (who are not regarded as Anglo-Indians).

Anglo-Indians realize that legally they are citizens with all the rights and privileges of other Indians; it is imperative, therefore, that they identify with India and assume all of the obligations and responsibilities that go with Indian citizenship. This, at least, is the "official party line." Although it is difficult to determine general consensus on this topic or to probe the intensity of their feelings as Indian nationals, there is reason to believe, judging from informal comments often made by Anglo-Indians, that some of them do not feel very strongly concerning their identity as Indian nationals. One Anglo-Indian school principal in Calcutta stated the dilemma of her own identity as follows: "My heart is in England, but my responsibilities are in India." Since then she has migrated to Great Britain.

The prejudices against them, real or imagined, or the prejudices that they themselves may hold against other Indians, are an obstacle to both group and individual identity. For Anglo-Indians who have left India and settled abroad a similar problem of identity again arises. Is it possible or even desirable to retain their self-identity as Anglo-Indians? Can they identify with, say, Great Britain, not merely as legal British nationals but also in the fullest psychological sense of the term?

For a minority people whose marginal position through the centuries has meant social and economic insecurity, who have been rejected from intimate social life of other groups, and who are aware of unfavorable attitudes directed toward them, it is reasonable to expect that symbols having significance for the Community should be cherished. Members of the Anglo-Indian group who have distinguished themselves serve such a symbolic function. The "display" of such symbols is the Community's answer to the stereotypes that Anglo-Indians are an inferior lot, incapable of producing men and women of outstanding ability. If the Anglo-Indian self-image reflects awareness of the others-image and induces a feeling of inferiority, for them to identify with Anglo-Indian men and women who have achieved distinction or success may compensate for these uncomfortable feelings. This may explain the prideful attention the Anglo-Indians give their folk heroes as Community symbols.

One of the images commonly held about the Anglo-Indian Community is that it has produced few or no persons of distinction except individuals who have achieved fame for their military or athletic accomplishments. This viewpoint is usually rejected by Anglo-Indians. Considering the comparatively small size of the group and the ambivalence experienced in the three centuries of its existence, it has, in their opinion, produced an impressive number of persons of distinction, or at least notable achievements. Usually these individuals are acknowledged by the general Indian public for their accomplishments, but seldom as Anglo-Indians.

Some of the Anglo-Indian chroniclers, such as Herbert A. Stark,[80] Cedric Dover,[81] and Frank Anthony,[82] while not entirely objective in their assessment of the Community's record of achievement, have nevertheless identified numerous persons who have notable records in various fields of activity. Some are cited for their business successes and benefactions. Some are eulogized for their contributions as leaders in the field of education and religion. Others reportedly had distinguished records in medicine and law, and several earned reputations as historians and journalists. A number of musicians and athletes have received wide recognition. The longest list of folk heroes, however, go to Anglo-Indians who have distinguished themselves in military service, whether to defend the British Empire or India itself. By demonstrating their military skills some have risen to the higher echelons of the services.

One folk hero that stands above all others as a Community patriot is Henry Derozio, who lived in the early years of the nineteenth century. Although he died at the age of twenty-three he had become fairly well known as a gifted poet, a teacher, a journalist, and a political activist in the interest of the Community. One Anglo-Indian author, Cedric Dover, refers to Derozio as "the greatest self-admitted Eurasian that his community has produced... Such a youth deserves the tributes that are paid to genius."[83]

---

[80] Herbert A. Stark, *Hostages to India* (Calcutta: The Calcutta Fine Art Cottage, 1926); *The Call of the Blood or Anglo-Indians and the Sepoy Mutiny* (Rangoon: British Burma Press, 1932); *John Ricketts and His Times* (Calcutta: Wilson and Sons, 1934).

[81] Cedric Dover, *Cimmerii? or Eurasians and Their Future* (Calcutta: The Modern Art Press, 1929); *Half-Caste* (London: Martin Secker and Warburg, 1947), Chapters 6-7.

[82] Frank Anthony, *Britain's Betrayal in India* (New Delhi: Allied Publishers, 1969). Chapters 4, 10.

[83] Cedric Dover, *Half-Caste, op. cit.,* p. 144. There are several collections of the poems and other literary works of Derozio, and at least one biography.

CHAPTER FIVE

THE ANGLO-INDIAN WORLD OF WORK

The contemporary occupational orientation of the Anglo-Indian Community can be properly understood only in light of the minority's known vocational history over a period of more than two centuries. Those living in the sphere of influence of the Portuguese and French were not seriously handicapped occupationally because of their mixed racial ancestry since they were judged individually rather than collectively, and color or other racial traits did not form a basis of selection or discrimination. But with the British it was a different matter. British policy, formulated and carried out by the East India Company, was one of fluctuation, ranging from complete acceptance through limited acceptance to virtually total exclusion in appointments to jobs.

Until 1780 the East India Company made no invidious distinction between the Anglo-Indians and the British. The result of such a flexible policy was that Anglo-Indians could be appointed to high civil or military posts in the services of the Company, provided they were individually qualified. But this policy was soon reversed. According to Goodrich, a new policy was formulated in which a distinction was made between Europeans of "pure blood" and those of mixed racial ancestry.[84] The new policy specified that "no son of a native Indian" could qualify for higher positions in the civil service or in the upper echelons of the military. This policy was extended to exclude from the civil or military services in the Company all persons not born of European parentage, i.e., both the mother and the father were to be European. There were a few occupational exceptions – musicians and farriers (those caring for horses in military organizations), for example.

The exigencies of the situation eventually dictated a modification of this exclusionist policy. Need for clerical workers who had facility in the English language resulted in admission of qualified Anglo-Indians to the "uncovenanted" or lower clerical posts in the Company. Although Indians were also permitted to occupy these low level positions, actually the Anglo-Indians eventually exercised a virtual monopoly of them. Although such posts became an important source of income for the Anglo-Indian Community, those holding them could not look forward to advancement into the higher grades whatever their qualifications or work records might be. These posts were reserved for the British.

The Rationale for Exclusionist Policies

There were several rationalizations for this exclusionist policy. The expulsion

---

[84] Dorris L. Goodrich, "The Making of an Ethnic Group: The Eurasian Community in India." Unpublished Ph. D. dissertation, University of California, Berkeley, 1952.

from military service stemmed from fears that Anglo-Indians, themselves racially akin to the Indian people, might support the Motherland rather than the Fatherland in case of an uprising against the British forces. Furthermore, as long as the East India Company maintained an open-door policy for the higher grades of the civil services, the appointment of an Anglo-Indian to a high position meant lessened opportunity for British officers. This restriction was imposed rather indirectly by revoking the policy of sending Anglo-Indians to Britain for special training. Finally, the stigma attached to persons of "mixed blood" who were sometimes "begotten in sin" afforded a moral basis for discrimination against the Anglo-Indians, who were indeed the kith and kin of the British. Religious prejudice may also have entered the situation; many of the Anglo-Indians were of Catholic persuasion whereas the British were overwhelmingly Protestant.

In addition to the above stated difficulties, there was the problem of defining the Anglo-Indian group collectively. Many viewed them as Europeans with some Indian blood; others defined them as Indians with some European blood. They were considered by some as natives of India like any other group indigenous to the Indian sub-continent, while others saw them as British subjects. As a "son of a native Indian," and therefore an Indian by one definition, the Anglo-Indian could not hold a high-level office in the East India Company, but as a European he could not hold a position reserved for indigenous Indians. Defined as an Indian he was unacceptable in the British military establishment; defined as a European he was not eligible for service in the armed forces of the Indian princes. These exclusionist policies succeeded in driving the Anglo-Indians out of civil and military positions, except for menial posts or low-level clerical positions.

In 1829 the Community by-passed the East India Company and presented a list of grievances to the British Parliament, outlining particularly the restrictions imposed on them in employment.[85] The fact that such a petition was directed to Parliament indicated that Anglo-Indians did consider themselves British subjects. In the Charter Act of 1833 it was specified that "no natural-born subject of his Majesty, who is a resident in India, should by reason only of his religion, place of birth, descent, color, or any of them, be disabled from holding any place, office, or employment" under the East India Company. Actually, the Charter Act had little immediate effect on the Anglo-Indian Community since their educational and occupational handicaps had reduced the number qualified to hold posts requiring much training or skill. But at least it was a moral victory and a minor breakthrough in the job situation.

Anglo-Indian and British Reciprocity

In the Great Mutiny of 1857, Anglo-Indians as a group demonstrated their loyalty to the British by fighting alongside the imperial forces in this abortive revolution by the indigenous Indians. The support given to the British tended to alienate them from Indian society even more than had been the case in the past.

---

[85] *Ibid.*, pp. 147-152.

The aftermath of this historic event severely affected the economic position of Anglo-Indians in India. As one informant remarked in an interview in Calcutta:

> "In the general amnesty offered after that upheaval, all posts were thrown open to Indians, and Anglo-Indians being the most convenient scapegoats were sacrificed on the altar of appeasement. Their economic plight now made them dependent on jobs controlled by the British. This was a god-send to the British, who were on the lookout for cheap but reliable manpower for the railways, telegraphs, and police. Anglo-Indians were particularly suited for these departments because of their facility in English, their proven loyalty, and the important fact that communications had to be firmly held if the British occupation of India was to be secured."

The latter half of the nineteenth century was a period of technological and economic expansion. Railways were built and put in operation. Telegraph lines were strung over the entire sub-continent. A modern postal system was developed. Customs facilities were established in the port cities. Police constabulary was reinforced. In all these undertakings Anglo-India played an important part.

In eloquent prose suggesting an emotional assessment of the contributions of the Anglo-Indian Community to the economic and technological expansion of India, Herbert Stark writes of the development of railways, steamship lines, and telegraphic communications in the latter half of the nineteenth century:

> Years had been spent in surveying the routes for the telegraph and railway system. The preliminary stage, as well as the work of actual construction, needed operators of various descriptions who were willing to endure the hardships, risks, and perils of pioneers. Such work did not appeal to Indians, whose knowledge of books had not given them a taste for the marshes and fens through which the rivers thread their way, for the solitude of remote places on the plains, for the dangers attending the penetration of forests and hills, for the privation inseparable from months spent in the wilds. Anglo-Indians therefore found no competition, and did work which but for them could never have been done in the country. They furnished the navigation companies with captains, second officers, engineers, and mechanics. From them were recruited telegraph operators, artisans, and electricians. They supplied the railways with station staffs, engine drivers, permanent way inspectors, guards, auditors — in fact, every high grade of railway servant. The expansion of the postal system, now possible owing to the organization of railways, threw one avenue open to them, and they were appointed to the more respectable positions.[86]

Throughout the latter part of the nineteenth century, and well into the twentieth, Anglo-Indians depended on the British for employment. It was a period of relative prosperity for the Community. But 1919 was a turning point. The Government of India Act that year specifically gave Indians a greater share both in legislation and administration, as well as in government posts. The Act meant increased competition for Anglo-Indians in fields which had been virtually monopolized by them. Relatively few Anglo-Indians had gone beyond high school or had received specialized technical training; hence they were disadvantaged in the competitive job market because many Indians, especially Hindus, had

---

[86] Herbert A. Stark, *Hostages to India* (2nd edition) (Calcutta: Star Printing Works, 1936). See also his *Call of the Blood* (Rangoon: British Burma Press, 1932).

impressive academic and professional credentials. Furthermore, the Indianization of government services was extended to minor posts, a sphere in which Anglo-Indians had held a virtual monopoly under the British imperial umbrella.

Job Competition with Indian Workers

Job competition, however, tended to be confined largely to the "clean" occupations — clerical jobs and minor supervisory functions. Such positions were highly prized by Indians, especially Hindus, because of their prestige value. For the middle class Indian whose education and cultural heritage had provided a non-manual orientation, manual work had little attraction; nor was he especially efficient in the skilled and semi-skilled jobs involved in new technological developments in transportation and communication. A desk job in an office had more appeal to him than a job as locomotive fireman or engineer. The solid reputation that the Anglo-Indians had earned in the skilled and semi-skilled manual occupations continued to give them a kind of unofficial priority in these areas. Even though their formal training was generally at a minimum, Anglo-Indians had a tradition of success in these fields, and their facility in the English language stood them in good stead. They took justifiable pride in their ability "to keep the trains running."

The occupational status system operated within the Anglo-Indian Community as it did in other Indian communities. Prideful of their technical competence and their reputation as good workers, Anglo-Indians looked with disdain on "coolie" labor or any other kind work that symbolized social inferiority. Seldom if ever did an Anglo-Indian voluntarily enter the ranks of the servant or coolie class. However, the lowest class of railway workshop jobs came close to coolie labor. And the Goans, from Portuguese Goa, many of whom are of mixed racial heritage, were, and still are, extensively employed as cooks, waiters, bearers, and other jobs of similar status.

These occupational traditions and the values associated with work roles have survived to the present. Even though other Indians have entered these occupations in increasing numbers, the traditional pattern of occupational preference and avoidance tends to survive.

Although Indianization of the economy continued during the years following the Government of India Act, the British nevertheless relied heavily on the Anglo-Indian Community in the strategic occupations associated with the railways, police services, postal, telegraph, and custom services.[87] Anglo-Indians in turn depended on the British for jobs in these fields. But as pressures were intensified to allocate more jobs to Indian nationals, the problem of unemployment, except for the World War II period, became increasingly acute. Moreover, the rising tide of Indian nationalism and the demand for an independent India clearly indicated that the years of the British imperial regime in India were numbered. Anglo-Indians fully realized that the preferential

---

[87] Owen Snell, *Anglo-Indians and Their Future* (Bombay: Thacker and Company, Ltd., 1944).

allocation of jobs in their favor would come to an end with Independence. But their reliance on the British protectorate had been so long and the influence of the system so pervasive that the prospective removal of the protective umbrella loomed ominous indeed.

Indian Independence and the New Social Order

The economic dependence of the Community on the British seemingly had its counterpart in a state of psychological dependence. The Anglo-Indians knew full well that Indian independence was inevitable, but the uncertainties concerning the place of the Community in the new dispensation were demoralizing. They were aware that their long and subservient relations with the British had made them widely unpopular among Indian nationals, many of whom questioned the loyalty of Anglo-Indians to Mother India. The least that could be expected was immediate termination of the preferential allocation of jobs in their favor. The policy feared by many was punitive retaliation by the new Indian government.

But their anticipations were generally wrong. The new regime, under the benevolent influence of Gandhi and Nehru, acted magnanimously in its policy concerning the Anglo-Indian Community. Rather than a precipitous termination of the preferential system, which undoubtedly would have had catastrophic effects on the Community, the government adopted a procedure for the gradual abolition of preferential job allocation to allow Anglo-Indians time to make an adjustment to the new order. Indeed, a transitional period of ten years was specified in the Indian Constitution to allow for an accommodation to the new order. The constitutional provisions were as follows:

> (1) During the first two years after the commencement of this Constitution, appointments of members of the Anglo-Indian community to posts in the railway, customs, postal and telegraph services of the Union shall be made on the same basis as immediately before the fifteenth day of August, 1947.
>
> During every succeeding period of two years, the number of posts reserved for the members of the said community in the said services shall, as nearly as possible, be less by ten per cent than the numbers of reserved during the immediately preceding period of two years:
>
> Provided that at the end of ten years from the commencement of this Constitution all such reservations shall cease.
>
> (2) Nothing in clause (1) shall bar the appointment of members of the Anglo-Indian community to posts other than, or in addition to, those reserved for the community under that clause if such members are found qualified for appointment on merit as compared with the members of other communities.[118]

This transitional period ended in 1960, after which it was clear that, in the labor pool, the Anglo-Indians would have to swim or sink. Artificial supports provided by the colonial regime were to be permanently removed. Anglo-Indians would be expected to share the vicissitudes of fortune, good and bad, with their fellow-nationals. By any reasonable assessment this was a fair and justifiable

---

[118] *The Constitution of India* (New Delhi: Government of India Press, 1963), paragraph 336.

policy. It was even more equitable than many Anglo-Indians had anticipated. Doubtless its formulation and adoption were in part due to the political strategy of Anglo-Indian leaders, notably Frank Anthony. Yet the policy did little to alleviate the economic deprivation that had befallen the Community. The blight of widespread unemployment and economic stagnation afflicted all of India in the post-Independence period.

Anglo-Indian Men and Work Roles

Broad occupational configurations have persisted for Anglo-Indians, although the concentrations in some of the traditional vocations have undoubtedly diminished since Independence. A government report for 1928-1930 indicated that some 14,000 Anglo-Indians, or about one-third of the male working population of the Community, were employed on the railways alone, with many others holding jobs in the telegraphs, customs, postal services, and medical departments.[89] The Census of India in 1931, the last of such census reports enumerating Anglo-Indians as a distinct group, indicated that about one-third of Anglo-Indian males were employed in transportation, and approximately 10 per cent in industry and 9 per cent in trade.[90] The broad categories employed by the census, however, are not very revealing as to the specific occupations of Anglo-Indians.

Many Anglo-Indians continue to fill traditional occupational roles. There are still the "railway colonies" in such cities as Kharagpur, Secunderabad, Bilaspur, Jhansi, Aubli, and Bangalore, in which reside the families of workers who perform a variety of tasks related to the maintenance and operation of the railroads. Gaikwad in his study observed that a high percentage of the employed workers in Bilaspur and Jhansi were in occupations related to railroading as recent as the 1960's.[91]

Data on occupations of Anglo-Indians were obtained from a sample of 168 case records of persons who had received some kind of support, or applied for it, in Calcutta from the early years of the present century to the 1950's.[92] The welfare recipients were asked to specify the job, or jobs, held by themselves, if a male, their fathers, their sons or sons-in-laws, and, if a female, their husbands. The picture that emerges from this array of jobs indicates clearly that the preponderance of occupations was in manual and clerical work. Of the 320 jobs designated, 99 were associated with the railways, mainly as skilled, semi-skilled, or unskilled work. Forty-eight supervisory or clerical jobs were mentioned, other than those related to the railway, and 16 were employed in the military and police services. Only 13 could properly be classified as professional, and of these, six were teachers, three

[89] *Report of the Indian Statutory Commission,* Vol. I (Calcutta: Government of India, Central Publication Branch, 1930), pp. 43-44.

[90] *Census of India,* 1931. Vol. I, Part II, Table XI.

[91] E. K. Gaikwad, *The Anglo-Indians* (Bombay: Asia Publishing House, 1967), p. 97.

[92] These data were obtained from a collection of welfare case records in the library of Dr. John Broomfield of the University of Michigan. These data should not, however, be considered representative of the entire Community since they were obtained from recipients of welfare and are probably weighted with occupations on the lower level of the structure.

were doctors, two were army officers, one was an electrical engineer, and one a veterinarian.

Technological and other developments in the post-Independence period have had the effect of dispersing Anglo-Indian manual workers into a wide variety of occupations. Skilled and semi-skilled male workers are now employed in almost every type of enterprise in a modernizing economy, both in civil and military establishments — mechanics, electricians, engineers, welders, factory operatives and foremen, miners, radio repairmen, airplane pilots and navigators, inspectors, even clerical personnel. A few have become professionals and semi-professionals, mainly teachers, officers in military organizations, and a scattering of lawyers, accountants, journalists, and the like. The Air Force, Army, and Navy have attracted Anglo-Indians in numbers out of proportion to the size of the Community.

The Work Situation for Men in Bangalore and Calcutta

Of 40 employed males interviewed in Bangalore, all but nine were directly or indirectly involved in technical or skilled manual jobs. The non-manual workers included six clerical personnel, a teacher, an accountant, and a physical training director. Since Bangalore is a major industrial metropolis it is not surprising to find such an occupational distribution in that city. Not one person among the interviewees was reported as an unskilled laborer. In other cities having a different type of economy there would be variations. But the dominant symbol in this city would be a workman's apron rather than a white collar.

In Calcutta, an Anglo-Indian technician commented that under the colonial administration the Indians did most of the unskilled work, the British held the administrative and managerial posts, while Anglo-Indians were the skilled workers and clerical personnel. This tradition so far as the Anglo-Indians are concerned has persisted, although there are many in the minor administrative jobs and a few in the major ones. Other Indians have replaced many of the British as major executives. Anglo-Indians have tended to cling to their traditional occupations, but in a highly competitive relationship to other Indians they generally have less job security than they enjoyed under the British. An Anglo-Indian manager of a small Calcutta factory producing oil drums reported that Anglo-Indian workers declined to take a job in the company because the work was unskilled, which they regarded as degrading, or at least beneath their cherished station in life. Another Anglo-Indian, a young man holding a major managerial post in a Calcutta factory, stated that 56 Anglo-Indians were employed in the plant, all in technical jobs. No other factory in the city employed as many Anglo-Indians, he said. The manager himself remarked that under the colonial regime he could not have risen to the level of a major executive. The company, however, was part of a foreign-owned enterprise.

However well qualified Anglo-Indian men are for employment in manual or non-manual jobs, the fact is that jobs are difficult to obtain, wages or salaries are usually low, and the opportunities for advancement often limited. One of the reasons for such an employment situation is the increasing numbers of Indian males who enter the competitive job market each year. Unless the individual possesses skills or knowledge having special economic value to prospective employers, military administrators, or government officials, his chances of employment are generally limited. This applies, of course, to all communities, not alone to the Anglo-Indian minority. Many Anglo-Indian boys just entering the labor market lack the qualifications for the kind of position traditionally acceptable to members of the Community.

Business and the Professions

Few Anglo-Indian men have entered the field of private business, except as salaried or wage-earning employees of corporations. The vocational tradition of the Anglo-Indian Community has oriented them in other directions. Under the British the opportunities for lucrative employment, and even economic security, did not lie in the field of business, nor have these opportunities greatly improved since then. Furthermore, other communities, notably the Parsees, Jews, and Hindus, with long experience in business, would probably make it competitively difficult for an Anglo-Indian to succeed in the business world.

The lack of necessary experience and sufficient working capital have placed a business career beyond the reach of most Anglo-Indian men. But a few do venture into the business world. A mechanic, for example, may establish a shop for the maintenance and repair of trucks or automobiles. A radio repairman owns and operates a small shop in Calcutta, and in the same city an electrician is the proprietor of a minor electrical business. Such enterprises, however, are not highly competitive with Indian commercial establishments.

The professions have not attracted many Anglo-Indian men. A major reason is that most of them have not attended a college or university, or been professionally trained in other ways, except for a military career. Under the colonial regime the vocational opportunities did not usually specify a high education. Generally the salaries or wages in technical work were as high as professional incomes. Hence Anglo-Indians reasoned that it was pointless to expend money and effort for a professional education when they could earn as much, or even more, in the protected manual or clerical occupations in which they had acquired special competence.

The many decades in which the entire Community was oriented to the manual and clerical occupations had the effect of stifling interest in higher education, or even in intellectual achievement in general. The British selected many young Hindu men of high ability to be trained in England for responsible positions as "gazetted" officers in the Indian Administrative Services, but, aside from a few Anglo-Indians who received officer training in a military school in England the Community was not seriously considered in this training program. The cost of education in preparation for a professional career was financially prohibitive for most Anglo-Indians. Many who did enter the professions, or were financially or otherwise qualified to do so, have migrated in large numbers to other countries.

THE ANGLO-INDIAN WORLD OF WORK

Anglo-Indian Women and Work Roles

Anglo-Indian women, like their menfolk, also developed exceptional proficiency in certain vocational fields and thereby earned a solid reputation for their skills. Those who entered the labormarket were attracted mainly to secretarial occupations, nursing, and teaching. As stenographers and secretaries they were especially useful to the British because of their competence in the English language as well as their occupational skills. Generally they had no hesitancy about accepting employment in an office among personnel who were mainly or entirely men — a work situation not usually acceptable to Hindu or Muslim women. Although Anglo-Indian women were not accepted as social equals by their British colleagues or superiors, they nevertheless had a symbolic function in an office setting in which female congeniality was an asset. They are often preferred as office secretaries dealing with confidential matters because they are not directly related to the major communal groups such as caste.

Anglo-Indian women eventually came to play an important role in the nursing profession, a vocation which Indian women were reluctant to enter because of the close relationship with male patients. Whereas an Anglo-Indian nurse might be willing to give a male patient a bath or massage, as part of a required work role, such a task would likely be embarrassing to a Hindu woman. As a result of their dominance of the nursing profession, especially in the better hospitals, Anglo-Indian women acquired a solid reputation for competence, a reputation which enhanced their demand as hospital and medical services were expanded to meet the needs of a modernizing society. The foregoing does not imply that Anglo-Indians completely monopolized the nursing profession. Actually, many Indian-Christian women also entered this field and were employed mainly in hospitals serving the lower-income population.

The other profession which attracted large numbers of Anglo-Indian women was teaching, mainly on the elementary level. In fact, women teachers recruited from the Community virtually dominated the elementary Anglo-Indian schools in which English was the medium of instruction, and many were also employed as high school instructors.

The occupational patterns during the colonial regime have tended to persist into the post-Independence period, although significant changes are occurring. As the Indian economy expanded and became increasingly differentiated, job opportunities for Anglo-Indian women have become more diversified. Aside from teaching or secretarial work in offices, in which their services continue to be in considerable demand, they are widely employed in jobs that require facility in the English language and ability to communicate effectively with the general public — hotel or office receptionists, telephone operators, salesladies in mercantile establishments, airline hostesses, performers in night clubs, and, for the uneducated or untrained, housekeepers and "governesses." Many poor Anglo-Indian women are employed in unskilled or semi-skilled work such as jobs requiring repetitive tasks on an assembly line.

The vocation in which Anglo-Indian women have definitely lost ground is nursing, mainly because of their inability to communicate effectively in an Indian language, or because Indian women are increasingly seeking jobs in this field. More and more the professional requirements include knowledge of at least one indigenous language to enable the nurse to communicate with non-English-speaking patients.

Many Anglo-Indian women are leaving the teaching profession because of low salaries. Actually, Anglo-Indian girls with limited secretarial training can commonly command a beginning salary higher than many professionally-trained teachers receive after years of service. As a case in point, the principal of a girls' school in Bangalore reported that she had recently hired a young secretary at 300 rupees (about 43 U.S. dollars) a month, but that many of her experienced teachers were receiving monthly salaries of 200 rupees or less. Such salary differentials have created a serious shortage of qualified teachers on the elementary school levels in Anglo-Indian schools.

Anglo-Indian women usually enjoy a more favorable work image than the men. Indeed, they have earned an enviable reputation as responsible and skillful workers, especially in the clerical occupations. Consequently, there is such a demand for their services that unemployment is not a serious problem for those who have been properly trained. These conflicting images have worked to the disadvantage, and often humiliation, of the Anglo-Indian men who may be forced to rely on their wives for family support.

The Selective System and the Job

Aside from the unbalanced economic nexus between available work opportunities and the supply of qualified workers, there are other factors that influence the individual's success or failure in employment. One is the leverage that certain Indian communities have in obtaining jobs for their members. Communal groups based on religion or caste, for example, frequently exert an influence in favor of their own members. And if members of such groups are in an administrative or otherwise commanding position to influence the selection of particular persons those identified with such communal groups have an advantage in the labor market. Indeed, many Hindus are in positions of administrative, political, or economic power to make or influence appointments. Conversely, few Anglo-Indians have such power or influence. The system obviously works to the disadvantage of the Anglo-Indian Community.

Members of large kinship groups are obligated to help their kinsmen whenever possible; if they are Hindus they are also under obligation to assist their caste brothers. Such an institutional structure affords an advantage in locating jobs and in obtaining employment. Thus the leverage that other communities may have in finding jobs for their members and influencing their appointment is not available to the Anglo-Indian. This is not to say that individual Anglo-Indians would fail to assist fellow-members in getting a job. Actually they do; and besides there are several organizations which perform this function for the Community. But the basic structural characteristics of Anglo-Indian society affords less leverage in the job market than do the built-in features of Hindu society. Since executives with authority to make appointments are usually Hindus, this community is in a potentially favorable situation.

Functioning of the system is therefore not so much a matter of actual discrimination as of preferential allocation of jobs on a communal basis. But the end results may be the same. A question was presented to a Catholic priest-educator in this way: "If two men, equally qualified, one a Hindu and the other an Anglo-Indian, apply for a position that is available, which would likely be selected?" The reply was, "If the appointive officer was a Hindu the person appointed would also very likely be a Hindu." There are, however, certain safeguards against such procedures. The Indian Civil Service theoretically functions without reference to communal membership or influences, but even that system falls short of its ideals in the selection of personnel. The military forces, however, emphasize that the selection and advancement of personnel occurs irrespective of communal identification. But this has been criticized by some Anglo-Indians as being more ideal than real.

Still another factor influencing the employment situation generally is the proverbial "vicious circle." Many young Anglo-Indians have been unable to obtain a job, or at least a position they are willing to accept. Older persons have often lost their jobs or otherwise been forced to take positions offering little remuneration in money or self-respect. Unemployment or painful downgrading is often accompanied by unemployability manifest in slovenly work habits, absence of work motivation, frustration, resentments arising from joblessness, and preoccupation with exotic (and sometimes erotic) behavior that affords transitory surcease from the harsh realities of life. The presence of unstable or unreliable persons has created an unfavorable stereotype among non-Anglo-Indians and even among some Anglo-Indians as well. This persistently unfavorable image has contributed to the difficulty in obtaining employment.

The reaction of Anglo-Indians and others to this situation tends, then, to become circular. A hotel proprietor in Bangalore may be fairly representative of certain employers concerning Anglo-Indian men. Said this proprietor, an Indian:

"I once hired an Anglo-Indian man but within a week I had to discharge him because of his indolence and general irresponsibility. I would not have another one on my property."

But he expressed satisfaction with the work of his female Anglo-Indian employees. Another employer, an Anglo-Indian manager of a factory in Calcutta, stated the situation somewhat more objectively:

"Anglo-Indian workers may be placed in two categories, those who are responsible, take pride in their work, and do a good job; and those who are irresponsible, unwilling to cooperate, decline to follow orders, and want to stop work at five o'clock on the dot. Although we make every effort to give them an opportunity, in the end we have to let them go. But the responsible ones profit by the training they receive in the factory and are never out of a job."

Still another Calcutta factory manager observed approvingly that Anglo-Indians in his employ were not only reliable workers but disinclined to join a labor union or go on strike. They were, he said, better workers than Hindus, who preferred clerical jobs "shuffling papers and signing names."

"The Cards Are Stacked..."

Anglo-Indians interviewed in various cities were generally agreed that the men were seriously handicapped either in obtaining a job or advancement in the position held. One of the common complaints was the alleged discrimination in promotions. It was repeatedly asserted that under the British regime Anglo-Indian personnel were seldom advanced to one of the higher ranks whatever their qualifications or work performance, and that this system is still widely followed in independent India. Said a retired railway officer in Bangalore:

> "There are many Anglo-Indians having the rank of a minor officer who are quite capable of performing the duties of higher officials. Unfortunately, these officers are never promoted to the higher grades. When promotions are made they find some non-Anglo-Indian officer and promote him. For this reason there is a lot of dissatisfaction among the Anglo-Indian workers who have been carrying out their duties for numbers of years."

A member of a panel discussing employment problems of the Community, himself an Anglo-Indian employed in a Calcutta private corporation, stated a somewhat different aspect:

> "When China attacked India in 1962 there was a big demand for the Anglo-Indians to go back into the military because the Indian government recognized their strategic importance. Before that time not much recognition had been given them. There was also a demand for them to go back into the telegraph and other strategic services."

Whether such discrimination actually exists, and if so its frequency and extent, we have no objective evidence other than verbal statements of individuals. But if there is job discrimination against Anglo-Indians or other communities it may be deceptively subtle rather than overt. An Anglo-Indian teacher in Bangalore was cynical about the vocational prospects for Anglo-Indians. He observed that they are not explicitly rejected when they apply for a position, but instead their applications are accepted. "Then excuses are found, or made up, to prevent or postpone their appointments; or, if appointments are made, the advancements are slow or else do not occur at all." He cited instances in which he was appointed on probation but was shifted to new posts before he could be advanced in any position. This he interpreted as an effort to disengage him, or at least to discourage him from continuing as a teacher. Realizing that the traditional image of the Anglo-Indian man was that of an unstable or irresponsible person, he had a strong determination to be a credit to the Community. But, he said, he never got to a high position in the system either as a teacher or administrator. A foreman in a Calcutta factory appeared embittered about the ironic turn of events that had worked to such a disadvantage to him personally and to the Community as a whole. He asserted that there was usually little opportunity for real advancement in government or private enterprise, especially if the boss was a Hindu.

The Workers Report in Bangalore and Hyderabad

The Bangalore survey (40 men and 12 women) included two questions concerning self-attitudes toward the job currently held:

"If you are employed, are you pretty well satisfied, or dissatisfied, with your job? Explain."

"If you are employed, have you received salary or wage increases, or promotions in rank, according to your idea of a fair reward for your work? Explain."

About half of the men expressed satisfaction with their job and the rewards for their work, and all but two of the women were satisfied. The reasons for dissatisfaction were variously stated, but were mainly concerned with inadequate remuneration or promotions. In some instances they reported that wage or salary increases were fair, or at least regular, but opportunity for advancement was limited; in other cases the situation was reversed; and a few reported that both remuneration and promotions were altogether inadequate. Some of them complained about favoritism as the reason for their dissatisfaction.

The following quoted statements may be representative of those satisfied with the job, or at least certain aspects of it:

"Fairly satisfied—the meager pittance of a salary and the future language question being the main problems." (woman teacher)

"Very satisfied. I started from the bottom, and with much encouragement I'm climbing fast." (mechanic)

"I am satisfied. I have come to the position of assistant foreman from the bottom mainly due to my ability." (factory worker)

"Satisfied up to a point, but ready to 'lay down tools, if an opportunity occurs." (miller)

"I consider my remuneration more than adequate as I am, in fact, highly paid by local standards." (woman confidential secretary)

"I have passed my tests in the Air Force and received my promotions regularly, including salary increases." (radar technician)

"I am satisfied as far as my remuneration is concerned, but dissatisfied with conditions of work and discriminatory attitude of my colleagues." (mechanic)

"So far I am satisfied, but now I have reached a stage where promotion is by selection, and I feel I will be discriminated against." (factory worker)

Those expressing unfavorable attitudes generally offered a variety of reasons for such dissatisfaction. Representative among these statements are the following:

"Wage increases and promotions are usually given to persons from influential families or to favorites." (woman purchasing officer in large company)

"With my experience I expect a far higher salary. Six years of service have not brought me the status I expected." (mechanic)

"Dissatisfied due to unfairness. Was treated fairly as long as I had an Anglo-Indian boss, but once he left there was a lot of partiality shown." (miller)

"Merits don't count. I do more work than I am paid for." (linotype operator)

"I am dissatisfied because of the meager salary with no prospects whatsoever. No salary or wage increases but the work continuously mounts (male clerk)

"Received annual increments due to efficient work done, but promotion withheld due to scheduled caste junior employees given preference." (locomotive engineer)

"I am dissatisfied because I feel that I am not given the opportunities I should have. The people concerned are not fair because they are trying to Indianize everything they come across." (male inspector in tool room of factory)

"I presume there is no future for any promotion. Our yearly increase is there, but where promotions are concerned our fair reward in work is doubtful since we are a minority and we have no backing." (male storekeeper)

One of the Anglo-Indian women included in the study reported both satisfactory and unsatisfactory experiences in employment. At the time of the survey she was employed as an office manager in a private firm, having been promoted from the rank of stenographer after a six month's probation period, and given generous salary increases.

"This firm," she reports, "appreciates the work put in by each member of the staff and rewards them accordingly. Before I secured my present job I had a lot of difficulty in two different appointments....

"In a government undertaking I worked for a period of one and a half years, having secured the job through very good influence. Even then I was kept down because I was an Anglo-Indian. Although I was given the designation of Personal Secretary, I received much less remuneration than my colleagues.

"I was treated with a lot of contempt because most of my colleagues were South Indian, and this community is the most prejudiced community in India, despite caste or creed.

"The main bone of contention between the subordinates and myself was that I never agreed with them on certain matters. This lead to a lot of unpleasantness with the head of the department, and when the question of promotions or increments came up my name never appeared on the list of recommendations.

"I was made to feel my position as a Christian everytime I applied for leave on a Christian festival. Though the leave was granted it was either with loss of pay or sick leave."

The Bangalore sample revealed that the length of time on the same job ranged from one month to 24 years, an average of approximately eight years. Whether the balance between expressed satisfaction and dissatisfaction would be different for other communities, say Hindus or Indian-Christians, in similar employment situations is uncertain. It seems probable, however, that Anglo-Indians who are unemployed, or who have irregular employment, with little or no economic security, would be even more dissatisfied than those holding jobs. A number of informal discussions with such persons elicited expressions of bitterness, hostility, and hopelessness, clearly indicating a feeling of being trapped in a situation not of their own making. Such feelings of alienation appear to be quite common.

Anglo-Indians who have been successful in their occupational careers, especially those who hold relatively high positions, generally express an optimistic view concerning employment opportunities for members of the Community. Some are critical of Anglo-Indians who have had unsatisfactory experiences. A high-ranking Anglo-Indian officer in a large firm in Hyderabad observed that some discrimination against Anglo-Indians does in fact occur, but that some of the difficulty lies with the workers themselves. He cited the experience of his company in hiring young men and expending considerable money in training them, only to have them leave the job and migrate to another country instead of remaining with the organization. He did not blame the company if it declined to hire Anglo-Indian workers, or promoted them slowly after they were actually hired, unless they showed some evidence of intention to remain in the firm. This policy, however, was interpreted by some as actual discrimination.

A woman member of the legislative assembly in Andhra Pradesh, a teacher by profession, expressed the feeling that occupational success depended in considerable measure on the individual. "I've told our boys and girls that they will have to pull up their socks and study as hard as other Indian boys and girls are doing." When asked if she had encountered any discrimination against Anglo-Indian boys and girls in getting a job, she replied in the negative, saying, "I'm glad to say that by and large we've been given a square deal." This viewpoint would probably resemble the "party line" of the top people in the All-India Anglo-Indian Association on the national and local levels.

Vocational Prospects for the Future

Thoughtful Anglo-Indians are of course concerned about the future of the Community in relation to employment opportunities, especially for young men and women just entering the world of work. A Calcutta high school instructor observed that, in view of the shortage of qualified teachers, the teaching profession offered attractive opportunities. The same respondent felt that the construction and operation of ships, such as marine engineering, held considerable promise for men who are mechanically skilled. Although there is no strong maritime tradition in India, he said, it is probable that this general sector of the economy will expand in the future, providing opportunities for young men with technical training or mechanical skill. (His own son was trained as a marine engineer).

There is some disagreement among Anglo-Indians concerning the opportunities for careers in the military services. Although Anglo-Indians are disproportionately represented in the military, and several have compiled distinguished records, a common complaint is that the military heroes are recognized but seldom identified, officially or in the mass media, as to their Community. In Calcutta, an Anglo-Indian army major, retiring from the services and with definite plans for migration to England, spoke bitterly of the situation as it bore on the career prospects of young Anglo-Indians. A few years earlier, he said, he would have recommended a military career to young men, but he had changed his mind and was extremely critical of what he considered to be discriminatory policies in the services. An Air Force medical officer in Hyderabad, also with definite plans to migrate to England, questioned the advisability of an Army or Air Force career for young men because of the fact that they are often shifted from one remote frontier post to another. In such a situation he believed that a normal family life would be very difficult.

There seems to be fairly general agreement that the traditional Anglo-Indian occupational specialties — railways, postal and telegraph service, customs, etc. — offer suitable employment for which Anglo-Indian men are generally well qualified, but with two serious limitations: Employment opportunities in these occupations are declining because of automation, and non-Anglo-Indians are competitively entering these fields. Various professions afford an opportunity for employment, but most Anglo-Indians are not qualified educationally for professional positions that have high educational requirements for admission.

For women, the occupations that afford the maximum promise are teaching and secretarial work, especially if a knowledge of English is required. A respondent in Kharagpur, himself a teacher, indicated that in addition to secretarial work, nursing, hair dressing, journalism, teaching, and care of children in private homes are perhaps the most promising occupations for Anglo-Indian women.

Student Aspirations and Expectations in West Bengal

Young people are not always realistic about their future jobs, especially when there is a wide range of options, as there are in urban environments. Limited confirmation of this proposition was clearly evident in a study of occupational and educational interests in West Bengal in 1964.[93] In the section of the questionnaire dealing with occupational interests two related questions were asked:

> 1. And now about your future job. What is the occupation you would like to follow when you are about 25 or 30 years old?
>
> 2. Sometimes we have difficulty in getting the kind of job we want. What kind of job do you think you will probably have when you are about 25 or 30 years old?

The response to the first question was interpreted as the level of occupational *aspiration;* the second answer as the level of *expectation*. Both questions called for the designation of a specific occupation. These occupations were subsequently classified according to a hierarchical scheme which seemed reasonably appropriate for this particular purpose.[94]

In Table I it is clearly evident that the male students, regardless of their

---

[93] The study was conducted under the auspices of the Association of Teachers in Anglo-Indian schools of West Bengal. The administration of the questionnaire and compilation of data were done by the teachers. The design of the questionnaire and analysis of the data were by the senior author.

[94] The methods employed in the study do not in all respects measure up to rigid standards of scholarly research. The persons administering the questionnaire in the classroom were generally inexperienced in research and did not always require the students to answer the questions completely and accurately. Of the 2,584 students (1,768 males and 816 females) who were asked to fill out the questionnaire, many did not provide relevant information for one or more questions. The percentage distributions shown in the accompanying tables are based on the number actually responding to specific questions. Furthermore, there was no way of determining the representativeness of the sample.

community identification, generally aspired to prestigious occupations, the percentages being 75 for the Anglo-Indians, 70 for the Hindus, and 69 for the "other" communities. If the professional and semi-professional categories are combined with the managerial and proprietorial class, almost nine-tenths of the male students aspired to that level. Only seven per cent of the male Anglo-Indians desired occupations below the professional and managerial class, a slightly lower percentage than was true of the Hindus and Others.

As might be expected, the level of expectation (the kind of job the students really expected to have) was somewhat below the aspirational level in the prestige occupations. This differential was similar for males in the three community categories, although less for the Anglo-Indians than for the other two. In view of the general employment situation in India, and especially the extent to which Anglo-Indians are handicapped educationally and otherwise from entering high-status occupations, it would appear that both their level of aspirations and their level of expectation are highly unrealistic in terms of the probable opportunities prevailing for them. This is indicated by the fact that 75 per cent of the Anglo-Indians aspire to be professionals or semi-professionals, and that 71 per cent expect that they will actually be occupied on that level when they are 25 or 30 years old. However, while only 5 per cent aspired to the skilled or semiskilled worker level, including the military and police, 13 per cent expected that they actually would find jobs in this general category. It is especially interesting that clerical and business occupations had little appeal to the male students.

Comparisons of male and female students are not always meaningful because vocations appropriate for young women may not be the ones customarily entered or aspired to by young men. Furthermore, the broad occupational classes shown in the tables may have a different content for each of the sexes; it is not likely that the category of skilled or semi-skilled labor would be of particular concern to girls or women. Nevertheless, certain comparisons may be valid.

The level of aspiration for professional and semi-professional occupations is much lower for Anglo-Indian girls than for girls representing the Hindu and Other communities — 27 per cent compared with 82 per cent for the Hindus and 67 per cent for the Others. An explanation for this difference has been considered earlier in this chapter. Whereas two-thirds of the Anglo-Indian girls aspired to clerical occupations, only one-fourth of the Others and 7 per cent of the Hindus desired to enter this vocational field. Interestingly, very few girls in any of the three groups desired to enter the business world as managers or salespersons.

The differential between aspirations and expectations was strikingly similar for all three groups. On the professional and semiprofessional level, 20 per cent of the Anglo-Indian girls *expected* to enter these occupations compared to 27 per cent who *aspired* to that level. The corresponding percentages for the Hindus were 77 and 82, and for the Others, 62 and 67. But the differential was reversed for the clerical occupations in all three groups. Whereas 75 per cent of the Anglo-Indian girls *expected* to be in clerical positions, compared with 66 percent who *aspired* to that level, the comparable percentages for the Hindus were 14 and 7, and for the Others, 34 and 27.

Table I

Percentage Distribution of Students in West Bengal Reporting their Occupational Aspirations and Expectations, by Community, Sex, and Occupational Class, 1964

Community and Occupation	Level of Aspiration Male	Level of Aspiration Female	Level of Expectation Male	Level of Expectation Female
Hindu				
A	71%	82%	62%	77%
B	16	7	17	2
C	12	1	18	2
D	*	7	2	14
E	*	2	1	2
F	*	*	*	3
	N=830	N=300	N=499	129
Anglo-Indian				
A	75%	27%	71%	20%
B	17	*	12	1
C	2	*	3	1
D	*	66	1	75
E	5	5	13	3
F	*	*	*	*
	N=153	N=128	N=91	N=84
"Other"				
A	69%	67%	57%	62%
B	19	2	24	1
C	10	2	11	1
D	*	27	4	34
E	2	2	4	1
F	*	*	*	1
	N=319	N=201	N=158	N=100

A = Professional and Semi-Professional
B = Managers, Executives, Proprietors
C = Salespeople, business personnel
D = Clerical workers
E = Skilled, semiskilled, Military, police
F = Unskilled, farmers, farm laborers
"Other" includes all other communities such as Muslims, Indian-Christians, Jews, Sikhs, Parsees, etc.
* = Less than one per cent

Students State Their Choices and Their Problems

A survey, conducted in 1958 by the Vocational Counseling Bureau in Calcutta, of 72 Anglo-Indian high school students (62 boys and 10 girls) revealed a pattern of vocational choices somewhat different from the preferences indicated in the West Bengal survey.[95] The vocation choices were as follows:

Boys

Mechanical apprentice	10
Marine engineer	9
Engineer	8
Marine officer	5
Marine rating (sailor)	4
Air Force man	4
Doctor	1
Artist	2
Teacher	1
Army man	1
Farmer	1
Accountant	1
Customs officer	1
Tea tester	1
Undecided	13
TOTAL	62

Girls

Doctor	1
Nurse	2
Secretary	2
Teacher	1
Undecided	4
TOTAL	10

The occupational listing in this survey gives a more detailed picture of the specific vocational choices than does the West Bengal study, since broad categories of occupations were used in the latter. Male high school students included in the survey were strongly oriented to engineering and mechanical work, especially in marine or naval posts. Since the four schools for training and employment of boys entering marine vocations are located in Calcutta, it is hardly surprising that this pattern of vocational preferences

The purpose of the Bureau's study was not only to ascertain the occupational

---

[95] The high schools represented in this survey were: St. Thomas' Boys' School, LaMartiniere Boys' School, St. Vincent's Technical School, and St. Patrick's High School, all for boys; and Loretto Convent (Asansol), Calcutta Girls' School, and LaMartiniere Girls' School, all for girls. Data were made available through the courtesy of the Bureau.

choices of Anglo-Indian students, but also to obtain other information about them to be used as the basis for vocational advisement. A major observation was that many students were unrealistic about their preferences or plans for a career, or were unimaginative or uninformed. Of the 33 students ranking above average in the aptitude tests, ten had no vocational plans, or their plans were not commensure with their abilities; seven had high aspirations but were having serious financial difficulties; only five had realistic vocational plans without any major problems. About one-fifth of the group wanted to migrate from India.

CHAPTER SIX

SOCIAL RELATIONS AND SOCIAL STRUCTURE

The principal conceptual approach in this study is that the Anglo-Indians were socially but not culturally marginal to the British during the days of colonial domination, and that they were (and currently are) both socially and culturally marginal to other Indian communities. This thesis has been supported by various kinds of evidence concerning attitudes, organization, and behavior that bear upon the relations between Anglo-Indians and others. The uncertainties that Anglo-Indians faced concerning their own position in India had a circular cause-and-effect significance on the relations with other communities and even on inter-personal relations within their own group. These uncertainties also involved the question of identity — identity both as perceived by others and by Anglo-Indians themselves. An excerpt from the 1923 annual report of the Anglo-Indian and Domiciled European Association states the issue from the viewpoint of the Anglo-Indians:

> We look forward with a feeling of insecurity and uncertainty because of the undefined position allotted to us. On the one hand we are told we are Indian, and yet un-Indian, while on the other it is impressed upon us that, though truly European, our position has been officially defined as "statutory natives of India" and that as a result there is equally a gulf between us and the European.[96]

Since the formal departure of the British from India the situation has changed considerably. Officially, at least, Anglo-Indians are accepted as Indian nationals with all the rights of full citizenship. Yet on a strictly personal level they are still regarded by some indigenous Indians as European in their sympathies and loyalties. This remains true despite the efforts of many Anglo-Indians to demonstrate their moral commitment as Indian citizens and their desire to serve the country. These lingering doubts, reinforced in some instances by cultural and behavioral differences, have in numerous ways affected inter-community and inter-personal relations.

Whatever may be the interests and inclinations of Anglo-Indians regarding their relations with other Indians, most of them, by choice or circumstance, come into regular contact with Indian "communities" or persons of non-Indian background. These contacts are as varied and complex as the persons and situations involved. Such encounters may be casual and fleeting, or prolonged and continuous. Some are informal, others are formally structured within an institutional or organizational framework. Their content may range from emotionally involved interaction to what can be termed objectively instrumental

---

[96] *Report of the Anglo-Indian and Domiciled European Association* (Calcutta: Anglo-Indian and Domiciled European Association, 1923), p. 3.

in purpose. They may vary according to the social stratum of the persons involved, to locality or region, or to the means of communication. Indirect contacts are often provided by the mass media, but for the most part the media focuses on personalities and events not relevant to the Anglo-Indian Community, which is seldom mentioned in the general English-language press

In most situations in which direct interaction across community boundaries occurs, Anglo-Indians are numerically in the minority. The attitudinal content of such intergroup relations may run the gamut from negative to positive, from grossly-distorted stereotypes to a realistic understanding of what the "others" are actually like. Like minority peoples in most societies, Anglo-Indians are probably better informed about the "majority" peoples of India than the reverse, but even their understanding may be somewhat limited or even distorted. Although situational contacts between Anglo-Indians and others do occur in abundance, the evidence of this study indicates that these encounters do not necessarily lead to intimacy.

Inter-Group Marriage

The Anglo-Indian Community had its origin in inter-racial relations between males of European origin and females of India ancestry. These ethnic origins go as far back in time as the early European colonizing and trading ventures or military conquests into India. In the initial stages of colonization, the British, through the East India Company, and the Portuguese, Dutch, and French, through their colonial regimes, generally looked with favor on inter-marriage between their male employees, whether civil or military, and Indian women. So far as the Portuguese were concerned, inter-marriage was always viewed in a favorable manner, even encouraged, probably for political and religious reasons. Beginning in the later years of the eighteenth century, the East India Company prohibited higher civil or military personnel from marrying Indian or Anglo-Indian women, although permitting, without encouragement, the rank-and-file soldiers or civil employees to marry across racial or cultural barriers.

Domiciled Europeans (i.e., Europeans habitually residing in India) often identified with the Anglo-Indian Community and married freely with that group. The taboos against inter-marriage, imposed by the British through the East India Company, applied also to marriages with Catholics, whether Portuguese, Anglo-Indian, or Indian converts. Goodrich concludes from her analysis that the prohibitions against formal inter-ethnic or inter-faith marriages had the effect of encouraging illicit relations, and that probably the majority of children born during the period when these taboos were most rigidly enforced were illegitimate.[97]

During the past century, no official restraints have been imposed to prevent marriages between Europeans and members of the indigenous Indian population, whether Anglo-Indian or not, but social restraints accepted both by Europeans and

---

[97] Dorris L. Goodrich, "The Making of an Ethnic Group: The Eurasian Community in India," Unpublished PhD dissertation, University of California, Berkeley, 1952.

Indians have had the effect of minimizing inter-racial marriages, especially marriages between Anglo-Indians and persons affiliated with indigenous ethnic or cultural communities.

Crossing racial and cultural boundaries through marriage or unconventional sexual relations has occurred through the centuries of Anglo-Indian existence, whatever may have been the restrictions against marital or extra-marital relations. Through this bio-social process newly-created Anglo-Indians have been added to the Community each year. This is in addition to the number of children born to Anglo-Indian parents in conventional or unconventional unions. The great majority of Anglo-Indians apparently marry within their own community, but each year numbers of marriages occur across community lines. Since census records of such marriages are non-existent, the number of actual exogamous marital unions is largely a matter of speculation.

Records of welfare cases obtained from agencies in Calcutta over several decades of the present century revealed a considerable number of inter-community marriages.[98] Of 141 Anglo-Indian welfare clients for whom the ethnic identity of their parents was reported, 109 said that both parents were Anglo-Indians; 13 said their father was an Anglo-Indian but the mother belonged to another community; while 19 reported that the mother was Anglo-Indian but the father was a member of another group. Nearly one-fourth of the parents of the clients were thus married to a person other than an Anglo-Indian. Most of the clients themselves were women, and of the 104 who had been married about one-fourth had husbands who were not Anglo-Indians. About half of the male clients reported they had been married to non-Anglo-Indian women. Probably most of these ccases of inter-ethnic marriages involved either Indian-Christian or "domiciled Europeans." Welfare clients could not be considered a representative sample of Anglo-Indians because they are mainly from the lower economic and educational levels of the Community, but at least there is some evidence that a sizeable proportion of the Anglo-Indian population has a spouse or parent belonging to another group.

Evidence from interviews with Anglo-Indians in India suggests that the number of Anglo-Indian girls marrying into other groups is greater than the number of Anglo-Indian men marrying Indian women. Probably the economic situation is the major determining factor in this differential marriage rate. Many Anglo-Indian men of marriageable age are either unemployed or simply do not have sufficient income to support a family without a supplement from the wife's earnings. Not only are Anglo-Indian women often reluctant to assume these additional marital responsibilities, but men in such circumstances probably have limited appeal to young women in other communities as well. Furthermore, the stereotype of an Anglo-Indian youth is that of an irresponsible and unstable person who does not make a conventionally desirable husband. On the other hand, Anglo-Indian girls stereotypically exhibit such attributes as self-sufficiency,

---

[98] These data were obtained from a collection of case records in the library of Dr. John Broomfield of the University of Michigan. Of the several hundred records in the collection, the data here reported represent a random sample of the total number.

initiative, and independence of thought and action — qualities which many Indian men find desirable in a prospective spouse.

The non-Anglo-Indian man, especially those of Western orientation, who has considerable social status and a comfortable income, may have a stronger matrimonial appeal to an Anglo-Indian girl than an Anglo-Indian boy having neither of these assets. As one informant in South India observed, "Many Anglo-Indian girls would prefer to marry an attractive Sikh or Hindu who holds a commission in the military services than an Anglo-Indian with neither job nor status, in spite of religious differences." But even for non-Anglo-Indian men to establish their marital eligibility in the eyes of Anglo-Indian women, there must be a common ground of Western culture, especially as it may relate to a functional knowledge of English and a Western style of life. The European or Indian-Christian generally meets these specifications more readily than men of other religious or ethnic affiliations. An informant in Calcutta observed that Anglo-Indian girls often preferred British husbands. Even men with low incomes or occupational status may offer what appears to be, to the Anglo-Indian woman, the attractive prospect of settling in Great Britain. A Catholic priest and school principal in Bangalore observed that many upper-class Hindu and Muslim parents were willing for their sons to marry Anglo-Indian girls but were not willing for their daughters to marry Anglo-Indian men.

Anglo-Indians interviewed in several cities in India generally were of the opinion that the number of girls marrying outside the Community had increased in recent years, and that many of these marriages were to men who, nominally at least, were of a different religion. However, none of the informants submitted any empirical evidence as to the relative success or failure of such marriages. Some of them did comment on the possible difficulties that could arise when the husband was a traditionalist in his religious beliefs and way of life. The principal of a Calcutta school remarked:

> The gap between the Anglo-Indian way of life and that of the orthodox Hindu or Muslim is very wide, and it is not easily bridged because Hinduism and Islam are both a way of life as well as a religion. If the girl marries an orthodox Hindu, she may be required to embrace the Hindu faith and change her name. Furthermore, she will experience a drastic change in family relationships, especially if the husband's family is a joint kinship arrangement in which the bride lives in her husband's parental household and is subject to severe restrictions imposed by the elders of the kinship group.

These difficulties would also exist if the girl married into a traditionalist Muslim family, with additional difficulties if she had to share her husband with one or more other wives.

The increasing tendency for Anglo-Indian girls to marry into other communities has created problems for Anglo-Indian men of marriageable age. They are often unsuccessful in attracting a suitable spouse, either of the same community or of a different group. Even when a marriage is consummated within the Community the husband may not have the financial resources to support his wife on a scale to which one or both of them aspire. Both, but especially the wife, may desire to maintain a European standard of living but on an Asian income, usually inadequate for the costs that are involved.

Such a situation commonly produces inter-personal strains and even conflict, especially if the husband feels humiliated by his inability to support a family and is dependent on his wife's earnings. On the other hand, the Anglo-Indian girl who cannot find a suitable spouse, either within the Community or in other groups, may be forced to become self-supporting. If she possesses occupational skills that are in demand, as many do, the prospects of obtaining a job are reasonably good. But if she has none of these skills, or is otherwise unequalified for a position, she may drift into illicit activities that afford some income.

Of 52 employed Anglo-Indians in Bangalore who responded to the question, "Have you, or any of your friends or members of your family, married outside the Anglo-Indian Community?" twenty-two reported that such out-group marriages had occurred in the family or friendship group.[99] Five were married to Goans, who may (or may not) have been of mixed racial ancestry, but were at least nominal Christians. One indicated that two of his sisters had married outside, one to a Muslim and the other to a Hindu. A female respondent reported that a cousin was married to a Punjabi (Indian), and that friends had married into the Muslim, Parsee, Hindu, and Sikh communities. A male respondent stated that two brothers, two sisters, and a "number" of nephews and nieces, were married to persons of British or American nationality. Another male respondent stated that he himself was married to a Parsee convert (presumably to Christianity), and still another reported that his aunt had married a Hindu convert.

In Calcutta, a divorced Anglo-Indian woman (a friend of the interviewer) was re-married to a Westernized Hindu who had discarded the religious beliefs of his parents. In another instance a young Anglo-Indian woman married the scion of a prominent Hindu family in Calcutta. A Catholic priest in Bangalore reported that of forty marriage ceremonies performed by him in the first half of 1967, two were marriages of Anglo-Indian girls to persons outside the Community, one to a Muslim, the other to an Englishman. Another girl had applied for permission to marry a Muslim. An Anglo-Indian Air Force officer in Secunderabad reported that his daughter is married to a Hindu, who is unorthodox in his religious beliefs. In Hyderabad, an Anglo-Indian employee of an American organization is the wife of a Muslim. Although these cases represent only a few people, they do support the view that a considerable number of Anglo-Indians are marrying outside of the Community.

Attitudes Toward Inter-Group Relations

Of the 52 Anglo-Indians included in the Bangalore survey, opinion on the topic of inter-group marriages was divided. In response to the question, "How do you personally feel about marrying *outside* the Anglo-Indian Community, either for

---

[99] The respondents did not in every instance specify the sex of the Anglo-Indian marrying outside the Community, but apparently the majority were women.

yourself or a member of your family?" twenty-two were unfavorable, 11 were favorable, and 19 either had no opinion concerning the issue or qualified their answers in such a way as to suggest an attitude of indifference — e.g., "it has its good and bad points," or "I don't think it would make any difference." Those who were favorable to inter-group marriages generally qualified their response by specifying that the spouse should be Westernized. Some replied that the success of such marriages depended upon the individual. One said, "Any Western community or nationality, a big YES! Anyone Eastern, acceptable, but with reservations." Another replied that "When women are married to persons of another community, they can be assured of a bright future because out of every one hundred Anglo-Indians you can find only one in a good position who can give the kind of treatment required for a smoothly-running home."

Those who held unfavorable attitudes toward intermarriage were often strongly averse to such marriages. As one viewed the situation, "Because no matter how highly an Indian is educated, their accent of speaking and expressing, and their habits, will never leave them." Another who disapproved of inter-marriages explicitly defined the problem as he saw it, "Disapprove foreigners. Because they hoodwink the poor girls with fantastic lies of the positions at home, make all the promises, get what they want, and then, 'I'll be seeing you, DARLING!' " Still another said, "I do not favor the idea of Anglo-Indians marrying outside the Community, as marriage in itself calls for considerable adjustments apart from the added adjustments two different communities would be required to adopt."

When the respondents were asked if there were any communities which they would particularly approve or disapprove for inter-marriage outside the Anglo-Indian Community, the majority favored marriage to persons of European heritage or the Christian faith; or conversely, were opposed to marriages with persons whose language, religion, or way of life differed from that of the Anglo-Indians. Explicitly or implicitly, the latter viewpoint referred to various Indian communities except, generally, Indian-Christians, Goans, or Mangaloreans, who are at least nominal Christians. One respondent said, "I should approve of Anglo-Indians marrying the Goans because they are like the Anglo-Indians — their ancestors were not British but French and Portuguese." Another approved marrying into "higher communities" but not "lower communities." "The former consists of educated and well-beloved Indians who know how to move about in our company." Presumably this respondent had reference to castes or other status groups in India.

Some of the respondents were specifically negative concerning other "communities". One disapproved of mariages with other Indians for the prejudicial reason, as he phrased it, that "a nigger will always be a nigger." Another disapproved marriage with Brahmins, observing that "Hinduism and Christianity are like East and West." An Anglo-Indian man opposed marriages to "Sikhs, Kashmiris, Hindus, and Biharis." Another expressly favored marriages with Europeans or Americans but not with Indians. "I approve of intermarriage with members of European or American communities because they possess the same culture and heritage as we do, but never with an Indian, because their so-called tolerance and Westernization is only a thin veneer which is easily stripped off." A female respondent stated positively that "the only Indian that an Anglo-Indian boy or girl can marry without any regrets is a Punjabi because this community has a Western outlook on life" and "is the only one which is tolerant of an Anglo-Indian and appreciates this Community for what it is."

Although the proportion of Anglo-Indian marriages to other Indians is still small, young Anglo-Indian adults do fraternize socially with their peers of other communities. This relationship tends to be largely, though not entirely, between Anglo-Indian girls and young men from the Indian-Christian, Hindu, Muslim, Sikh, or other groups. These associations seldom terminate in serious romances or marriages, but rather tend to be limited mainly to recreational activities such as attendance at movies, dances, night clubs, informal house parties, and the like.

One of the common complaints among Anglo-Indians is that Indian men are often interested in Anglo-Indian girls only as objects of sexual exploitation. An informant in Kharagpur stated that "we have come to accept them (other Indians) in our dance halls, but we do not like this." Another informant, in Calcutta, observed that they frequently "crash" social functions, without an invitation, for the purpose of meeting Anglo-Indian girls. "If the function is a dance," he said, "Hindu, Muslim, or Sikh boys attend to dance with the girls. Anglo-Indian men have no opportunity to dance with, or otherwise know very well, girls of other communities." This respondent also commented that social isolation of a class nature is almost as great; that Anglo-Indians of low status have little opportunity to meet informally, on a basis of social equality, persons on the higher social and economic levels.

Differential Inter-Group Relations

Intimate social life of Anglo-Indians tends to be largely with others of the same community, although there are many exceptions. Responses to a questionnaire from 52 employed residents of Bangalore supports this generalization. When asked to identify by community the three persons (excluding members of their own kinship group) whom they regard as closest friends, three-fifths (32) specified only Anglo-Indians. Seven of the respondents mentioned as closest friends two Anglo-Indians and one outsider, while eight respondents specified one Anglo-Indian and two from other communities. Only one of the respondents included no Anglo-Indian among his best friends, and four reported that they made no distinctions as to community. The form of the question, however, reveals nothing as to the content of these intimate inter-personal relations, nor does it exclude additional friendships beyond the three that are specified.

Additional evidence from the same survey tends to support the foregoing data. In response to a question concerning informal social activities, about two-fifths stated that they participated only with Anglo-Indians, but slightly over half mentioned that other communities were included in such activities as going places with friends, visiting, or having parties in homes. Of those who do participate socially with non-Anglo-Indians, several did not specify the group but employed such expressions as "Anglo-Indians mostly," "generally," or "usually," or mentioned only Christians such as Indian-Christians, Goans, or Hindu converts. However, a few are catholic in their choice of associates, as indicated by such responses as: "People of all communities, but particularly Christians brought up in an Indo-Anglican style," or "My social activities are not restricted to any particular group or community — they belong to Hindu, Christian, and Muslim communities."

The tendency for many Anglo-Indians to associate only or mainly with others of the same community is by no means peculiar to this group; it is, indeed, characteristic of other ethnic peoples as well. The comments of two respondents offer a possible clue to the explanation of this tendency: "I associate for the most part with Anglo-Indians, since occasions in their midst are the most enjoyable," and "I do go out with friends from other communities, but whatever you do with them you are still made to feel different. You do what they do and act as they act ... definitely does not give one any pleasure in trying to mix."

Personal interviews with Anglo-Indians in various Indian cities, and observations of their social behavior, tend to confirm the foregoing findings. An Anglo-Indian woman living in a middle-class residential district of Bangalore said that she and her family do not mix socially with their Brahmin neighbors; their interaction is limited to a morning or evening formal greeting. A young widow employed by a hotel in Bangalore and residing in a district occupied by Hindus and Muslims, said that she and her family had no intimate contacts with their neighbors. On the other hand, some Anglo-Indians pridefully acknowledge that their friends include members of other communities and that they have friendly relations with neighbors. An executive in a major corporation in Hyderabad said that his family resides in a large compound with fellow-employees and that they are on friendly terms with all their neighbors. The asserted self-identity of himself and his wife is Indian, not merely Anglo-Indian; symbolic of the family's Indian identity his wife usually wears a *sari*. A Bombay Anglo-Indian businessman reported that his children have many friends from various communities, contrasting this situation with his own childhood in which his parents shielded him from intimate contacts with Indian children.

The separatism that so often characterizes relationships between Anglo-Indians and others may or may not reflect crude ethnocentric sentiments of the communities involved, depending on specific situations and the attitudes of individuals. Cultural factors may also be either divisive or integrative. Persons sharing a common religion and mother tongue, or a similar style of life, are more likely to be psychologically and socially close than those in which religion, language, and life-style are strikingly different. For this reason Anglo-Indians commonly find that associations with Indian-Christians, Goans, or others having a similar cultural heritage are more satisfying than with Hindus or Muslims whose religion and way of life are rather formidable barriers. Because of prohibitions concerning behavior in the preparation and consumption of food, for example, Anglo-Indians and orthodox Hindus or Muslims cannot satisfactorily dine together in the homes of either. Eating without benefit of table utensils, as Hindus and Muslims generally do, may be offensive to Anglo-Indians, while the serving and consumption of beef or pork is unacceptable to most Hindus or Muslims. Hindus are commonly vegetarians, while Anglo-Indians are usually non-vegetarian. These cultural practices and values in association with numerous other variations become, therefore, a barrier to intimate interaction.

Language

One of the barriers to social interaction between Indian communities or regions is language. Under the British regime the English language served the needs of Anglo-Indians in a satisfactory manner since it was the official *lingua franca,* and therefore was adequate for communication in most work situations and in school. Anglo-Indians did not usually make the effort to become fluent in an indigenous language and were thus unable to communicate effectively with other Indians not conversant in English; nor could they enter fully into the social life of the Indian people or comprehend many subtle meanings embedded in Indian culture. This meant that their relations with other Indians were often tangential. They still are. The post-Independence education requirement that all students in school study an indigenous Indian language may help to lower the barriers, but achieving language facility is arduous for Anglo-Indians who generally are not strongly motivated toward the mastery of an indigenous language. The language barrier thus prevents Anglo-Indians from participating freely in various collective undertakings even if they are otherwise qualified; and, by the same measure, non-English-speaking Indians are likewise prevented from participation in certain spheres of Anglo-Indian life.

Infiltration and Seepage

The two-way process of infiltration and seepage is a feature of many groups and societies, whether distinguishable by cultural or physical characteristics, or both. Individuals may, for a variety of reasons, seek to enter such groups, either publicly or clandestinely, and if successful, change their identity and undergo new social experiences. By the same token, individuals may abandon their own communities and in so doing may or may not strive to enter another group. Literature is replete with examples of this phenomenon: the expatriate, the religious convert, the immigrant seeking a new national identity, the Hindu searching for a different caste identity, the American Negro striving to "pass" as a Causcasian, and so on. This process of infiltration and seepage is likewise characteristic of change in the Anglo-Indian Community. The number and types of persons who seek to enter or leave a community is determined by several factors, including the comparative status of the group, conditions of life and work within it, opportunities that exist outside, scalability of the barriers against infiltrators, and the values of those involved.

Infiltration by outsiders has probably occurred throughout the long history of the Anglo-Indian Community, although specific information is sketchy in that the nature of the process defies accurate record-keeping. The prevailing opinion among Anglo-Indians who were interviewed is that infiltration occurs in considerable volume, but whether it is increasing or decreasing is not clear. One informant in Bangalore expressed the opinion that it is decreasing because today there are few advantages to be gained by identifying with the Anglo-Indian Community. An informant in Calcutta stated that infiltration probably occurred in Bombay in greater volume than in any other Indian city because of the presence of larger numbers of Goans, Mangaloreans, and other South Indians who themselves may be of mixed Portuguese and Indian ancestry. Presumably some of the infiltrators are Indian-Christians with English names; even Hindus or members of other Indian communities reportedly have sought to identity with the Anglo-Indian Community.

Name changes is one of the means by which persons may establish a new community identity, or even bolster his social position without necessarily changing community. An informant in Calcutta mentioned an individual who changed her name from Nath, a common Indian family name, to Nott in her effort to become recognized as an Anglo-Indian. Frank Anthony observes a tendency for many Anglo-Indians to look with favor on British or Irish names in preference to names of Portuguese derivation.[100] Sometimes the Portuguese names were Anglicized. Thus D'Silva becomes Silver, Da Costa becomes Coster, Rodrigues is changed to Rodericks, Perreira to Perrier, Fernandez to Fern, or D'Cruz to Cross. A few Anglo-Indians even have Jewish or Armenian names, possibly the result of inter-marriage in which the progeny of these unions were assigned to the Anglo-Indian Community.

Infiltrators are motivated by various reasons for entering the Anglo-Indian Community. In the labor market they may find it advantageous to pose as an Anglo-Indian in seeking a job requiring certain skills or experience. Some apparently feel that an Anglo-Indian identification is an advantage in obtaining a potential passport to migrate to another country. Others seeking welfare benefits provided by the Community, or scholarships to enable their children to attend an Anglo-Indian school, likewise may find identification as an Anglo-Indian an advantage.

Anglo-Indians are said by some to have certain distinguishing characteristics of speech, mannerisms, and physical appearance; hence spurious claimants to membership in the Community are, accordingly, identifiable by those who are sensitized to these traits. If, however, Anglo-Indian officials are to certify with assurance the proper qualifications for membership, a birth certificate is generally required as evidence. Such information is not always available in India, where vital statistics are known to be incomplete and often inaccurate.

Persons who regard themselves as "authentic" Anglo-Indians generally resent these incursions into the Community and view the infiltrators as interlopers, undeserving of the Community's benefits and prerogatives. The economic effects of infiltration are a matter of concern to some because the infiltrators may lay

---

[100] Frank Anthony, *Britain's Betrayal in India* (New Delhi: Allied Publishers, 1969), p. 371.

claim to jobs or welfare benefits that might otherwise go to persons recognized as authentic Anglo-Indians. Those who are proud of their Anglo-Indian heritage and are dedicated to the ideals of the Community are particularly resentful of interlopers who have no proper claim to membership. Even Goans who seek to identify as Anglo-Indians, even if they lay claim to dual racial heritage, are sometimes regarded as spurious claimants. There has thus developed a status order in which Anglo-Indians with English family names reportedly achieve a modicum of prestige associated with British ancestry.

One of the functions of the All-India Anglo-Indian Association, through some of its local branches, is to evaluate the credentials of individuals applying to the Association for assistance and to eliminate those whose ancestry cannot be properly authenticated. Anglo-Indians applying for passports and in need of official identification may, if their birth certificates are in proper order, be certified by the local organization. These standards and rules of certification have apparently been modified in recent years.

Through the process of seepage many leave the Community, either temporarily or permanently, presumably because they believe that identification as Anglo-Indians is a handicap. Some apparently are embarrassed to be known as an Anglo-Indian and either identify with some other group or strive for anonymity in their social relations. Others avoid the Anglo-Indian label in the labor market, believing that their chances of employment or promotion in salary or rank are better if they change their identity, at least in the work situation. This does not necessarily mean that their psychological identity has changed, but only the overt manifestations of identity. A Calcutta informant said that her son, employed in a Kerala firm, "passed" as an Indian-Christian at work but otherwise retained his family and Community ties. As a former student and teacher in England, she was self-identified as a Christian while overseas. A number of Anglo-Indians of fair complexion have been known to pass as Westerners in Europe, America, or India.

Intermarriage also provides a mechanism for an Anglo-Indian woman to change her identity if her husband belongs to another community. Probably the greatest seepage involuntarily occurred along this line among the children or young adults of dual racial ancestry who were absorbed into the general Indian population when their European or Anglo-Indian fathers did not assume responsibility for their upbringing and the burden was therefore placed on the Indian mother.[101]

Those who are loyal to the Community and are emotionally involved in its affairs often view with concern the tendency of some to change their community identity or abandon India altogether. They feel that the future of the Community will be determined, in considerable measure, by the efforts of individuals willing to work for the common good, both of the Anglo-Indian people and of India as a whole. Probably most Anglo-Indians, however, are tolerant of those who shift their community identity, especially if the change of identity has not been made

---

[101] Dorris L. Goodrich, *op. cit.,* p. 5.

to the discredit of other Anglo-Indians. Reginald Maher expresses this point of view in his brief account of a young Hollywood star who concealed her identity as an Anglo-Indian because she apparently feared that disclosure of her dual racial heritage would damage her professionally. "To blame her for thus abandoning her people would be quite unfair," he writes. "Except a heroine fired with a pride in and love for her people, nobody would have acted differently. She was in danger of having thrust on her the reeking mantle of the odious Victoria Jones of *Bhowani Junction.*"[102]

Social Differentials

India is a highly stratified society. Viewing the entire social order in perspective, one perceives a complex hierarchy of groups and persons arranged in a status system, with various determinants of status. Within many communities there is also a status order in which individuals are distributed according to the values that are attached to the functions they perform, the possessions they have, their physical or cultural attributes, their behavior, and the like. The Anglo-Indian Community as a whole does not rank high in the status system of India, although by any reasonable criteria it probably ranks above some communities, such as the "untouchable" castes. Aside from barriers restricting social interaction between organized groups, class barriers also have a limiting influence on interaction and social participation. Just as many Anglo-Indians do not have the financial resources or cultural attributes required to obtain admission to numerous organized groups, by the same measure they are isolated socially and perhaps spatially from other Indians who are more generously endowed with these possessions or attributes.

A picture of the stratification system, obtained from an analysis of the era when the British were an integral part of the social system in the sub-continent, presents a unique perspective. Because of their power and influence, coupled with their affluence, the British ranked at the top of the status hierarchy, save for a few privileged Indians such as native princes and great landowners. This intrenched position of power and wealth provided the underpinnings of a prestige system whose strata were virtually closed to outsiders not having the proper social credentials. Anglo-Indians were rigorously excluded from British "society," however much they may have admired the British and aspired to be like them, even to associate with them. They thus occupied an in-between position in the social structure, from which they could "look up" to the British and "look down" on other Indians. But upward mobility into the British segment was a virtual impossibility, and downward mobility into Indian society, as they would view it, was not desired. Since the withdrawal of the British from India the structural aspect of stratification has changed, but the values maintained by Anglo-Indians have been modified only slowly.

Religion in India has both a divisive and integrative influence on social life. As

---

[102] Reginald Maher, *These Are the Anglo-Indians* (Calcutta: Swallow Press, 1962), p. 40.

we have observed earlier, the Christians (Anglo-Indians and Indian-Christians) are culturally distinct from Hindu, Muslim, and other communities, and these cultural differences are reflected in social distinctions and often isolation of one community from another. But within the Christian population there are differentials based upon doctrinal, organizational, and even biological elements. Indian-Christians sometimes view the Anglo-Indians as a community whose members are only their "half-brothers." Both Indian-Christian and Anglo-Indian communities are fragmented into numerous denominations and sects whose religious beliefs and practices are sometimes suspect by those in different groups. They worship in different churches, socialize mainly with persons of their own religion, and even have a style of life that may keep them apart rather than bring them together.

Within the Anglo-Indian Community there are differentials of status and power which tend to isolate the "haves" from the "have nots." Some of the organized groups (clubs, for example) are prestigious, open only to the elite who have the funds necessary for membership or participation in various activities. These organizations are centers of influence since the power elite generally gravitate to them. This is especially true of the All-India Anglo-Indian Association, whose membership includes most of the prominent Anglo-Indians in positions of power. There would be considerable overlapping, for example, in the memberships of the Rangers Club of Calcutta or the Gidney Club of New Delhi and the All-India Anglo-Indian Association.

Economic differentials within the Community are generally associated with *social* differentials and therefore constitute a deep cleavage in the group. It is well known that a large portion of the Community is mired in poverty and forced to reside in the slums under degrading conditions. This class cleavage is itself a barrier whose effect has been to isolate the lower-classes from middle- and upper-class Anglo-Indians, to alienate them from the main-stream of Anglo-Indian society, and to create a "communication gap" between them and their fellows in more comfortable circumstances.

The lower stratum consists not only of a "hard core" for whom destitution has become an involuntary way of life, but also the downwardly mobile who have seen better days. Among the long-time denizens of slums, the preponderant feeling seems to be that of apathy and defeatism, often coupled with expressions of self-pity and complaints about their mistreatment and misfortune. Sometimes there appears to be a sullen acceptance of their fate in a world in which they feel powerless. Those who have more recently experienced such degradation, whose memories of a better life are still fresh, likewise feel engulfed by forces over which they have no control, and embittered toward those whom they hold responsible for their hard luck. Many blame the British for abandoning them, the Anglo-Indian leaders for ignoring them, and other Indians for discriminating against them.

In the absence of data providing a comparison of the economic position of Anglo-Indians and other Indians, or a comparison of Anglo-Indians "then" and "now," or even Anglo-Indians in different localities, it is not possible to establish trends in income or employment. However, a sample survey conducted in Calcutta in 1957-1958 reveals clearly the economic situation at that time.[103] The survey involved interviews with persons representing 491 households for a total of 2,116 individuals, or an estimated 10 per cent of Calcutta's Anglo-Indian population at that time. Even though the incomes for the Community as a whole are low, commensurate with the income level of the Indian population in general, there is a fairly wide gap between the highest and lowest income classes. The income distribution is indicated by Table II, adapted from the original tables and tabulations.

Table II

*The Percentage Distribution of
Monthly Household Incomes in Calcutta*[104]

Monthly-Income Groups in Rupees	Dollar Equivalent*	Number of Households	Percent of Total
50 or less	$10 or less	36	7.3
51-100	10 to 20	77	15.7
101-200	20 to 40	118	24.0
201-400	40 to 80	124	25.3
401-750	80 to 150	80	16.3
750 or over	150 or over	56	11.4

* Dollar value of the rupee was approximately 21 cents at that time. Owing to currency devaluation its present value is about 14 cents.

The views that middle or upper income Anglo-Indians have concerning the "under dogs" of their Community vary considerably, depending largely on the values of particular individuals and their intellectual grasp of the situation. Some have compassion for those who, in their opinion, have been victimized by social forces or by indifferent or unscrupulous persons. Some even have dedicated themselves to the task of assisting, in whatever way possible, Anglo-Indians imprisoned by the complex web of economic and social circumstances. A Calcutta journalist, for example, has dedicated himself to the cause of the Community as a whole and particularly to the destitute. A businessman in the same city, also a leader in Community affairs, organized a club primarily for the benefit of Anglo-Indian youth, especially those whose opportunities for constructive recreation were limited by their impoverishment. Many others, sympathetic in their attitudes toward the unfortunate, contribute time and money toward the alleviation of economic distress. Most of these activities, however, tend to be palliative and are therefore limited in their rehabilitative effects.

Anglo-Indians in comfortable circumstances often personalize the situation and place the blame on individuals for their own misfortune. One leading educationist in Calcutta stated that Anglo-Indians under the British regime developed the habit of spending money recklessly with little or no concern for the

---

[103] *Pilot Survey of the Socio-Economic Conditions of the Anglo-Indian Community, 1957-1958* (Calcutta: Baptist Mission Press, 1958).

[104] *Ibid.,* Table 3.1, p. 10.

proverbial "rainy day," and that this pattern of behavior has persisted. When, after Independence, they were forced to rely upon their own resources, they had no savings and often no jobs. A similar point of view was expressed by a white-collar worker in Calcutta: "We Anglo-Indians are so dashed profligate; as soon as we get one rupee we start planning how to spend the ten rupees we hope to get. We have felt compelled to maintain a certain standard of living, and that costs money, often more than we can afford." Another white-collar worker rationalized the situation by remarking that "every community has its dregs. Some Anglo-Indians are too proud to take a low-pay job, or too proud to beg. They will always remain poor... For those wanting to go to work the opportunity is there. You can't pick and choose. There are some people who are just drones. How they live I don't know." Similarly an Anglo-Indian leader in Bangalore dismissed the problem of destitution mainly as the consequence of profligacy among the "undeserving" poor.

Impoverished Anglo-Indians are undoubtedly aware that others interpret their plight in such personalized terms, and this awareness may tend to widen further the "understanding gap" between the higher and lower social classes. As observed in another section of this book, criticisms of the top leadership of the Community and of the All-India Anglo-Indian Association indicate a rather widespread feeling that those who are socially and economically secure are without compassion and are therefore not deeply interested in the welfare of those at the bottom. On the higher levels of the social structure, however, there is a general approval of the top leadership. A well-to-do informant in Calcutta, speaking of the president of the All-India Anglo-Indian Association, said, "Frank Anthony today presents the most intelligent view of the Anglo-Indian Community and of all India as well... We couldn't have found a better leader." And a knowledgeable educator in Kharagpur said, "The top hierarchy is working perfectly. But in our state I fear that those who should be able to serve well have lost the 'common touch.' "

Social Mobility

Contrary to popular notions, India is a dynamic society in which social change is occurring in almost every facet of the social order. Inevitably these changes have the effect of altering the social and economic positions of individuals, families, and even entire communities. In this respect the Anglo-Indian Community is no exception.

By the third decade in the present century, competition for jobs became intensified, reducing the near-monopoly of certain occupations that Anglo-Indians had enjoyed. Undoubtedly this made it increasingly difficult for them to maintain an acceptable standard of living. Except for a period of virtually full-employment during World War II, the post-Independence period has been one of increasing economic hardship during which large numbers of persons have been either unemployed or employed at incomes inadequate for the maintenance of a standard of living to which they had been accustomed in earlier years. These persons were in a position wherein the mobility escalator was moving downward, leading to the slum and conditions of penury and privation.

This is not to say that the mobility escalator was moving downward for everyone; undoubtedly many people were able to hold fairly remunerative jobs and otherwise maintain a desirable standard of living. At the same time there were a few whose economic position had improved during these years. Whether the mobility patterns paralleled those of other Indian communities it is not possible to say, but it may well be that inflation and unemployment characterizing the Indian economy affected other communities in much the same extent that it has the Anglo-Indians.

The survey conducted in Calcutta by the Anglo-Indian Survey Committee, mentioned earlier in this chapter, reveals fairly well the employment situation in 1957-1958. Of 1,207 persons 14 years of age or over who stated they were "in need of employment," the following data, classified by sex and age, resulted from the survey:

Table III

*Percentage Distribution of
Anglo-Indian Adults in "Need of Employment"*[105]

Age Groups	Male	Female	Total
14-17	14.0	17.5	15.9
18-50	16.9	39.5	33.4
51-60	31.5	32.3	31.9
60 plus	38.2	34.3	36.2
Total average	27.0	36.4	31.8

Of the total number of Anglo-Indians in the sample, approximately one-third were in need of work, representing about one-fourth of the males and slightly over one-third of the females. The two zones of Calcutta having the highest percentage of persons in need of work were Dharamtolla (43) and Entally (38), both having concentrations of impoverished residents. Although it is generally conceded that Anglo-Indian women commonly have better opportunities than men for employment this generalization probably is valid only for those who have secretarial or nursing skills which are in short supply. Whether the percentage of Anglo-Indians in Calcutta in need of gainful employment is valid for the Community in India as a whole is problematical; doubtless the proportion varies according to the locality or region. At the same time there are no comparable data for other Indian communal groups, even in Calcutta.

An overwhelming majority of the persons interviewed in the survey believed that the "socio-economic position of the Community is much worse than it was twenty years ago."[106] Of 430 adult respondents, approximately nine out of ten

---

[105] *Ibid.*, adapted from Table 6.2, p. 20. The number of persons in "need of employment" is not necessarily the same as the number of unemployed persons. The survey revealed that 55.8 per cent were gainfully occupied. The remainder (44.2 per cent) were either "in need of work," or for some reason were unemployable or did not desire a job.

[106] *Ibid.*, p. 2.

viewed the situation as less favorable than two decades earlier. Whether the worsening of economic conditions for Calcutta Anglo-Indians specifically, or other Indians in general, implies an increasing number of downwardly mobile individuals is uncertain. Knowledgeable Anglo-Indians can point to examples of individuals or families who have become destitute since Independence; at the same time others can identify individuals who have been upwardly mobile in terms of income and occupational status, while positions of many appear to have changed little or not at all. The balance is not entirely clear, but the overall picture does seem to indicate that downward mobility has exceeded upward mobility in volume, although mobility in either direction may be selective in terms of education, occupational skills, and individual abilities.

Interviews with Anglo-Indians in several cities revealed a preponderance of opinion that the Community as a whole has experienced an economic decline since Independence. In Patna, the participants in a panel discussion agreed that as far as income and standard of living are concerned the Community had lost ground in the post-Independence period. This may, however, have been true of other communal groups as well, especially those groups which are relatively small in numbers. A radio technician in Calcutta said he believes that the economic situation has been worsening for Anglo-Indians and that the prospects for improvement are poor because of increased competition for jobs and the spread of unemployment. Another informant discussed the matter in a similar vein, saying that many have been forced down the social structure, and that those who have been downwardly mobile are not likely to move up again.

Undoubtedly many workers have changed occupations without any appreciable increase or decrease in income or social status – what is generally known as horizontal mobility. There are also instances of upward mobility in which individuals have been upgraded in the occupational structure through promotions in rank or increases in income. Upward mobility on the occupational ladder is probably characterized by low velocity and short distance movement (generally true of workers everywhere). There are, however, instances of impressive occupational successes. A young Calcutta industrialist, for example, occupied a relatively important post in 1964, having risen from a low position in the social structure. Commenting on the general situation, he said that although the Community "does grouse a good deal about the lack of opportunities for upgrading, the situation is better now than it was in earlier days." He possesses a viewpoint commonly held by successful businessmen, contrasting with the outlook of the unsuccessful or downwardly mobile worker.

What appears to be a preponderance of downwardly mobile persons is undoubtedly the result of numerous contributing factors or conditions. The depressed condition of the Indian economy is undoubtedly an important factor, possibly the basic one. Increased competitiveness for jobs that at one time were virtually monopolized by Anglo-Indians is another. Some members of the Community would presumably prefer to be unemployed than to accept menial jobs that might entail a loss of status, at least in their own eyes. Inadequate educational qualifications or training for certain positions has prevented many

Anglo-Indians from moving up in the occupational structure, or have perhaps even been responsible for their occupational descent. Anglo-Indians do not ordinarily belong to labor unions; hence little use is made of this kind of organization for upgrading or protection from loss of job. Because Anglo-Indian males generally have more difficulty than females in obtaining employment, or holding jobs they already have, it seems reasonable that downward mobility in terms of income or occupational status is greater among men than among women in the Community. Finally, there is the possibility that discrimination in employment or promotion in salary or rank may have the effect of forcing individuals downward in the socio-economic structure, or at least blocking or decelerating their upward movement.

Upward social mobility most commonly occurs when individuals are motivated toward the achievement of goals representing an elevation of status. Aspirations of individuals to attain these goals may be modified by the strength of their motivations and the realism of their objectives. Often the actual expectations fall short of the level of aspirations. In the survey of students in Anglo-Indian schools of West Bengal, the results of which were tabulated in another chapter, it was learned that the expressed levels of both aspiration and expectation for Anglo-Indian students were high — as high as the aspiration-expectation levels for Indian students in other communities.

What the data do not show is the intensity of motivation of the students to attain these goals, or whether the levels were a matter of phantasy or of serious intent. The fact remains, nevertheless, that the students did set their occupational goals fairly high, the majority aspiring to vocations on the professional or administrative levels, however unrealistic their aspirations and expectations might be. Whether these aspirations will eventually be translated into actual mobility strivings, successful or unsuccessful, can only be known when, as adults, they confront the world of work.

CHAPTER SEVEN

ORGANIZED LIFE OF ANGLO-INDIANS

India is a land in which various "communities" maintain a degree of exclusiveness through organized groups which erect barriers confining membership and participation to individuals of a particular religion, caste, language, occupation, region, or racial heritage. Such organized collectivities are usually manifestations of an ethnocentric sentiment, and exist to protect the members or facilitate their efforts to achieve certain group or individual objectives. The All-India Anglo-Indian Association and various Anglo-Indian clubs are examples of such organized exclusiveness. Somewhat comparable are Indian organizations (Hindu, Muslim, Parsee, Sikh) which normally admit to membership only persons of a designated religious identification.

There are numerous organizations in which Anglo-Indians are admitted as members and participants along with members of other communities. Some of these are open to all, irrespective of race, religion, or other attributes; some have selective membership policies, admitting certain group representatives but excluding others, either explicitly or implicitly. Labor unions in India have an open-door policy, admitting Anglo-Indians along with other Indians regardless of community identity, provided they qualify for membership on other specified grounds. Certain welfare organizations, however, restrict membership to "Christians," whether Anglo-Indian, Indian-Christian, or "domiciled European." The East India Trust Fund, which has administrative supervision over a number of organizations such as "homes" for the aged or disabled, is such an organization. Within these establishments the residents are generally isolated from all non-Christian peoples, with the occasional exceptions of organization employees.

Anglo-Indian schools in which students and teachers generally represent a considerable range of communal affiliations is another relevant example of heterogeneity. Christian churches likewise have a membership of Anglo-Indians and Indian-Christians, and may even be attended by persons representing non-Christian communities. In many organized work situations Anglo-Indians likewise associate with other Indians on the basis of presumed social equality. Inter-personal relations within these organizational structures undoubtedly vary, from intimate to formal, depending on the attitudes of the interacting persons and the particular circumstances.

Social organizations function as repositories of and/or transmitters of culture and in these respects may be either integrative or disruptive, bringing people together or keeping them apart. The cultural components of an organization may center around religious ideologies and practices, or, for that matter, beliefs and behavior in any sphere of life. The religious beliefs and practices of Anglo-Indians as manifest in certain organizations provide barriers to interaction with Hindus or

Muslims (or other communal groups) whose organizations become repositories of a quite different body of religious doctrines or cultural traditions. Likewise, barriers erected by other communal groups often limit interaction with Anglo-Indians. Such exclusion, however, does not necessarily imply inter-communal animus. Since Anglo-Indians and Indian-Christians are not separated by religious differences they may hold common membership in certain organizations such as churches; but they may nevertheless be separated by "blood ties," communal feelings, and style of life.

Psychological and Organizational Components of Community

A "community" has two essential components. One is a psychological element in which individuals come to think of themselves as a distinctive collectivity whose members share a common or similar set of interests, values, and cultural elements. The second is a formal or informal set of organizations whose functions are to satisfy certain needs and desires of its members in the various affairs of social life. Goodrich is of the opinion that the Anglo-Indian group ceased long ago to be merely a disparate aggregation of individuals having certain distinctive physical characteristics and became a community in which the members viewed themselves collectively as a people apart.[107] This community self-awareness emerged slowly, the result, at least in part, of discrimination against them by the British and rejection by other Indians. As observed in another chapter, the British did not consider them *bona fide* Europeans, and the populations of India did not generally consider them acceptable Indians. The psychological and social need for a clear identity presaged the gradual development of an ethnocentric outlook which made possible a sense of belonging.[108]

A "community consciousness" and *esprit de corps* can perhaps best be nourished and strengthened within the framework of social organization. At least a social organization can operate as a means through which such feelings are encouraged. The early years of the nineteenth century saw the emergence of an organized community life within the Anglo-Indian minority. Tenuous and unstable as the initial organizations almost inevitably turned out to be, they nevertheless provided a basis for collective social action and participation in organized social life. Probably many organizations that came into existence under colonial conditions survived only a short time, leaving no authentic documentary records. As Goodrich points out, many of them emerged under crisis conditions and declined when the immediate crisis had passed and the situation was altered. Some appeared as a reaction to threats against the group as a whole or its individual members. Others were undoubtedly born of a growing sense of deprivation and a realization that the survival of the community necessitated organized defensive action by the Anglo-Indians themselves.

---

[107] Dorris L. Goodrich, "The Making of an Ethnic Group: The Eurasian Community of India." Unpublished PhD dissertation, University of California, Berkeley, 1952, p. 7.

[108] *Ibid.*, pp. 67-112.

Organizational Antecedents

This is not to say that Anglo-Indians were completely excluded from all forms of organized activity. The Christian churches admitted them, if not always as social equals with the Europeans who dominated these organizations but at least ideologically as members within the fatherhood of a Christian God. In the eighteenth century, before proscriptive policies were adopted by the East India Company, they were usually admitted to the European schools in India on an equal basis with the children of European parents. It was not until late in that century that they were denied some of these privileges. They were also alternately admitted to, or excluded from, military organizations, depending on the prevailing climate of British opinion and the trend of events. All of these organizations were dominated by Europeans who formulated policies to their own liking and were not necessarily for the benefit of Anglo-Indians, who were often *persona non grata* but nevertheless tolerated. It became increasingly clear to Anglo-Indians that their survival as a collectivity meant organized action by and for Anglo-Indians themselves. For a group whose long dependency on Europeans had drained their potential resourcefulness for independent collective action, the establishment of community-oriented organizations was a difficult task.

As the leaders became increasingly concerned about the general welfare of the Community, organizations were established to assist the needy. Among these groups was the East Indian Amelioration Fund designed to help families in Bombay to find employment in agriculture, mechanical trades, and commerce. Similarly, in Madras and Hyderabad, the Philanthropic Association was formed for the purpose of establishing new settlements of Anglo-Indians in a variety of locations previously untouched. J. W. Ricketts, a prominent early leader of the minority, formed a similar organization, the Commercial and Patriotic Association, whose objective was to promote activities in agriculture, trade, and general welfare of the Anglo-Indian Community. Most of the ameliorative organizations established usually did not endure very long during this period and were consequently unable to attain their stated objectives. But at least they afforded valuable experience for the leaders. An example was the Patriotic Association, subsequently known as the United Association of India, whose objective was to provide a medium for the expression of grievances concerning disabilities of the Community.[109]

Throughout the nineteenth century various organizations came into existence. Some of them were designed exclusively for Anglo-Indians; others had a broader membership basis and admitted Europeans, Indian-Christians, or even other Indians. Several associations were established in the latter decades of the nineteenth century and early years of the twentieth. One of the first organizations was the Eurasian and Anglo-Indian Association, established in Bengal in 1876.

The Anglo-Indian and Domiciled European Association of Southern India was

---

[109] S. R. Mehrota, "The British India Society and Its Bengal Branch, 1839-1846," *Indian Economic and Social Historical Review*, p. 146 (June, 1957).

founded in 1879.[110] A few years later, around the turn of the century, the Imperial Anglo-Indian Association was organized, but with the death of its founder it went out of existence, to be revived later as the Anglo-Indian Empire League. The function of this new group was to integrate the various associations that had come into existence within India.

Later, in the 1920's, the Anglo-Indian Association of Bengal changed its name to the Anglo-Indian and Domiciled European Association, All-India and Burma, with the noted leader, Henry Gidney, as president. Here again an effort was made, this time with considerable success, to consolidate the various associations that had sprung up in India. This organization was "parent" of the present All-India Anglo-Indian Association, presently the dominant Anglo-Indian organization in India.

The Anglo-Indian and Domiciled European Association of South India has been a competitor over the years, refusing to amalgamate with the "All-India" organization. Instead, this Madras-based body insists that a federation should be formed which would ultimately allow considerable autonomy of each association. Leaders of the South India organization believe that their group would be dominated so completely by the All-India Association that its distinctiveness would be lost and ultimately it would cease to function effectively in the interest of the Anglo-Indians in the southern region. Members of this unit have also expressed concern about the possible loss of their financial assets, considered to be quite large, in the event of such a merger. The association in South India, for example, has established a school in Villupurum.

Another southern organization, the Union of Anglo-Indian Associations of Travancore-Cochin State (now Kerala), organized in 1953, has federated with the Madras-centered association, but presently it has chapters only in Kerala. The Union of Anglo-Indian Associations represents, in the main, a community of mixed racial ancestry, Portuguese and Indians, commonly known as Feringhees. Leaders of the Union urge that the Feringhees be accepted for membership in the Anglo-Indian Community, but the All-India Association has declined to open its doors to them because of the fact that their mother tongue is Malayalam rather than English. This viewpoint is stated by Frank Anthony,[111] president of the All-India Association, as follows:

> ... without our schools and without our language, English, we cannot be an Anglo-Indian community. We may be like the Feringhees of Kerala, who claim to be originally of Portuguese descent but who have merged with the lowest stratum of the Indian Christian community, with their mother tongue as Malayalam.

During the first half of the present century numbers of other associations and committees were established to serve the various needs of the Anglo-Indian Community. Among these were the Anglo-Indian Study Circle, the Anglo-Indian

---

[110] E. K. Gaikwad, *The Anglo-Indians* (Bombay: Asia Press, 1967), p. 35. Some of the data concerning various early communal organizations are from the same source. See also Frank Anthony, *Britain's Betrayal in India* (New Delhi: Allied Publishers, 1969), p. 394.

[111] "Mr. Anthony's Presidential Address," *The Review*, 57 : 39 (November-December, 1966).

Youth League, and the Britasian League. The Anglo-Indian Civic Union was an *ad hoc* committee on which the main Anglo-Indian organizations were represented and which was intended to protect persons and property in the turbulent days prior to Independence when anti-British sentiment was strong, and later when Hindu-Muslim conflicts created hazardous conditions in West Bengal. The Political Advisory Board (later changed to Anglo-Indian Advisory Board) was comprised of elected representatives from organizations which would be empowered to decide matters of public policy to be supported by the Anglo-Indian Community. As a consequence of changing social and political situations after Independence this board ceased to be functional and therefore went out of existence, and with it most of the organizations it supposedly represented. In the following pages two organizations will be considered in some detail.

The Britasian League

The Britasian League, organized in the 1930's, with headquarters in Calcutta, was notable for its ambitious program concerning the resettlement of Anglo-Indians, its energetic campaigns to generate a spirit of community responsibility among the members, efforts to create an interest in agriculture, and plans for the development of cooperative agricultural and industrial marketing facilities. Its official journal, *The Britasian Gazette,* along with numerous propaganda tracts, preached the gospel of a back-to-the-land movement, but with emphasis on industrial development as a concomitant to agriculture.

One of the resettlement schemes sponsored by the Britasian League was an agricultural project known as McCluskiegunj, named in honor of a prominent philanthropist, E. T. McCluskie, promoter of colonization projects who, as early as the 1920's, had planned an agricultural colony to be located near Ranchi, some two hundred miles west of Calcutta. About 7,000 acres were to be made available to Anglo-Indian settlers, the land to be distributed in five-acre plots to settlers who would organize a colony of proper and permanent residents. Although the project was launched with considerable fanfare, with promoters announcing that a new day was dawning for the Anglo-Indian people, the project itself was unsuccessful. Many of the 300 families settling in the colony became disillusioned, or perhaps bored with rural life, and returned to their urban habitats. Today only a few families remain, marooned in the backwaters of what was once a widely-publicized utopian scheme.[112]

The Britasian League had a strong nationalistic orientation. This is clearly evident in the promotion of a "homeland" for Anglo-Indians. It even had a "national anthem," the first stanza of which follows:

For we are Britasian Citizens
Yes, we are Britasians all.
No longer need we search or roam

---

[112] Another colony was planned at Jhargram, also near Calcutta, under different auspices, but it lacked internal cooperation and unity and also failed. Other unsuccessful colonization projects were at Whitefield in Mysore State and Mogra near Dehra Dun.

Seeking for a place to call our home
We have a homeland rich and fair
Pearl of the ocean blue

This "homeland" was to be the Andaman and Nicobar Islands, in the Bay of Bengal off the eastern coast of India. The proposal was to obtain permission from the government to reserve these islands for the permanent settlement of Anglo-Indians, Anglo-Burmese, and Malaya-Eurasians so that they could have full freedom to follow their own way of life and to work out independently their own destiny within the framework of the British Commonwealth. A special committee, known as the Britasian Colony Committee, presented a formal request in 1945 to the Government (then British). Although presumably supported by many Anglo-Indians it was opposed by influential leaders in the Community, neither was it supported by the British government. Apparently the leaders did not consider the plan viable because financial support was not assured. There may have been other reasons. At least it was never formally approved.

All-India Anglo-Indian Association: Structure and Functions

The All-India Anglo-Indian Association, referred to earlier in this chapter, has for a half-century been the most influential organization to represent the Anglo-Indian Community on a nationwide basis. Most of the Association's long history has been under the leadership of two men, Sir Henry Gidney, who died in 1942, and Frank Anthony, his successor, who has held the imposing title of president-in-chief in addition to his position of respect as a member of the *Lok Sabha* (lower house of Parliament). By 1970, the Association had over 70 affiliated units, or "branches," located in all sections of the country. Each local branch has complete autonomy in the selection of its corps of officers and committee personnel, and is free to determine the functions of the local organization. However, the local associations have traditionally supported policies formulated in the higher echelons of the national organization, and for this support have received certain benefits, such as educational scholarships for Anglo-Indian children.

The national organization holds an annual convention which is attended by officers and delegates from many local branches. Aside from the social activities of this occasion, the agenda includes an address by the president and also provides an opportunity for discussion by the delegates of the major problems facing the Community, principally issues and policies relating to education and language. Formal action may be taken on resolutions offered by delegates or by the national officers.

On the local level the "branches" also have periodical meetings to consider matters of immediate concern to their members. In addition to the formalities of a presidential address, reports of committees, and the selection of "office-bearers" for the following year, consideration is given to such matters as scholarships for local Anglo-Indian youths and assistance to needy members.

The national association has provided facilities through which the general

Community has been able to attain certain objectives in the furtherance of its own ameliorative policies as well as the defense of its own interests. It has been, both in theory and to a considerable extent in practice, a shield for the protection of the Community against disruptive or antagonistic forces. Perhaps its most important function has been the support of Anglo-Indian schools through scholarships and other forms of assistance for Anglo-Indian students. Through its leaders it has spearheaded efforts to continue English as a medium of instruction in Anglo-Indian schools. Earlier, when the political position of the Community in independent India was in doubt, it defended the right of the Anglo-Indian minority to special representation in the national and state legislative bodies. It maintains a central employment bureau in Delhi, in addition to employment services in some of the local branches, and has collected funds for the benefit of the needy and for national defense and drought relief in times of emergency.

The annual conclaves of the All-India Anglo-Indian Association are functionally important in coordinating and publicizing the activities of the various local branches, clarifying the issues confronting the Community, and specifying the organization's policies concerning these issues. Probably the latent function of strengthening and maintaining *esprit de corps* among the members of the Community is the most important function of all. As in the case of the national meetings, an important function of local branches is to create and reinforce a sense of identity of the members through shared participation in common undertakings, including meetings and social affairs.

The All-India Anglo-Indian Association, with its numerous branches over the country, supplies the structural elements to maintain the Community as a functional entity.[113] The national association may best be viewed in its relation to national leadership, for it is largely through the medium of this organization that the leaders have been able to obtain mass support in the dissemination of ideas and the formulation of policies. Few, if any, other well-known minorities of dual or multiple racial heritage have been able to develop an organized community life to the extent achieved by Anglo-Indians, whether the Eurasians of Indonesia, the Burghers of Ceylon, the Anglo-Burmese of Burma, the Mestizos of Latin America, or even the Coloureds of South Africa. The charismatic leadership that has emerged on the national level, while effective in promoting the interests of the Community and directing it through difficult situations, has nevertheless so dominated the Community as to reduce the prospects for the emergence of other influential national leaders or changes in the policies of the organization. The expressed adulation of the long-time president, apparently not discouraged by the leader himself, has some of the characteristics of a "cult of personality."

Anglo-Indian Association Membership

The All-India Association and its constituent branches by no means represents *all* of the Anglo-Indian Community. The total membership actually includes only

---

[113] The competing Anglo-Indian associations, while divisive in their influence, nevertheless supply structural elements that also strengthen the Community.

a fraction of the total adult population. Of 52 employed adults in Bangalore who were asked by Gist about membership and participation in the Association, approximately half (27) said they did not belong, and of those who were members, 12 reportedly did not participate in any of the activities. Out of an Anglo-Indian population of 10,000 in Bangalore in 1967, only about 400 were members, approximately the same ratio of membership to total population two decades earlier. Wright found in his New Delhi study that of 176 adults interviewed, 47 per cent of the males and 42 per cent of the females were members of the Association. As in the Bangalore survey, the sample is probably not statistically representative of the entire community.

Many Anglo-Indians have serious misgivings about the Association and its national leadership. When the Bangalore non-members were queried as to basic reasons why they did not belong, a few stated that they did not have time or had merely neglected to do so, and perhaps would join later; but most of them were doubtful of its advantages or were critical of its policies. The following are representative expressions of their attitudes:

I do not feel that my family and myself will receive many benefits.

In the past we (the family) belonged, but since we feel the subscription fees are being put to better use in other ways, we don't belong now.

I do not belong to the Association because I was never helped in any adverse circumstances, such as financial aid.

When my family wanted to join the All-India Anglo-Indian Association we found that another association was formed calling itself the Mysore State A. I. Association. This confused us, as they were rivals, so we kept clear.

The so-called Anglo-Indian Association in India today is being run by non-Anglo-Indians who have anglicized their names, usually from old tombstones, and as such do not have either the views or interest in the Anglo-Indian Community.

Anglo-Indian Publications

Although numerous Anglo-Indians have followed literary and journalistic careers, only a few periodicals or newspapers have been published specifically in the interest or behalf of the Community. The first of these was *The East Indian*, organized and edited by the youthful Henry Derozio, an Anglo-Indian poet and publicist, in the early years of the nineteenth century.[114] In 1879, *The Anglo-Indian* was established as the official organ of the Anglo-Indian and Domiciled European Association in South India.[115] Undoubtedly the most influential journal at present is *The Review*, published under the auspices of the All-India Anglo-Indian Association. Started in the 1920's as *The Anglo-Indian Review*, the name was changed subsequently to *The Anglo-Indian Review and Railway Union Journal*; later, it was renamed *The Review*.[116]

[114] Cedric Dover, *Half-Caste* (London: Martin Seiher and Warburg, 1943), p. 153.
[115] E. K. Gaikwad, *op. cit.*, p. 35.
[116] *Ibid.*, p. 36.

The Review, the principal communications link between the various branch organizations, and between the national leaders and individual members, carries as a front-page banner the statement, "India's most widely circulated monthly." This journal is also a channel through which information about the Community reaches others, notably political personalities in the central and state governments In a very real sense the magazine is a highly personalized house organ of the president, whose speeches, photographs, and activities occupy considerable space in each issue. Except for presidential and other addresses at the annual meeting of the All-India Anglo-Indian Association, together with reports of discussions by the delegates, the periodical is, for the most part, a compendium of information about the activities of Community leaders, meetings of the branches, and social festivities such as Christmas parties, New Year's celebrations, the May Ball, athletic events, and even the celebration of the president-in-chief's birthday.

The Review also focuses attention on individual Anglo-Indians who have been awarded recognition for one reason or another. Photographs of individuals who have distinguished records in military service or in athletics are conspicuously displayed in the magazine. They are the contemporary folk heroes of Anglo-Indian society. Other persons considered worthy of publicity in the magazine are attractive young women selected as May Queen in what might be considered a beauty or popularity contest, and occasionally Anglo-Indian youth who have outstanding records in scholarship. But the main focus is on the president-in-chief, Frank Anthony, whose moral and political influence extends far beyond the authority of the presidential office.[117]

Critiques of the Association and Review

Because of limited information it is difficult to evaluate the effectiveness of the national association and its various branches in terms of the functions which are supposedly performed. Criticisms of the organization by Anglo-Indians would indicate that performance may fall below the level of expectations based upon publicity in *The Review.* Two prominent Anglo-Indian leaders in Bombay reported that the local branch in that city discontinued its employment bureau because it was not functioning effectively. Instead, its activities (in 1964) centered around education and charity. Two clerical workers declared that the local branch in Calcutta was not an effective organization, that its functions were limited primarily to job placement and helping Anglo-Indians establish their community identity when applying for a passport.

A critical evaluation of the All-India Association and *The Review* was made in a letter, by an Anglo-Indian correspondent, to the editor of a Bombay newspaper, in which the shortcomings of the organization, including its house organ, are enumerated. The Association has failed to create enthusiasm among Anglo-Indians, he says, because nothing tangible is done:

---

[117] The magazine is edited in the office of the president-in-chief of the All-India Anglo-Indian Association.

1. To bring about a fusion of the several Anglo-Indian associations now existing ... or at least a compromise to work in coordination in the larger interests of the Community.

2. To cater to the intellectual, cultural, and recreational needs of the Community, particularly the younger generation, rather than running the inevitable dances, whist drives, and the pernicious habit of gambling termed "tombola" or "housie."

3. To probe into their problems, particularly the less fortunate ... offer a solution, particularly for the education of the children.

4. To re-orient their outlook in matters of employment, to help in the launching of small-scale or cottage industries on their own volition or on a cooperative basis.

5. To educate the youth in the community's past, present, and future, instead of extolling, parrot-like, the leadership of Mr. Frank Anthony ...

The writer is critical of *The Review,* saying that it could be made into a stimulating and useful journal by dealing with many topics of importance to the Community and with problems which are of general concern to all of its members. The publication of the president's speeches in Parliament, he says, and the items about meetings and social activities of the branches, do not create enthusiasm among the members or motivate them to deal with the problems that they now confront.

In New Delhi, an Air Force clerk reported that he belonged to the Association, and supported it, although in a reluctant manner. Both he and his wife, who is also employed, complained that they are expected to donate to "purses" to be presented to Frank Anthony, the president, on special occasions, commonly on Anthony's birthday. An unemployed man, residing in New Delhi, said, while commending Anthony for his fight to continue the English language, that the Association needs new leadership to replace the "old guard" which has tended in recent years to become dictatorial and impervious to new ideas.

However, many Anglo-Indians do not share these criticisms, but rather express confidence in the Association and its leadership. A working mother in New Delhi, for example, asserted that those who criticize the Anglo-Indian leadership are not well-informed and do not have a "feeling of belonging" to the Community. Certainly there is no other person who has successfully challenged the authority and leadership of Frank Anthony. When he does eventually retire from his present post it is possible that a new leader might chart a different course for the Association.

Any national multi-functional organization like the All-India Anglo-Indian Association can scarcely measure up to the demands and expectations of all persons identified with the Community. It is structured as a federation of local associations scattered widely over the country, each having autonomy in carrying out certain functions. At the same time there is considerable centralization in which the national president has a strong voice in formulating policies and providing guidelines for collective action. The Association might be compared with the so-called "strong mayor" type of government in numerous American cities in which the body politic is duly represented by democratically-elected officials but in which the mayor exerts considerable influence in decision-making and as a symbolic leader. Such organizations invariably develop internal strains and generate unrest because they are unable, or are so judged, to satisfy the needs and interests of everyone.

So it is with the All-India Anglo-Indian Association. Dissenting voices are often heard, and "palace revolutions" have even been proposed or undertaken, but so far the Association has been sufficiently responsive to the needs of the Community, or at least of its influential members, that it remains a viable organization. As a prominent former resident of Calcutta stated the matter, "While the performance (of the Association) may be uneven, in the last few years greater emphasis has been placed on efforts to improve the economic lot of the Community rather than on 'relief', and the larger funds now available to the central office is making it possible for money to be diverted to measures of practical self-help".

Organized Participation of Anglo-Indians

Anglo-Indians participate rather extensively in formal associations, but membership and participation tend to be limited mainly to persons on the middle- or upper-income levels. If low-income persons participate in an organized group it is likely to be the church, especially if they are of the Catholic faith. Only a few persons on the low-income levels who were interviewed claimed to be members of the Anglo-Indian Association. Either they cannot afford the membership fees and related expenses, or they feel alienated from the people who are members. Although middle- or upper-class Anglo-Indians probably do not participate in formal organizations as much as Western peoples on a comparable social level, they do nevertheless have numerous associational connections.

Among the 52 employed adults in Bangalore who responded to a questionnaire concerning membership in formal organizations, nearly three-fourths (36) indicated that they were members of one or more organizations. Approximately half (27) were members of churches or church-related groups, or both. Among the church-oriented organizations were the Catholic Club, St. Patrick's Youth Club, the International Young Christian Worker's Movement, the Sacred Heart Church Club, and the Christian Family Movement. The fact that most of the respondents were of the Catholic faith suggests an explanation for the number who were members of church-related groups. Slightly over one-fourth of the respondents (14) were members of labor unions, and there was a scattering of persons who had membership in service organizations, sports clubs, and dramatic societies.

Membership in formal organizations generally depends on factors or conditions relevant to a particular situation. Aside from financial ability to pay the membership fees and other expenses, there are other factors such as the existence and accessibility of organizations, or the opportunities for unorganized social activities. The size of the city or town may be a factor, since large cities may offer a wider array of organizations and activities than smaller cities, which often afford limited opportunities for organized social life. The extent to which Anglo-Indians participate or hold memberships in organized groups may vary from one locality to another.

The Family

At the risk of oversimplification it may be said that three types or models of family or kinship groups prevail in India. One is the classical joint or extended family which, in its ideal-typical form, consists of a male household head and his wife; their adult married sons and their wives and children; their unmarried sons and daughters; and brothers of the famiy head and their wives and unmarried children. There are, of course, many variations of this pattern. Normally it is a three-generation family unit, but in some instances it may consist of four generations. Members of the kinship unit may or may not live in the same household, depending on the circumstances.

A second type is the modified-extended family which consists of persons related by blood, marriage, or adoption who recognize and maintain a network of inter-personal kinship ties with others not ordinarily residing in the same household. Like the classical joint family model, the modified-extended family may include members of two or more nuclear units whose members interact, in various ways, with other kin who normally reside in separate households and who may be remotely situated from each other. Inter-personal connections with kin may serve the function of satisfying social and emotional needs, or instrumental functions in the form of mutual assistance in one form or another. But the modified-extended family is not as highly institutionalized as the classical joint family; inter-personal ties with kin are more a matter of individual choice than a group-imposed obligation. The nuclear family, not the kinship circle, is the basic unit.

A third type is the isolated nuclear family which consists of husband, wife, and children living in the same household. In its ideal-typical form this model maintains no close personal ties with other consanguineal or affinal kin beyond the immediate family group.

Whereas the classical joint family system is widely prevalent in the Hindu population of India, the Anglo-Indian family characteristically resembles the modified-extended family pattern in which the members usually maintain personal connections with their biological or affinal kin beyond the immediate family unit consisting of husband, wife, and children. We have no data on the number of Anglo-Indians who belong to isolated nuclear families, but if Western cultures afford any guidelines the proportion of families representing this model is fairly low. The fact that Anglo-Indians are members of an ethnic minority occupying a marginal position in Indian society suggests that kinship ties are reinforced by their strong feeling of community identity.

The Anglo-Indian modified-extended family, ordinarily consisting of husband, wife, and children, and sometimes including other dependents such as parents of the husband or wife, permits more individualized behavior of its members than is true of the classical Indian joint family. As in the West, young adults are free to have dates without a chaperon, and the selection of a spouse is mainly an individual matter, unlike the indigenous Hindu system in which marriages are customarily arranged by older members of the kinship group. Young married couples generally set up housekeeping apart from their respective parental families, in contrast to the prevailing practice in the Hindu system in which the bride goes to live with her husband in his parental household. Low divorce rates reflect the influence of the Catholic church, of which a large proportion of the Anglo-Indians are members. As observed elsewhere, Anglo-Indian girls are sometimes reluctant to marry men of their own community because they see themselves, in the years ahead, as the main support of their family. Said an Anglo-Indian girl in New Delhi:

> My mother works as a secretary, but my father hasn't worked for over two years. It isn't his fault; he just can't get a good job. The man I marry will have to have a good job. I may work for a few years but not forever. My mother taught me that much.

Organized Characteristics of Social Welfare

Welfare services for the benefit of Anglo-Indians are carried out through the medium of numerous organizations, some functioning under the aegis of the Anglo-Indian Community, others provided by organizations serving a wider clientele. In the absence of an effective public welfare system in India, services to needy persons or families are largely in the hands of private agencies supported by donations from individuals or local institutions. Numbers of agencies restrict their clientele to persons of the Christian faith without reference to racial heritage or nationality. Such agencies would therefore provide services for Anglo-Indians, almost all of whom are Christian.

The East India Charitable Trust, with headquarters in Calcutta, is responsible for the financing and management of numerous welfare operations in West Bengal, Bihar, Assam, and Orissa. Organized in 1950 to coordinate and direct various charitable activities, the Trust manages several residential institutions, provides financial or other forms of assistance to individuals or families in distress, contributes financially to various organizations offering welfare or medical services, and finances numerous scholarships for indigent children or youth. As Christians, Anglo-Indians are eligible for benefits provided by the Trust. Some of the homes are partly self-supporting by means of sales of articles fashioned by the residents or by production of vegetables grown in the institution's gardens. The institutional function of the Trust in Calcutta alone is indicated by the following establishments or organizations that are maintained and supervised:

> *Tollygunge Homes.* Provides residential and medical facilities for 60 elderly European or Anglo-Indian persons of any Christian denomination.
>
> *St. Mary's Home and Hospital.* Accommodates 65 elderly European or Anglo-Indian women of the Protestant faith.

Mary Cooper Home. Affords accommodations for 34 elderly European or Anglo-Indian persons, of either sex, who are Protestant.

Lavinia House. A "rescue" home for European or Anglo-Indian girls.

E. I. C. T. Nursery School. Provides day care for 50 young children of working mothers.

St. John's Baby Clinic. Provides clinical services for prenatal and postnatal care of mothers and their babies.

Women's Friendly Society. Employs Anglo-Indian and Indian-Christian women in making garments, profits from the sales of which are used for charitable purposes.

The Anglo-Indian Association Calcutta Canteen and Boys' Hostel. Serves free meals to indigent Europeans and Anglo-Indians, and maintains a hostel for 50 Anglo-Indian boys.

The Sherwood House Trust. Provides financial support for 50 female orphans, of British parentage, while attending school.

Church-sponsored organizations in various cities likewise serve the Community. The Convent of the Good Shepherd in Bangalore maintains a school and boarding facilities for the accommodation of children from indigent families, many of whom are Anglo-Indian. Indigent members of the Anglo-Indian Community are served by the welfare facilities of the Roman Catholic Church, Salvation Army, and the World Council of Churches. These services are generally available to individuals or families without reference to race, religion, or nationality. Bengal Christian Council has supported a bureau of vocational and educational counselling providing service to students and teachers in the Anglo Indian schools. Through the Welfare Committee considerable sums are spent for medical aid and relief of Anglo-Indian families unable to provide these services for themselves.

Organized Cooperation

Throughout the relatively long history of the Community in India, Anglo-Indians had little experience in business and industry, except as employees of commercial enterprises or government. If they exhibited little aptitude for, or interest in, careers in business it was partly because the opportunities were always limited. Other Indians with long experience as tradesmen virtually monopolized the managerial and proprietorial posts in private business. The economic security that Anglo-Indians enjoyed as monopolists of certain occupations seemingly blunted their motivation to succeed in private competitive undertakings. At any rate, why, in their judgement, should they incur the risks of private business undertakings when as employees they could be sure of a steady job at good pay? Given this economic background it is not surprising that Anglo-Indians were slow to establish cooperative organizations in their own interest and under their own management. But a beginning has been made.

Under the leadership of a prominent member of the Community, the Christian Cooperative Credit Union was formed in Calcutta in 1953. Patterned after credit unions in the United States, Germany, and Canada, the union has become an organization with considerable financial resources, providing both opportunities for investments and loans at moderate interest rates.[118] From this initial undertaking several other cooperatives have been established, including a cooperative nursing home, a pharmacy and laboratory, cold storage facilities, a training school for welding, and a bakery. In addition, a cooperative housing society has undertaken to provide land or proper apartments to the members on an "own your own home" basis. Tracts of land are acquired by the organization, then divided into residential plots and sold to members of the Community under a long-term amortization plan. The same principle is followed in the construction and disposition of private residences. The future of these enterprises is still uncertain.

Cooperative societies have received endorsement in principle, but not financial support, of the All-India Anglo-Indian Association, provided they are established in cities having relatively large concentrations of Anglo-Indians. The Community, through local branches of the Association, has recently established cooperatives in other cities. Asansol has a cooperative union, and a women's industrial cooperative has been organized at Coimbatore. Although some of the cooperatives have been successful, several undertakings have either failed or had limited success. In order to provide a substantial membership base most of the cooperatives have included other Christian communities in addition to Anglo-Indians.

Political Organization and Leadership

As a collectivity Anglo-Indians do not participate extensively in the political life of India except in quasi-political activities relating to the Community. Such action commonly takes place through the Anglo-Indian Association or similar organizations. Although the political leaders representing this minority in the national and state legislative assemblies have generally identified with the Congress Party, supporting many of the policies of that party, the rank and file tend to be indifferent to political matters that do not seem to be immediately relevant to the needs and problems of the Community. Generally they accept the political values and party identity of their leaders without becoming directly involved themselves in strictly political activities or confrontations.

Minority parties, whether to the right or the left, or even the middle, have had little appeal to Anglo-Indians although they may not be satisfied with their lot in India; but even these people generally fail to strive cooperatively to alter the situation either by political means or by direct action. They seldom participate in organized protest movements except, on occasions, as members of labor unions that go on strike. They tend to look with considerable misgiving on mass demonstrations and other forms of direct collective action as unwarranted behavior of undisciplined persons. This aversion to organized political activity

---

[118] Starting with 40 members and a capital of 2,000 rupees in 1953, by 1968 the union had increased to 3,435 members and the capital to about one and one-half million rupees.

appears to be a by-product of the long history of dependence on the British to whom they were obedient and on whom they relied for the major decisions in the affairs of life. Of the values that Anglo-Indians cherish, obedience and loyalty rank high. These values can, of course, be translated into political inactivity. A resident of Patna expressed the opinion that one reason Anglo-Indians were not extensively involved in political activities is that they wish to avoid any risks of retaliation that might be brought against the Community.

The All-India Anglo-Indian Association, and to some extent other communal organizations, do function as a kind of surrogate for political parties and political activities. As a small minority within a vast population in which Hindus exercise dominant political control, Anglo-Indians feel politically helpless at the polls and therefore rely almost totally on their own leaders and their representatives in the national and state legislative bodies. Even these representatives are not elected by popular vote, but are rather nominated in political caucuses and officially appointed to the offices by the president of India (for the two representatives in the *Lok Sabha*) and by the state governors (in the legislative assemblies). Representation in the state legislative assemblies is not guaranteed but is at the discretion of the state governor. States having concentrations of Anglo-Indians (Andhra Pradesh, Madras, Mysore, Bihar, Maharashtra, Uttar Pradesh, Madhya Pradish, and West Bengal) have, since the new Constitution was adopted in 1950, had representatives in the legislative assemblies.

Yet at least the form and processes of democratic procedure are observed in the selection of political representatives for the Community. This procedure may, however, vary from one state to another. In West Bengal, according to a well-informed member of the Community, the first step in the selective process is the ascertaining of persons who are willing to stand for nomination, after which an investigation is made of their qualifications for office and their previous activities on behalf of t.e Cmmunity. "First of all," he said, "we go around and ask people if they would like to stand for nomination. If so, their names are presented to the selection board for consideration. They are then investigated as to their points of view on various questions, whether or not they are a college graduate, and what their work record has been." How well the selection board represents the political wishes and interests of the rank and file is perhaps debatable.

Anglo-Indians are certainly not completely indifferent as to all political or civic matters. Much depends on the nature of particular issues. Perhaps the issue about which Anglo-Indians are most deeply concerned is the status and future prospects of their mother tongue, the English language. Although such issues are not settled by popular vote in which public opinion can be registered, members of the Community believe that certain Indian politicians in positions of power desire to terminate the use of English as a medium of instruction in schools. Anglo-Indian opinion against these alleged attacks is solidly crystallized. Yet, there is little that, as individuals, they can do except to assure their Community's legislative officials of their support.

On other issues there is less unanimity of voting behavior or expressions of political opinion. One informed Anglo-Indian leader in Calcutta reported considerable "bloc voting" on some issues, but on other issues a diversity of voting behavior. There is undoubtedly an awareness that even with bloc voting the Community is so small that its political influence at the polls is negligible, except perhaps in certain localities in which it conceivably could hold the balance of power in elections. Probably most Anglo-Indians are so conditioned to relying on the leadership of Frank Anthony that they seldom assert themselves collectively on public issues except those of direct and immediate concern to the Community.

Religious Organization

That all Anglo-Indians are Christians, at least nominally so, is generally recognized. Although the Community has existed alongside peoples of other religious faiths — Hindus, Muslims, Sikhs, Parsees, Buddhists, Jews — there is no evidence that Anglo-Indians have embraced any of these religions (although some may have actually done so, without any record of the conversion being kept or made available). The Community itself, however, represents a diversity of Christian denominations. There is no church that one can say is exclusively for Anglo-Indians.

Anglo-Indians of Catholic persuasion are probably in the majority, with the others distributed among numerous non-Catholic denominations such as the Church of England, Methodist, Baptist, Presbyterian, and various evangelical sects, including the Salvation Army. As in most countries, the Catholic church is structured to include satellite groups over which the church itself exercises extensive control. Aside from performing certain religious functions, these organizations provide the facilities for social, recreational, cultural, or athletic activities, or even social services of an ameliorative nature. Probably the majority of middleclass Anglo-Indians participate in these organizational functions. The Protestant churches are also organized along multi-functional dimensions, but the controls allow for considerable freedom of action and thought.

The most prestigious Protestant denomination is the Church of England, which tends to attract Anglo-Indians of the middle or upper classes. Located in or near the slums are the evangelical sects whose simplistic theological appeals attract Anglo-Indians with limited education or fundamentalist religious convictions. These churches commonly provide material assistance and spiritual comfort to the alienated, the destitute, the rejected. For financial and other reasons membership and participation in church and church-related activities are less extensive among these people than among Anglo-Indians with more financial resources and broader cultural and educational backgrounds. Persons who were interviewed generally believe that Anglo-Indians are church-goers, whether Protestant or Catholic. This observation is probably more applicable to middle-class people than to those on the lower social and economic levels.

The foregoing materials in this chapter indicate that the Anglo-Indian minority is a community both in its organizational features and in the social-psychological elements of community life. Not all of the organizations in which Anglo-Indians are members or participants are exclusively for this minority, but their existence, and the functions they perform, provide the framework through which community sentiment can be expressed and community activities carried out. Yet these organizations, if they are exclusive, to tend to isolate the Anglo-Indian from other Indians and perhaps contribute to his alienation and therefore marginality. But there is also a tendency for Anglo-Indians to share their organized life with other Indians, generally through joint memberships and a commonality of interests and experiences. These observations suggest, at least superficially, that the integration of Anglo-Indians into the broader fabric of Indian society is proceeding apace.

CHAPTER EIGHT

EDUCATION

In the following discussion of Anglo-Indian education the marginal position of the Community in Indian society is revealed especially in the development of educational institutions. Anglo-Indian schools have traditionally followed the British plan in which the content of the curriculum and the medium or mode of instruction are Western, a fact that has tended to set Anglo-Indian education apart from the prevailing educational institutions within India. These institutional differences have reinforced the cultural and social marginality of Anglo-Indians, although since Independence this marginality has been reduced by changes in the curricula of Anglo-Indian schools.

Eighteenth Century Education

During the initial period of colonialism in India the education of Anglo-Indian and European children was largely concentrated in missionary schools. The early Catholic schools were located primarily in the South, in the Portuguese sphere of influence. Established in considerable measure to propagate the Catholic faith, the schools were open to all children of Europeans residing in India, including those of Anglo-Indians. Early educational efforts of the British East India Company in behalf of the Company's civil and military personnel were ostensibly to counteract the influence of Catholic missionaries by propagating the Protestant faith. The institution of Protestant education occurred in Madras, but other European schools were started in Bengal and Bombay in the early years of the eighteenth century. Admitted to these schools were children of Indians who had been converted to Christianity, as well as children of British, Anglo-Indian, and Portuguese parents. Most of these schools were established by missionaries or chaplains of the East India Company.

Many educational leaders of this period were motivated either by the desire to propagandize the doctrines of Christianity or to further the imperial interest of the British in India by emphasizing educational functions consonant with the need of the ruling powers. It was primarily education for God, King, and Empire. The following communication, part of an appeal for funds for a school in 1784, came from a British member of the Society for the Promotion of Christian Knowledge:

> The Society has received information that there is a considerable number of children born annually in the British settlements in the East Indies of fathers who are Europeans and mothers who are natives. That of this description there are born annually not less than 700 at Madras and on the Coast of Caromondel ..... that the fathers of these children being usually soldiers, sailors, and the lower order of people, too often neglect their offspring and suffer them to follow the caste of their mothers ..... that if a Christian education were bestowed on them their manners,

habits, and affections would be English, their services of value in the capacity of soldiers, sailors, and servants, and a considerable benefit would accrue to the advantage of this Kingdom and tend to give stability to the settlements.[119]

The position of the East India Company toward education of Anglo-Indian children was one of calloused indifference, but Company officials who could afford to do so often sent their mixed-blood offspring to England for an education. Goodrich cites evidence that there was some "color selection," that those of fair complexions were more likely to be sent because they had a better chance of getting along in color-conscious English society than did darker individuals.[120]

Nineteenth Century Education

Many European schools founded after the turn of the nineteenth century made no allowance for Anglo-Indian children, who were regarded as Indian, not European, by the British.[121] By this time the Anglo-Indian Community had come to realize that it must assume considerable responsibility for the education of Anglo-Indian children, although the Community's finances were not sufficient to support adequate schools without outside assistance. Two notable schools were founded in 1823, one under the sponsorship of the Church of England and named the Calcutta Grammar School, later to become St. Paul's School; and the non-denominational Parental Academic Institution, later to become Doveton College, with one branch in Madras, the other in Calcutta.[122] The Calcutta Doveton College continued to exist for nearly a century. Recognizing that the Community must depend in considerable measure on its own efforts and resources, the leaders in Calcutta organized the Apprenticing Society and established a marine school for the training of young men who, hopefully, might find employment in an expanding oceanic trade.[123]

From 1835 onward the British government, which had taken over the functions of the East India Company in India, undertook an educational program that emphasized the education of Indians who possessed the potential abilities needed for the civil services. This policy was designed especially to encourage bright young Indians to attend English-medium schools in order to develop facility in the English language and an understanding of the colonial system, thereby becoming more valuable to the Empire in matters of governance. Anglo-Indians were not included in this scheme, but instead were usually passed over when appointments were made to the higher echelons of the civil or military services.

Consonant with the plans of the British to extend and expand education on all levels was the establishment of a university system. At the middle of the

---

[119] Frank Penney, *The Church in Madras* (London: Smith Elder and Company, 1904). Cited in Dorris L. Goodrich, "The Making of an Ethnic Group: The Eurasian Community in India," Unpublished PhD dissertation, University of California, Berkeley, 1952.
[120] Dorris L. Goodrich, *op. cit.*, p. 205.
[121] *Ibid.*, p. 100.
[122] *Ibid.*, p. 141.
[123] Herbert A. Stark, *Hostages to India* (Calcutta: The Calcutta Fine Art Cottage, 1936), p. 133.

nineteenth century the universities of Calcutta, Bombay, and Madras were founded, but students and faculties were drawn mainly from other Indian communities. These universities, and others that came later, had little direct influence on the Anglo-Indian Community. Most Anglo-Indians were either financially unable or intellectually unprepared to attend a university even if they had been interested in doing so.

European education was given an impetus in the latter half of the nineteenth century, after the Sepoy Mutiny, when a plan to reward the Anglo-Indian Community for its support of the British provided for the education of Anglo-Indian children. This plan, formulated in the 1860's by Bishop Cotton, Metropolitan of the Church of England in Britain and India, specified that the schools were to be supported jointly by the government and the church. It has often been referred to as the Magna Carta of European education in India. The principles of the plan provided that the schools would be started by the churches and administered by them, but with government financial support if specified standards were maintained. The pattern of this system still prevails; it has had far-reaching influence on Anglo-Indian education in India.[124]

During the last half of the nineteenth century a number of schools were established which were accessible to the children of Anglo-Indian or European parents. The character of the schools varied considerably. Some were designed for the elite and well-to-do; some for middle-class children; others for the benefit of poor families.[125] A few were located in "hill stations," or summer resorts, such as Ootacamund, Darjeeling, Kalimpong, and Coonoor, but mainly they were in the larger cities having concentrations of Europeans and Anglo-Indians.

Among the well-known institutions that still exist are the two LaMartiniere schools, one located in Calcutta and the other in Lucknow. Financed initially from funds contributed by a Frenchman who gave his name as well as his money to the schools, these institutions were established primarily for the education of Anglo-Indian and European children. Continuing to this day as Anglo-Indian schools, they have tended to become more and more educational institutions for elite Indians, Europeans, and Anglo-Indians. St. Xavier's College, established and operated both in Calcutta and Bombay under the auspices of the Roman Catholic Church, is nominally an Anglo-Indian school but with a student clientele representing various communities in India. The Bishop Cotton Schools, with separate facilities for boys and girls, were established in the 1860's in Bangalore, Nagpur, and Simla under the sponsorship of the Anglican church. Similar is Christ Church School in Bombay; St. Thomas' School and Calcutta Boys' School in Calcutta; and St. John's School and Baldwin School for boys and girls in Bangalore.

An educational program that has been widely publicized in recent years is the

---

[124] From correspondence with Austin D'Souza, Inspector of Anglo-Indian Schools in West Bengal, 1969.

[125] Austin D'Souza, unpublished manuscript concerning the history of Anglo-Indian education in West Bengal.

Frank Anthony Public School plan. The All-India Anglo-Indian Education Society has projected an educational program providing for approximately twenty "public" schools to be established in various cities during the 1960's and 1970's. By 1970 three schools, all bearing the name of the president of the Association, had been established in Delhi, Calcutta, and Bangalore. Like many other private Anglo-Indian schools, they mainly serve the well-to-do in various communities, rather than families with low incomes, the exception being a few students on scholarships. Some of the profits accruing from the operation of the schools are channeled into the scholarship fund of the All-India Anglo-Indian Association of which the Anglo-Indian Education Society is a subsidiary.

Contemporary Trends in Education

After the turn of the twentieth century numbers of changes occurred in the system. For one thing, the term "Anglo-Indian" replaced "European" as a broad classification. Possibly this change was made because the term had commonly been applied to Europeans who permanently resided in India and was therefore synonymous with "domiciled European." When the term "Eurasian" was replaced by "Anglo-Indian" with reference to persons of joint European and Asian ancestry, it created some confusion as an institutional label because of the implication that the schools usually functioned for the exclusive benefit of Anglo-Indian children. Such was not the case. Although a few schools were founded for the sole benefit of the Anglo-Indian Community, they are not presently restricted to any particular racial or cultural group.

The Anglo-Indian school is distinctive mainly for the nature of its curriculum and the medium of instruction. Throughout the present century these schools have been undergoing a continuous process of change. Early in the present century the basis of student selection was liberalized, but even then not more than one-fourth of the students could be from communities other than European or Anglo-Indian. This ratio has now been revised; in most of the schools that operate the majority of students are neither European nor Anglo-Indian, but instead represent other communities in India. Actually, the number of Anglo-Indian students in the majority of schools is relatively small, in some instances less than five per cent of the total enrollment. Proportionally and numerically, Hindu students are usually predominant, a situation that might be expected since the Hindu community represents the largest segment of India's population.

The new Indian government established at the time of Independence affirmed its intention to protect the rights of the Anglo-Indian minority, as well as other minorities. The Constitution, adopted in 1950, specified certain safeguards, including recognition and support of Anglo-Indian schools. Financial support by the national and state governments was to extend over a period of ten years, ending in 1960. These financial grants were available only to those schools whose student admissions included at least forty per cent from communities other than the Anglo-Indian minority. Most of the states, however, continue to provide some financial support to these schools.

Altogether there are some 300 Anglo-Indian schools in the country which are recognized and licensed by the government department of education in the states where they are located. A few of them are government-owned and operated, but for the most part they are private institutions which are financially self-supporting or supported in part by religious orders, secular foundations, or individuals.

Changing Functions of Anglo-Indian Schools

With the imminence of Independence and the departure of the British, a critical reappraisal involving the role of the school in India was undertaken to equip the Anglo-Indian system of education to meet the challenges of the post-war period. Even before World War II a group designated as the Anglo-Indian Study Circle, in a report on the state of Anglo-Indian education, concluded that the schools had not been sufficiently effective in developing a sense of Indian citizenship among the students, nor had they created a sense of community pride or solidarity.[126] The study group recommended that the curriculum be brought in line with modern educational developments, that such subjects as Indian history and culture be integrated into the program, that the study of Indian languages be made mandatory, and that such prevocational courses as domestic and manual arts be a part of the training.

An official report by the Barnes Commission, appointed in 1944 to review the Anglo-Indian system, made similar assessments and recommendations. Anglo-Indian schools, according to the report, should retain their separate identity and not be merged into the general system of education. At the same time they should be more closely synchronized with the main currents of Indian life by including in the curriculum such subjects as Indian history, geography, literature, and indigenous languages. The report also urged that the schools place less emphasis on exclusively academic studies, traditionally a feature of English education, and more emphasis on subjects having direct vocational relevance. Students wishing a strictly vocational education should attend technical schools. In a speech before the *Lok Sabha* in 1970, the Anglo-Indian representative, A. E. T. Barrow, strongly emphasized the need for vocational schools for young people who desire to further their education but who have neither the aptitude nor the needed motivation to do successful work on the university level.[127]

Continuing efforts are made by educational personnel to improve the quality of education in Anglo-Indian schools. In 1958, the Council for the Indian School Certificate was established, with representatives from various educational bodies and institutions. The Council is not merely an examining body but is concerned with various curricular matters, the development and maintenance of facilities such as laboratories, and the improvement of instruction. A majority of the

---

[126] *Ibid.*
[127] *The Review*, 62 : 15-17 (April, 1970). See also Frank Anthony, *Britain's Betrayal in India* (New Delhi: Allied Publishers, 1969), chapter 13. In this chapter Anthony reviews in considerable detail the history of Anglo-Indian education in India.

Anglo-Indian schools are affiliated with the Council, but other English-medium institutions are also included in the cooperative program.

Because English is the mother tongue of Anglo-Indian children and youth, they attend schools in which the English language is the medium of instruction. Furthermore, the Community, or the schools themselves, may provide special benefits, financial or otherwise, enabling Anglo-Indian children to attend these schools. Although many of the schools have only a token enrollment of Anglo-Indian students and therefore do not serve the needs of the Community very well, others do attempt to meet these needs by providing instruction to students for low-income situations.

For all practical purposes, therefore, Anglo-Indian schools are the only type of educational institution serving the interests and needs of the Community. To some extent admission of Anglo-Indian students is on a most-favored basis. This policy means that numbers of children from other communities may in fact be excluded to provide space and instruction for Anglo-Indian students. Such a policy merely indicates that Anglo-Indian schools, and the Community in general, recognize their special responsibility for the education of Anglo-Indian children. In this respect it is no different from schools that serve the special needs and interests of other communities in India.

Institutional and Student Support

The system of scholarships and other subventions has spelled the difference, for many Anglo-Indian students, between little or no schooling and considerable formal education. The All-India Anglo-Indian Association raises sizeable funds to be distributed as scholarships or grants-in-aid to enable students to attend school or college. Some 150,000 rupees were earmarked for scholarships in 1964, and this amount was to be increased each year.[128] By 1968 some 300 Association scholarships were annually awarded, largely for training in colleges, universities, or technical schools. In addition, local chapters of the Association often provide some financial assistance to students. State governments usually make financial contributions to Anglo-Indian schools (as well as others), allocating monthly payments or lump sums to institutions for helping students in need of special assistance, especially those who must be provided food, lodging, and clothing. In 1966, for example, Anglo-Indian schools in Maharashtra State were allotted 30 rupees per month for each "boarder," and for each Anglo-Indian student enrolled an annual grant of 100 rupees was made to the school.

Scholarships and other forms of educational assistance may be classified into two categories: (1) Those designed specifically for Anglo-Indians and/or "domiciled" Europeans, and (2) those in which Anglo-Indians are eligible to compete with other communities. A survey, conducted in Calcutta in 1957 by the Vocational and Educational Counselling Services, listed and described the scholarships and other forms of educational assistance available to a considerable

---

[128] *The Review,* 54-55 : 12 (November-December, 1964).

number of young persons in West Bengal.[129] The Education Society, a unit of the Anglo-Indian Association, has for a number of years awarded scholarships annually to needy students.

The numerous scholarships and other forms of educational assistance available in West Bengal may give the impression that the amount and kind of financial aid to students are sufficient to meet all the needs. The fact, however, is not this at all. Some of the scholarships and stipends are scarcely within reach of many students; often the students themselves cannot qualify for them; and many do not, because of additional expenses, provide enough assistance to enable destitute or otherwise indigent students to attend school. Explicit requests by Anglo-Indians for scholarships are reported to be less than the number available. A somewhat comparable financial situation is one in which a surplus of loan funds may exist in banks and loan companies but cannot be used by many impoverished families because they do not qualify for one reason or another.

Institutional Stratification

The institutional hierarchy which has developed within the Anglo-Indian school system reflects, in a way, the economic stratification of the Community and its place in the social structure of Indian society. There are, for example, a few sub-types distinguishable yearly by the numbers and status of Anglo-Indian students enrolled, and by the functions the schools perform for the Community.

The elitist schools ordinarily have a small enrollment of Anglo-Indians because the high tuition fees are often prohibitive and because academic standards are too rigorous for many students. Generally the elitist schools tend to attract students from the higher economic strata, whether Hindu, Parsee, Indian-Christian, or other communities. Most of the Anglo-Indian students in these schools, however, are recipients of financial assistance. The ratio of these students to the total enrollment in the elitist schools is usually small. In 1964, Anglo-Indian students represented only about 10 per cent of the enrollment in the Calcutta Boys' School, 15 per cent in Christ Church School in Bombay, and about 20 per cent of the students in the Lucknow and Calcutta LaMartiniere schools. About 15 per cent of the students in St. Joseph's European High School in Bangalore were Anglo-Indians in 1967, 10 per cent in St. John's High School, 13 per cent in Cathedral School, 7 per cent in Bishop Cotton Girls' School, 2 per cent in the Baldwin Boys' School, and less than 10 per cent in the Frank Anthony School.[130]

Anglo-Indian representation in low-status schools is sometimes higher than in middle-or upper-class institutions. About three-fourths of the students in St. Patrick's School and Orphanage in Bangalore are Anglo-Indians, approximately 100 of which are boarders – indigent students who receive board or lodging, or both. The percentage representation of students in this school is highest of any in the city, although nearby St. Ann's School also has a large enrollment of

---

[129] *Stipends and Scholarships for Anglo-Indian Youth*, No. 2, 1957.

[130] All of the foregoing data on the representation of Anglo-Indians were obtained from personal interviews with teachers or school officials.

Anglo-Indians, many of whom are indigent. St. Paul's School in Calcutta, located in a populous low-income district, has an Anglo-Indian student population exceeding half of the total enrollment – the highest percentage of any school in Calcutta. In fact, there are about a half dozen schools in Calcutta that especially serve the low-income families of the Community and which, therefore, assume much of the burden of educating the indigent. St. George's School in the Nilgiris, South India, has an Anglo-Indian student population approximately 60 per cent of the total. The average for Anglo-Indian schools in Mysore State in 1964 was 8 per cent.[131] Most of the Anglo-Indian students are supported by funds contributed by churches or foundations.

Whatever the current distribution may be, it is generally believed that the Anglo-Indian representation in many schools has declined since Independence. This decrease has apparently been most pronounced in the primary and secondary school levels. Drop-outs and non-attendance may have contributed to the decline, but probably more important has been the heavy out-migration from India.

Numerous Anglo-Indian schools charge tuition fees beyond the financial reach of most Anglo-Indian families. Enrollment fees in these schools generally range from 25 to 75 rupees a month, depending in part on the educational level of the students, whether primary, secondary, or college. There are usually other expenses as well. Some of these schools operate at a financial profit, which may be used to finance scholarships for Anglo-Indian students, permitting them to attend a school which otherwise would be too expensive. Christ Church School in Bombay is an example. Many of the students in this school are from Hindu, Indian-Christian, Parsee, Muslim, or other non-Anglo-Indian families that can usually afford high educational costs. The policy, in other words, is to tax the rich or well-to-do for the benefit of indigent students, notably those from the Anglo-Indian Community. One rationale for the high fees in these schools is that superior salaries can be paid, thus attracting superior teachers who will be the principal components of a distinguished educational institution.

Disadvantaged Students and Educational Costs

From sheer economic necessity most Anglo-Indian students attend schools having tuition fees ranging from 10 to 25 rupees a month (about $1.50 to $3.50). If these schools are located in or near low-income districts occupied by Anglo-Indian families many of the students must depend on scholarships provided by the Anglo-Indian Association or some other organization. Such schools are occasionally combined with orphanages for destitute and homeless children. The St. Patrick's school and Orphanage in Bangalore is an example of such an institution. Although the tuition fee is only 13 rupees a month, almost all of the students receive assistance, in the form of waived fees or scholarships, or both. Generally these students are from indigent or disrupted families, or from a home environment otherwise unfavorable to conventional learning and behavior. Homeless students are usually given full board and lodging, although the limited

---

[131] *The Review*, 54-55 : 29 (December-January, 1964).

facilities in many schools make it impossible to furnish such accommodations for all those in serious need. Students who cannot be accommodated may be provided a noon meal, and for indigent students school uniforms may also be issued free of charge.

A unique institution in the Anglo-Indian educational system is Dr. Graham's Homes, a combination school and home maintained for indigent and homeless children and youth. Founded in 1900 by a Presbyterian missionary whose name the institution bears, and located at Kalimpong in the Himalayan highlands of West Bengal, the institutional policy is to admit needy individuals, from infancy to youth. Although the majority of admissions are Anglo-Indians, the institution accepts other children from India, Bhutan, Sikkim, and Tibet without reference to race or religion. The religious orientation of the institution, however, is Christian, but with opportunities for religious worship in a different tradition. Because the guests are usually without financial resources of their own, support comes mainly from the outside, chiefly in the form of contributions from individuals and groups, or from special agencies. The institution is so organized, however, that students, through a work-study program, can contribute indirectly to their own support. A sampling of 52 "alumni" who had resided in the home at various intervals indicated that the average length of residence was 11 years, with a range from 5 to 18.[132]

Enrollment fees charged by many schools are insufficient to maintain superior institutional, instructional, and other services. Hence they are forced to depend to some extent on various sources of assistance. The Christian churches, both Catholic and Protestant, provide considerable support, either in cash or services. The Cathedral School in Bangalore receives annual donations from the Christian Children's Fund, an American philanthropic organization. St. Ann's School, an integral part of the Good Shepherd Convent School, not only receives support from the Catholic Church, but also food contributions from such organizations as CARE. In some localities Parent-Teachers Associations, or their equivalent, make contributions for the benefit of needy students.

Student Needs Exceed Facilities

However adequate or inadequate the school facilities, the quality of instruction, and the scholarship system may be, many Anglo-Indian children of school age either do not attend any school, or attend so irregularly that the learning process is seriously hampered by frequent interruptions. A common complaint of school officials and teachers is that educational facilities are so limited that the schools cannot accommodate all the children of school age, that they have reached their capacity, even though the educational needs of many students are not met. There are conflicting reports about the adequacy of the scholarship system, especially scholarships made available by the All-India Anglo-Indian Association for its service to numerous local branches. One viewpoint, expressed by several

[132] *The Kalimpong Homes Magazine,* 4 (July and December, 1961), (July and December, 1962), and (July, 1963).

informants, is that the Association scholarships are awarded almost entirely to children whose families are members of that organization, that they are commonly given to children who do not seriously need them, that the "have nots" are generally overlooked in the allocation of these benefits.

On the other hand, leaders of the Association report that the requests for scholarships often fall short of the number available. The implication is that the shortage is lack of student or parental interest, not in opportunities. That the number of applications allegedly falls short of the number of scholarships available may be inadequate information for students concerning possible financial assistance, or indifference to education on the part of parents who urge their children to leave school and seek a job.

Irregular or non-attendance of young children presents an especially serious problem, partly because they are usually not eligible for scholarships however much they or their families may need financial assistance. Furthermore, compulsory school attendance laws enforced by municipal officials have not become an integral part of the Indian social system. In large cities the number of school-age children who get their education on the street rather than in the classroom is not known, but school officials are generally agreed that the number is considerable. In many instances they are on the street because there is no space available in the already-crowded classrooms. Even those who are in school may have so many distracting experiences at home that their reaction to scholastic work may be one of apathy. Several elementary teachers reported in interviews that children often came to school without breakfast and therefore, because of acute hunger, could not concentrate on school work. In some instances, parents reported that they could not afford money for school uniforms, usually required of students, and therefore could not send their children to school, even though they wished to do so.

Disadvantaged Schools and Their Problems

Teachers and officials at schools in which underprivileged students make up a fixed percentage of the total enrollment that is fairly large reported that these schools lacked the capacity and facilities to accommodate all the children or youth in need of an education. The principal of St. John's School in Bangalore observed in 1967 that enrollment for 1968 had already been terminated because of space limitations. Emphasized particularly was the need for hostels to accommodate orphans or other young persons whose home environment is unfavorable to their mental and moral development. Then there is the problem of providing guidance and protection to young persons when they leave school to enter the world of work. A parish priest at one of the convent schools in Bangalore reported his plans for a hostel to accommodate young persons, no longer in school, until they became established in a job or settled in a home. His efforts to finance the hostel had met with limited success.

Because many students leave school without the anchorage of a home or job their exposure to anti-social influences become a serious problem for society as a whole and for the Anglo-Indian Community in particular. Teachers and school officials frequently stated that a crucial need of disadvantaged schools was for more boarding facilities for neglected, abandoned, or homeless students. The principal of an Anglo-Indian school in Bangalore reported that numbers of her girls desired to enter the profession of nursing, but that the moral hazards they often encountered in hospitals while in training made this a doubtful career. She had reference to the risk of being sexually exploited by male workers in the hospitals.

Even with financial benefits from various sources many Anglo-Indian schools confront insuperable difficulties. Classrooms are commonly crowded, and teachers are overworked and underpaid. In so-called convent schools the salary question is not crucial since the teachers ordinarily are nuns whose remuneration is mainly in kind rather than in cash. But for schools in which the teaching staff is salaried, the problem of attracting and retaining superior teachers, or of maintaining teacher morale, and indirectly student morale, is serious. In some of these schools, especially in the South, teachers may receive as little as 100 rupees a month.

Elite schools invariably face a dilemma concerning the education of Anglo-Indian students. If they set the enrollment fees high enough to meet the cost of an institution with high scholarly standards, most Anglo-Indians cannot afford to attend; if they set the fees at a level which the majority of the students can afford, the income of the school is not sufficient to maintain a quality institution. A realistic compromise has been to waive tuition fees in the case of a few students, or to obtain scholarships from outside sources for their support.

As in the past, relatively few Anglo-Indians at present expect or plan to attend a college or university. The explanation commonly advanced by parents or young adults is that a college education is financially unattainable. Such an explanation is probably valid because the low incomes of most families do not permit the kind of expenditures that a college education entails. A policeman in Patna observed that it would cost about 75 rupees a month to send a youth to college, and that the incomes of most families are not sufficient to permit such an outlay if they maintain a decent standard of living. Even the costs of a high school education are comparatively high in relation to most family incomes, since a majority of the English-medium schools are private and therefore charge tuition fees.

It appears likely that the economic handicap, however important, is in some instances more a rationalization than reality; that the absence of a tradition of higher education and the lack of serious interest in college training may have been more important than the lack of financial resources. Parents are often not only unable but also unwilling to make the sacrifices necessary to send a son or daughter to college. One Community leader said that some of the younger Anglo-Indians did not attend college because they were reluctant to spend the time and money for such an education only to experience job discrimination later on. A Calcutta educator stated the viewpoint held by many Anglo-Indian youth, "Why should I want to continue living off my parents instead of going out and finding a job?" "Higher education" for many means technical schools in which vocational training can be readily translated into a job.

The acute shortage of qualified teachers in the Anglo-Indian schools has been a matter of considerable concern to the Community. This shortage has occurred in spite of the fact that salaries are higher than in public (government) schools. Many well-trained and experienced teachers have migrated from India since Independence, leaving a gap in the ranks of educational personnel. Because of low salaries and unfavorable working conditions in many schools, talented young persons are often reluctant to enter a teacher-training college to prepare for a career in education.

School administrators and teachers generally agree that Anglo-Indian students, as a group, have a less impressive scholastic record than Hindus or other students of comparable age in the same school. This reflects differences in the strength of intellectual motivation, and can scarcely be explained convincingly on the basis of hereditary limitations. In fact, their motivational weakness for solid achievement in academic subjects, or their limited interest in such matters, undoubtedly reflects the social influences of what might be called the Anglo-Indian sub-culture. This sub-culture and its corollary values can best be understood when viewed in historical perspective.

For many decades Anglo-Indians served British imperial interests in India through their occupational roles in developing and operating such strategic institutions as the railways, telegraph and postal services, police forces, and the like. For these services they were amply rewarded monetarily and through a near-monopoly of jobs were assured of considerable economic security. These jobs were generally mechanical or clerical in nature, and although a degree of literacy was necessary they did not ordinarily require college or university training. In fact, a skilled mechanic could generally command a higher income than many professionals.

The rewards available to Anglo-Indians were therefore not dependent on higher education or intellectual inquiry and interest. Rather, the tradition was that of "hewers of wood" and drivers of locomotives. But it was a prideful tradition, not in intellectual and cultural achievement but in achievement of a more mundane character.

That tradition has persisted. It became, and still is, an important aspect of community and family culture, profoundly influencing the interests of Anglo-Indians, young and old. If, as their thinking went, they could command a good wage with only limited occupational skills, why should they expend the necessary effort to achieve success in academic subjects demanding considerable intellectual discipline, hard work, time, and money? The immediate gratification of a lucrative job took precedent, for many, over unappealing rewards for scholastic attainment and the uncertain promise of a satisfactory vocation later on. Unlike many Hindu or Parsee families, in which there is a strong tradition of learning and academic achievement, the majority of Anglo-Indians have been motivated toward a different success model. This undoubtedly accounts in some measure for the unimpressive intellectual performance of so many Anglo-Indian students in school, at every level, and for their indifference to a college or university career.

These social and cultural elements are by no means the only factors curtailing the educational experiences of many. Economic components are also important. Many Anglo-Indian families live under conditions of extreme destitution and over-crowding in the home.[133] Children in such families are handicapped in school, not only because their social environment is inimical to effective learning but also because many are handicapped by problems of health and malnutrition, and by distractions due to tensions and crowding in the home.

Over the past century Anglo-Indian youth have shown a preference and aptitude for technical work of a practical nature. Many of them, after completing their studies on the elementary school level, obtained technical training as apprentices in large engineering establishments, especially railway workshops, throughout the country. Usually they completed these apprentice courses, in three to five years, with considerable success, and some became qualified for senior supervisory or managerial posts in the expanding technology. A former resident of Calcutta comments on this educational experience of young Anglo-Indians:

> On the basis of this initial training and experience, many attained higher professional diplomas both in India and abroad. In special schools (St. Vincent's at Asansol or Don Bosco at Liloah) where technical courses at the high school level were established in the 1950's, Anglo-Indian students, whose levels of literary performance had been indifferent, attained above average success.[134]

Student Academic Preferences and Aversions

A survey of students in English-medium schools in West Bengal in 1964-1965 made it possible to compare Anglo-Indian students with Hindus and others with reference to their educational interests and aspirations.[135] The evidence is clear, in-so-far as generalizations can be made from these data, that Anglo-Indian students are less oriented to strictly academic disciplines than are other students. To determine their preferences concerning the subjects in school, the following question was asked:

What type of subjects do you like best in school?
1. Subjects in which you have to study to learn, such as mathematics, science, and literature; or
2. Subjects in which you have to work with your hands, such as carpentry, metalwork, needlework, or cooking.

Table III illustrates the results of this question. Subject matter preferences of the Anglo-Indian students differ markedly from either the Hindu community or the "Others."[136] Two-thirds of the Hindu boys, and half of the "Others," preferred

---

[133] See especially chapter 9, "Styles of Life".
[134] Personal correspondence from Dudley Francis, March 26, 1971.
[135] This survey was conducted under the auspices of the Association of Teachers in Anglo-Indian schools of West Bengal. The design of the questionnaire and analysis of the data were by the senior author.
[136] Percentage figures for the "Other" category do not convey a clear picture concerning any one of the communities included. It seems probable that there were important differences between the communities included, i.e., Parsees and Jews generally are strongly motivated in academic disciplines, perhaps more so than Muslims or Sikhs.

regular academic subjects, compared to only one-third of the Anglo-Indians. On the other hand, only 4 per cent of the Hindus and 9 per cent of the "Others" gave their preference as non-academic subjects, while one-fourth of the Anglo-Indians liked these courses. In the case of girls the pattern was strikingly similar. The Hindus especially showed a preference for the solid academic subjects but expressed no strong liking for those courses involving manual work.

Table III

Percentage Distribution of 1,671 West Bengal Male Students and 923 Female Students According to Subject Preferred, by Community, 1964

	N = 1,051 Hindu	N = 216 Anglo-Indian	N = 404 Other*
	Males		
A	63%	32%	51%
B	4	26	9
C	33	42	40
	100	100	100

	N = 489 Hindu	N = 145 Anglo-Indian	N = 289 Other*
	Females		
A	47%	23%	37%
B	13	36	24
C	40	41	39
	100	100	100

A = Regular academic subjects
B = Non-academic subjects involving hand work
C = Like both types

* "Other" includes all other communities such as Muslims, Sikh, Indian-Christian, Jewish, Parsee, etc. (Percentage data above refers only to those supplying information in the questionnaire. No data were furnished by 132 boys and 125 girls.) Of the total number of students responding, 361, or about 13 percent, were Anglo-Indians.

Students were also asked to indicate the subjects, if any, which they disliked or wanted to give up. The most striking difference was the study of an Indian language. Although nearly half (48 per cent) of the Anglo-Indian males expressed dislike for this subject, only 10 per cent of the Hindus and one-fourth of the "Others" were negative toward the study of an Indian language. For the girls the percentage distribution was similar.

The strong occupational orientation of Anglo-Indian students is revealed in responses obtained from other inquiries in the survey. Of those who expressed a liking for school and stated the reason, nearly two-thirds (63 per cent) of the male students replied that they considered an education important in preparation for a job, compared with about two-fifths (42 per cent) of the Hindus and slightly over half (52 per cent) of the "Others." However, only 15 per cent of the Anglo-Indians liked school because they enjoyed reading and studying, compared with one-fourth (26 per cent) of the Hindus and one-fifth (22 per cent) of the "Others." The pattern for the girls was similar, except that only 8 per cent of the Anglo-Indian females liked to read and study compared with one-third (35 per cent) of the Hindus and one-fourth (24 per cent) of the "Others."

Many Anglo-Indian students dislike school, for one reason or another, and it is these who probably represent the majority of drop-outs. Of the male students stating the reasons for disliking school, nearly half (46 per cent) indicated that they found studying difficult or uninteresting, compared with about one-fifth (22 per cent) of the Hindus and about two-fifths (41 per cent) of the "Others." The pattern for the girls who responded was similar, the percentages being 57, 30, and 25, respectively.

An aspect of school life that does not follow the general pattern is sports. Athletic events have a strong appeal to Anglo-Indian students, both male and female. Indeed, many of them excel in such athletic activities as basketball, cricket, and soccer. Intramural contests in Anglo-Indian schools is an important and popular school activity. This is also true of dramatic and musical activities, in which Anglo-Indian students commonly exhibit considerable talent, and certainly a great deal of interest.

The occupational orientation of Anglo-Indian students is manifest in their responses to still other questions in the survey. When asked their reasons for studying hard in school, if they felt this was desirable, all three categories stated overwhelmingly that it is "one way to get a job," but the Anglo-Indian male students having this point of view were proportionately more numerous than the others. Almost nine-tenths (88 per cent) gave this as the reason compared with three-fourths of the Hindus and the "Others." Students who stated that it would be difficult or impossible to continue in school also showed a strong occupational orientation. A somewhat higher percentage of Anglo-Indian students than of Hindus and "Others" said they needed to get started in an occupation.

The foregoing data, and limited generalizations based upon them, apply only to students actually attending school when the study was made in West Bengal. A comparative study restricted to "drop outs" might give a somewhat different picture concerning their academic likes and dislikes as well as the nature of their interests and reasons (or rationalizations) for leaving school. Probably the "drop outs" are more negative toward academic matters than are students actually in attendance.

Anglo-Indian students commonly experience emotional difficulties because of conflicting pressures that create for them a serious dilemma. As one well-informed school principal of an elitist school in Bangalore observed, if the student aspires to a high-status occupation and attends a school with high standards of scholarship, he often falls behind and eventually drops out. But if he does not attend high school, nor even obtain a technical education, he is seriously handicapped in obtaining a job commensurate with his aspirations. In either case his position is one of frustration. This school principal expressed the view that, in his school, the frustrations of these students are commonly manifest in behavior problems. Such a reaction may also be characteristic of students who feel stigmatized by the support they receive from "freeships." Anglo-Indian students reared in families having a tradition of education usually perform quite well scholastically. The fact is, however, that most of them do not have such a home environment, and this factor is commonly reflected in poor academic performance.

Nothing in the foregoing data would justify the conclusion that Anglo-Indians invariably do inferior work in school or have no intellectual interests or aspirations. Indeed, some have creditable or even outstanding scholastic records. All that can be deduced from the West Bengal study is that many are indifferent to those aspects of formal education not relevant to their own values and interests. By tradition and socialization they are strongly oriented toward pecuniary and narrowly vocational objectives or toward extra-curricular activities that are more recreational than academic.

Educational Handicaps in a Competitive Society

In the opinion of numerous persons, there is an increasing tendency among parents to emphasize the importance of formal education and to urge their children to continue in school. Many parents are aware that a successful breakthrough into the upper levels of the occupational structure will involve college or university training. Respondents generally agreed that a small increase in the number of Anglo-Indians attending institutions of higher education has occurred over the past few years. One educator, a high school principal in Bangalore, estimated the increase at about one per cent a year. The president of the All-India Anglo-Indian Association estimated that about 10 per cent of Anglo-Indian youths are studying in institutions of higher education.[137] This, he says, is a higher percentage than is true of any other community except the Parsees, but he provides no empirical evidence that such is the case.

The problem is not solely a matter of encouraging Anglo-Indian youth to attend a college or university, or even a technical school. It involves the matter of motivation and aptitude on the part of children and youth, those who are socially, culturally, and economically disadvantaged and who are socially indifferent or resistant to learning in a school situation. It involves also the matter of home environment and parental influence, or interpersonal relationships with parents and peers who might be instrumental in stimulating an interest in learning or in encouraging students to intensify their efforts in school. It even involves curricular and pedagogical changes that are relevant to the needs of the Anglo-Indian Community and of Indian society as well.

The mature adults generally recognize the importance of formal education in their own lives as indicated by the responses of 52 Anglo-Indians in Bangalore

---

[137] Frank Anthony, *op. cit.*, p. 437.

who were requested to supply information on a questionnaire. When asked if they ever felt handicapped because of lack of education, two-thirds of the respondents, all employed, stated that they had at one time or another felt at a disadvantage. Some of the respondents indicated that financial circumstances prevented them from obtaining more education—an explanation that may have been partly rationalization. The average numbervof years they had attended school was 10, with 6 as the minimum and 17 the maximum. Twenty had been school dropouts. Among the reasons expressed for feeling handicapped were the following:

> Future prospects in my career are not so bright since I do not have a college education. (11 years)
>
> I was unable to get the jobs I aimed for as my qualifications were inadequate, due mainly to the fact that I did not realize the importance of higher education in my youth, and my parents' inability to finance me for much longer than they did. (13 years)
>
> With my present education I find it difficult to get a better job. (8 years)
>
> Education has been my handicap because when the good posts I have tried for have been given to others it is because they have higher degrees, not higher ability. (11 years)
>
> I feel handicapped because I cannot face educated people with their ideas. (9 years)
>
> A university education with specialized training in, say, company secretaryship would have fetched me a better job. (14 years)

On the other hand, 18 reported that they did not feel especially handicapped educationally, and some of them reported the reasons:

> Thank God I am able to hold my own with the most educated of persons. (14 years)
>
> Since English is my mother tongue, and very much in vogue here, I have felt at an advantage. (13 years)
>
> Being one of the privileged few Anglo-Indians who possess a university degree, and that with an extremely good pass, I have been able to meet other educated Indians on their own ground. (17 years)

Most of the Bangalore respondents reported that they had experienced no serious difficulties in obtaining a job, but some who did have difficulty attributed it to actual discrimination. Among these were such statements as the following:

> Lack of a University degree when I applied for an assistant editor's job with a children's magazine. I had had a children's book published and had written over one hundred stories, articles, and serials which were published for Indian magazines.
>
> It was difficult when I first left school, probably because of the community to which I belonged and the lack of influence I commanded, and my qualifications were not outstanding enough to overcome these disadvantages.
>
> I have been unlucky. I have tried and am still trying. I have been called for interviews and have successfully passed exams, but with no luck.
>
> I have always had difficulty in obtaining a job, for in spite of my high educational qualifications and high recommendations the jobs have always been given to Hindus, and especially to those of the same caste of the interviewing officers.

Educational Distribution in the Anglo-Indian Community

The distribution of the Anglo-Indian Community according to levels of attained education indicates a high percentage of literate persons, even though few members of the Community have a college education. Gaikwad found in a sample of adult Anglo-Indians in three Indian cities that the percentage of persons who held a degree or had attended college ranged from 2.5 per cent in Bilaspur, 5.1 per cent in Bangalore, to 6.4 per cent in Jhansi.[138] Of 260 persons interviewed in Delhi by Wright, ten per cent reported they had "some" university or college training, and 4.2 per cent held university degrees.[139]

At the other end of the educational spectrum, the percentage of illiterate Anglo-Indians is relatively small. Gaikwad found in his survey that 5.6 per cent of the adult Anglo-Indians in the Bilaspur sample were illiterate or had not attended school, 6.5 per cent in Jhansi, and 5.2 per cent in Bangalore.[140] Gaikwad's data also indicate that, for the three cities, a large percentage had attended high school or elementary school. Wright's survey in New Delhi revealed that only 1.8 per cent of the respondents said they had never attended school, and slightly over one-third had been in school eight years or less. Almost two-fifths had attended school for 9 to 12 years. A Calcutta teacher active in educational affairs estimated that the number of illiterates in the Community did not exceed two per cent of the total Anglo-Indian population.

Considerable emphasis on education, but education at the lower or middle levels, has always been a feature of Anglo-Indian values. If, in earlier decades, the Community was to retain a favorable position in the occupational system controlled by the British and if they had sufficient learning to communicate effectively in their occupational roles, an elementary education was a minimal requirement. Opinions of numerous persons interviewed in this investigation indicate that the Community has lost ground educationally since Independence, although a concerted effort is being made to upgrade the quality of instruction in many Anglo-Indian schools and to inculcate the children and youth with positive educational values. There are reports, unverified, that illiteracy has actually increased since Independence. Actually, the number of illiterates may have remained fairly constant, or even decreased, although proportionally there could have been an increase due to selective out-migration which has tended to skim off the better-educated.

The Regulation System

Anglo-Indian schools are generally under the jurisdiction of a state director of education who supervises all government-regulated schools conducted by private

---

[138] E. K. Gaikwad, *The Anglo-Indians* (Bombay: Asia Press, 1962), pp. 143-146.

[139] Roy Dean Wright, "Marginal Man in Transition: A Study of the Anglo-Indian Community in India." Unpublished PhD dissertation, University of Missouri, Columbia, 1969, p. 79.

[140] E. K. Gaikwad, *op. cit.* Non-attendance does not necessarily imply illiteracy. Individuals may be literate by self-instruction or by tutoring in their own families. Since illiteracy is so difficult to determine by operational measures, data are probably very imprecise. Also, respondents may be reluctant to admit that they are not literate because of the general stigma which may be attached to illiteracy.

bodies. In West Bengal, for example, supervision of these schools is vested in the inspector of Anglo-Indian schools. The Interstate Board for Anglo-Indian Education attempts to maintain uniform standards of scholarship in the system. The All-India Anglo-Indian Association maintains a department whose function it is to provide guidance and support for Anglo-Indian schools. The main function of one of the two Anglo-Indian representatives in the *Lok Sabha,* himself an education specialist, is to help adapt the educational program to current needs and problems of the Community. He was replaced in 1971 by another educator.

In view of the disparity among Anglo-Indian schools as to salaries and professional qualifications of teachers, the cultural and economic backgrounds of students, and the physical equipment of school plants, maintaining uniform standards of scholarship is difficult. Standardization of requirements is also a function of the Council for the Indian School Certification Examination, which has superseded the Senior Cambridge Examination, formerly prepared under the authority of Cambridge University. This examination is not only used by Anglo-Indian Schools but by many others, including the Air Force Schools and Indian private schools which have English as a medium of instruction.

Curricular Changes and the Language Issue

The Anglo-Indian school system in the course of its evolution has had to make adjustments to conditions in independent India. Indeed, it has been necessary to come to terms with the political, cultural, and social expectations of Indians as well as of Anglo-Indians. Throughout most of the history of Anglo-Indian schools they were not a direct part of the social life of India's people, but a back eddy removed from the main cultural stream of the time. There were really no prominent places in the curriculum for Indian literature, art, history, philosophy, music, dance forms, religion, and language. All this changed in more recent years. The main themes of Indian culture have become more or less integrated into the school curricula. The objective, as propounded by a prominent educator in West Bengal, is to provide a blending of the cultures of East and West through the medium of education.

Language is a case in point. English is the medium of instruction in all Anglo-Indian schools, but the study of Hindi, the national official language, is now required, and in addition the study of a regional language is compulsory. This is the so-called "three language formula." As a result of these requirements Latin and French have disappeared from the curriculum. These new requirements have occasioned considerable concern among members of the Community because Anglo-Indians generally have lacked any serious interest in mastering an Indian language and have shown scant aptitude for language study other than English. Yet it is no longer a matter of choice.

English is, of course, functional for Anglo-Indians. It is *their* mother tongue. But the uncertain future of English in the curricula of Anglo-Indian schools is a matter of considerable concern to educational leaders and many others. Although the Community had been given official assurance by the national government that English could continue to be the medium of institutional instruction, certain ardent nationalists in government prefer that it be replaced by an Indian language. Should this occur, Anglo-Indian leaders see only disintegration ahead for the Community since its most important bond of unity is the English language.

Furthermore, Community leaders view with apprehension the proposed plan requiring all colleges or universities to adopt as the medium of instruction the regional language in which the institution is located. Such a plan would apply to numbers of colleges in which English is presently the instructional language. In the opinion of educational leaders, Anglo-Indian students attending college would be seriously handicapped if the instruction and literature were in a language in which they had limited proficiency. They also point out that Anglo-Indian schools attract many Indian students — Hindus, Muslims, Sikhs, Indian-Christians, Parsees, and others — who want to master the English language. Some of the parents of these children, the leaders often assert, are actually "enemies" of the English language (probably for political reasons) but nevertheless want their own children to become familiar with the medium. Hence some students in Anglo-Indian schools are themselves children of upper-class Indians who have not always been kindly disposed toward these institutions and English language as a medium of instruction.

The issue of English versus an indigenous Indian language as a medium of instruction in schools having traditionally employed English was the major subject of discussion in a convention held in Madras in 1967 to consider the place of English in India's educational system. Among the three thousand participants were several distinguished educators and statesmen.[141] As might be expected, the participants, including those representing the Anglo-Indian Community, voiced support of English and the right of Anglo-Indian schools, or any others, to employ the English language in their curriculum.

Shortly afterward a committee of Indians, meeting in Bangalore, drew up a formal statement expressing their collective views on the subject[142] In its report to the Minister of Education in the national government the committee cited as evidence of the support of English a study conducted in 28 colleges by Bangalore University in which 91 per cent of 8,508 students favored English as a medium and only 9 per cent desired the regional language. The committee also stated that preference for English "is not limited to colleges, but extends to secondary and even primary schools. The denial of choice of English medium is denial of maximum educational and employment potential and is indefensible. We recommend that students at all levels of education should have free choice of English medium and the state should not limit it in any way."[143]

The issue is far from settled. For years the titular leader of the Community, Frank Anthony, a member of Parliament, has carried on a campaign for the right of the Community to employ English in the schools. "If, because of the compulsion by the Hindi chauvinist phalanx," he stated in a public address, "English is driven

---

[141] *The Review,* 58 : 8-18 (November, 1967).
[142] *The Review,* 59 : 13-14 (February, 1968).
[143] *Ibid.,* p. 14.

out because there is no foreseeable or acceptable substitute, there will be chaos in education and inevitable political disintegration."[144] And on the occasion of his presidential address in 1966 he reminded his lighteners to "Remember this, without our schools and without our language, English, we cannot be an Anglo-Indian Community."[145]

[114] *The Review*, 58 : 5 (August-September, 1967).
[115] *The Review*, 57 : 39 (November-December, 1966).

CHAPTER NINE

STYLES OF LIFE

The idea of a distinctive Anglo-Indian "way of life" is probably a myth more than a reality. Anglo-Indians vary a great deal as to tastes, interests, values, income, education, occupation, and other cultural and social attributes. Yet, because they have a common heritage of language, religion, and various elements of Western culture, and because there is a common bond of self-identity as Anglo-Indians, certain cultural uniformities have developed so that, generally speaking, an Anglo-Indian "sub-culture," with all of its variations, is in many ways distinguishable from Hindu, Muslim, Sikh, or Parsi culture. But in a very real sense this sub-culture is a blend of Eastern and Western culture in which the many cultural strands are woven into a fabric whose psychological and behavioral manifestations and material elements give the community a distinctive *gestalt*.

Acculturation and Life Styles

As long as the British remained socially, politically, and economically dominant in India, and maintained a rather distinctive style of life, the Anglo-Indian *modus vivendi* was buttressed by British power and economic support. If Western life styles were viewed with disfavor by Indians having strong nationalistic feelings, the Anglo-Indians had visible models in the British and their culture. But woven into the fabric were numerous components rooted in Portuguese culture. This is not to say that they were merely imitators of the British and Portuguese; rather, they were socialized into Western culture which, because of historical circumstances, was oriented more toward Britain than Portugal. Nevertheless, Portuguese influence persists, as evidenced, for example, by the spread of Catholicism among Anglo-Indians and Indian-Christians. Situated in a society in which most of the people were Hindus or Muslims, the Anglo-Indians were influenced in various ways by these major cultural groups, although this influence was far less than that exerted by the Europeans.

Yet the fact that many non-Anglo-Indians, especially the newly rich, themselves adopted portions of Western culture had the effect of softening the criticisms and enhancing the acceptability of Western (mainly British) cultural patterns and styles of life. Some of the Western cultural forms adopted by Indians became a kind of bridge connecting Anglo-Indians and other Indians, serving in the same way that Anglo-Indian adoption of certain aspects of Indian culture had helped to bridge the gap from the opposite direction. Probably the gap between Anglo-Indians and Indian-Christians, a much larger minority, was bridged more effectively than the gap separating Anglo-Indians from other Indian communities. The bonds of a common religion are vitally important in the Indian sub-continent.

Through the centuries there has been a considerable degree of acculturation to Indian society. Historically, the styles of life characterizing the Anglo-Indian sub-culture have always placed the Community in a marginal position, one in which the cultural and behavioral differences were wide in certain aspects of society but narrow in others. The acculturation or integration of Anglo-Indians into Indian society has depended on several conditions, including their felt needs to be integrated with other Indian communities, the satisfactions which acculturation could offer them, and their acceptability in the economic and social life of the indigenous population. The extent and character of their acculturation and integration, the degree of their social acceptability, and the nature of their self- or others-identity provide a rough gauge of Anglo-Indian marginality. A Calcutta clergyman (non-Anglo-Indian) who is intimately familiar with the vicissitudes of the Anglo-Indian Community summed up the situation in an interview:

> One of the difficulties is that the Anglo-Indians are living between two cultural worlds and not really wanted in either, but wanting nevertheless to be a part of the European world — wanting this very strongly — and also wanting, but less strongly, to be a part of the world of Indian culture. They accepted European culture almost *en toto*, but are slowly, almost reluctantly, becoming a part of the Indian world. This has made it difficult for them, has made them feel insecure; and much of their behavior, and even some of their disorganization, may be explained in terms of this conflict and its insecurities. England and the West must cease to be the mecca for Anglo-Indians; if they are realistic they will identify with India, accepting as much as possible of Indian culture, especially language.

Since any level of living has many component elements, each of which may have considerable symbolic significance for social status and self-images, a disparity between the idealized and the real is a source of dissatisfaction. This is particularly true of the Anglo-Indians in India, many of whom have experienced economic adversity and are unable to maintain the standard of living to which they were accustomed in earlier years, or at least the standard to which they have been socialized to consider adequate. Their financial inability to enjoy a Western *modus vivendi* has created problems of personal adjustment and is a source of frustrations which sometimes lead to deviant or hedonistic behavior. The spirit of immediate gratification, "let the future take care of itself," widespread among Anglo-Indian youth, tends to run counter to the Weberian "Protestant ethic" of hard work and frugality which appears to be characteristic of certain other communities in India.

These hedonistic values are often manifest by extravagant expenditures required in keeping up appearances and acquiring certain status symbols, or in frivolous behavior that is dysfunctional from a strictly economic standpoint. Whatever the explanation in social-psychological terms, excessive alcohol consumption by many persons, not only young but adult individuals as well, is probably a symptom of disillusionment and frustration produced by poverty, unemployment, and other conditions generating an acute sense of deprivation.

Housing and Home Life

The furnishings of Anglo-Indian homes can be said to symbolize a Western style of life and the social position, in India, of families that have acquired these possessions. The physical features of such homes are by no means uniform, varying according to the educational and income levels of the occupants, their tastes and interests. As one might expect, middle- and upper-income families generally reside in houses or apartments that are comfortably spacious and at the same time having the essential amenities for modern living. The decor and furnishings bear the earmark of Western, and particularly British, interior styling: among the middle classes there is the ubiquitous overstuffed living room furniture, mahogany or oak tables, floor coverings that may have been fabricated in a European mill, all commonly intermingled with furnishings or decorations of indigenous origin. Wall pictorial displays often include portraits of the occupying family or other relatives, sentimental religious pictures or inscriptions, photographs or drawings of familiar Indian or European landscapes, portraits of Indian or British notables such as Gandhi, Nehru, Churchill, or even the British royal family.

The homes of affluent or educationally sophisticated families commonly show evidence of discriminating tastes in the display of interior decorations and equipment. Separate bedrooms are provided for members of the family, and there is usually a minimum of housing congestion. Some of the larger housing units, however, are located in congested residential districts. Many workers who are employed by government agencies or private corporations which furnish living quarters for their employees — Binny Mills of Bangalore, for example — live in comfortable or even relatively luxurious quarters. The following cases refer to Anglo-Indian families who are luxuriously or comfortably housed:

> Mr. and Mrs. K. live in a luxurious apartment on the near south side of Calcutta. Mr. K. is reputed to be one of the wealthiest Anglo-Indians in India, and is the owner or manager of extensive properties (partly an inheritance of his wife). He also owns a string of race horses which represents a financial investment as well as a sporting activity. The house is luxuriously furnished and discriminatingly decorated, with numerous *objets d'art* acquired in their extensive travels in India and abroad. A spacious compound provides a setting for social gatherings. The meals are prepared and served, European style, by Indian servants.

> Mr. and Mrs. M. live in a modest residence in Kharagpur, a railway center some 75 miles west of Calcutta. Mr. M. is employed as a technical supervisor in the railway shops, and in this position has a fairly good income. The house is comfortable although not luxuriously furnished; it is orderly and scrupulously clean, a characteristic of most Anglo-Indian homes. The interior decorations do not show evidence of discriminating cultural tastes; rather they are perhaps fairly typical of the tastes of working class families with good incomes.

> Mr. and Mrs. R. occupy a comfortable flat on the near north side of Calcutta. Mr. R. is a manager of a small factory employing a considerable number of semi-skilled workers. Judging from the style of home life, the family has an income sufffcient to afford numerous luxuries. The house is not only comfortably furnished, but the occupants own such objects as a gramophone and numerous records of popular music,

a radio, and a guitar. As in other households in this general economic class, the domestic work tasks are performed by Indian servants.

> Mr. and Mrs. H., residents of New Delhi, are both gainfully employed, he as a clerk, she as a secretary in a government agency. They have four children between the ages of four and eleven. Their residence is a four-room apartment, with an additional room for the family cook and his wife, who looks after the children while the parents are at work. Mr. H. belongs to the Gidney Club, whose meetings he and his wife attend once or twice a month. They attend Catholic church services regularly, go to two or three English-language movies each month, and associate freely with neighbors, some of whom are not Anglo-Indians. Mrs. H. owns two saris but seldom wears them, preferring Western attire. Mainly their food is prepared and served European style, but they regularly eat curries and rice. Neither is fluent in an Indian language.

At or near the bottom of the social structure are the slum dwellers who often live in congested residences in equally congested neighborhoods. Many of the houses in such areas are without modern sanitary toilets, running water, or electricity; indeed, the furnishings may be limited to a few primitive cooking and serving utensils, one or two beds, and a few rickety chairs – or perhaps no chair at all. Winding streets, often scarcely ten feet in width, are little more than corridors lined by one- or two-room hovels whose dark interiors more nearly resemble a dungeon, in the classical sense, than a residence.

The incidence of contagious diseases, such as tuberculosis, is high in these areas, and the risk to property and life is considerable. The district centering around Ripon Street in Calcutta can be cited as one such example. Here are concentrated large numbers of Anglo-Indians who, for the most part, are destitute, forced by circumstance to live under excessively adverse conditions. Many are supported by public or private welfare agencies. The following cases are examples of the conditions of home life of such families:

> Mr. J., age 40, lives with his wife and two small children in a two-room flat in a congested slum of Calcutta. At the time of the interview, Mr. J. was employed at 65 rupees a month, having spent 13 years in the Indian navy – but had no retirement benefits from his naval service. His pregnant wife, formerly a nurse, was unable to work because of a cardiac condition. The children attended school irregularly because of the risks of going alone through the congested district and adult escorts were not always available. The family received partial support from an Anglo-Indian welfare fund, with slender prospects for a general improvement of living conditions. The quarters consisted of a combined "living room" and kitchen, meagerly furnished, and a single bedroom.

> Mr. and Mrs. S., in their thirties, live with their two children in a one-room flat in a Calcutta slum. They were recently married, Mrs. S. having been widowed in a previous marriage. Mrs. S. is a Christian and Mr. S. is a Muslim. At the time of the interview Mr. S. had a menial job in the Bengal Club at a monthly salary of 60 rupees. He had an irregular employment record, which was due, by his own admission, to heavy drinking and a resentful attitude toward authority in the work situation. The "living" room was large enough only for two beds; there were no chairs or other household furnishings. Cooking was done on a primitive stove just outside the door of the living

room. The flat had no toilet facilities or other modern amenities. Yet the interior was clean and orderly.

Three Anglo-Indian families consisting of 23 persons occupy a two-room house in Bangalore. The senior adults are unemployed, but some of the junior adults hold menial jobs at low wages. Two unmarried daughters, one with two children and the other with one child, live in the household. Both are employed at wages of 25 and 40 rupees a month, respectively, while their parents take care of the children. An atmosphere of self-pity and resentment seems to reflect a feeling of hopelessness—of being trapped without any avenue of escape.

Mr. and Mrs. R. reside in a one-room apartment in the Chandi Chowk section of Delhi. Mr. R., in his fifties, is presently unemployed. At one time he worked on the railways, but was discharged in 1959 and has been unable to find regular employment since then. Mrs. R. works as a dishwasher in a restaurant, receiving 64 rupees a month. Their living quarters, located in a congested section of the city, are meagerly furnished. Both are members of the Roman Catholic church, but seldom attend services, except two or three times a year to receive communion. They say that they would attend more often, but that they feel unwelcome. Neither belongs to any social club, nor do they engage in formal social activities. Mostly their recreation is visiting informally or playing cards with friends, although they do see their adult children fairly often. Their food is mainly vegetables, but occasionally they serve meat, usually when the children come for a visit. Both Mr. and Mrs. R. wear Western attire.

A survey of 2,116 Anglo-Indians in Calcutta included information about 491 households in that city in 1957.[146] The sample, representing about 10 per cent of the Anglo-Indian population of Calcutta, was drawn randomly from several districts in the city. One of them, Entally, is a congested slum area occupied mainly by extremely poor people. The other areas (Park Street, Dharamtolla, and "Other") represent a considerable range of incomes, quality of housing, and neighborhood environment.

Forty per cent of the residences of the Entally sample were classified as "huts," compared with approximately six per cent of the houses in the other districts. In terms of floor space, most of the residents lived in congested quarters. The average floor space in the occupied houses was 36 square feet in Entally, 65 in Dharamtolla, 99 in Park Street, and 107 in the "Other" zones. Nearly half of the Entally residents received their water supply from street taps, but less than 13 per cent of the residents of the "Other" districts obtained water from this source. About three-fourths of the Entally residents lived in areas having open sewers, but less than half of the families in the "Other" districts relied upon such drainage facilities. Most of the residences and neighborhoods fell below what was considered to be reasonable hygienic standards, as judged by the investigators; the percentages being 90 for Entally, 72 for Dharamtolla, 64 for Park Street, and 49 for "Others." Although housing conditions as these may be found in other cities, probably a higher proportion of Calcutta's Anglo-Indians live in sub-standard housing than those residing elsewhere.

---

[146] *Pilot Survey of Socio-Economic Conditions of the Anglo-Indian Community, 1957-1958* (Calcutta: Baptist Mission Press, 1958), pp. 12-15.

Food Habits and Preferences

Anglo-Indians are thoroughly conditioned to Western food preferences and drinking-dining behavior. The kinds of food they eat, methods of food preparation, and the style of food consumption definitely show the influence of a Western way of life. As a general rule, they are non-vegetarians; if there are deviants it is probably because they cannot afford the price of meat. Since they have no taboos against the consumption of beef, pork, fowl, or fish (except as exerted by Western religious influences, e.g., Lent), interdining with orthodox Hindus or Muslims obviously presents certain difficulties. Yet the influence of Indian culture is apparent in their acquired taste for curries and domestic "sweets" as well as their extensive consumption of rice or food products made with a rice base.

The actual behavior involved in the preparation, serving, and consumption of food resembles traditional British culture more than the indigenous cultures of India. Facilities for the preparation and serving of food generally reflect the purchasing power of the family — whether a relatively primitive or a modern food technology. Artifacts used in the consumption of food tend to resemble those of Western peoples. In the middle-classes these include serving dishes, proper cups and saucers, porcelain plates, and such utensils as knives, forks, and spoons.

Table manners likewise show the influence of the West. At regular meals within the home, middle-class Anglo-Indians almost invariably sit on dining-room chairs at a dining table, often at pre-arranged places for members of the family or invited guests. The behavioral aspects of food consumption — the proper way to use a knife, fork, or spoon, or the acceptable way to serve others — resemble the European style of eating. The traditional Indian practice of eating solely with one's hands, without benefit of table utensils, is socially unacceptable, and for some downright offensive. These behavior patterns also create a cultural and psychological obstacle that actually makes difficult intimate interaction between Anglo-Indians and Indians who follow the traditional mode of food consumption. The early morning tea seems to be a part of the British cultural legacy, just as soup is usually an introduction to the evening meal.

Wine or other alcoholic liquor is sometimes served as an *aperitif* before meals, and the cocktail social party has become widely accepted by Anglo-Indians who adhere to middle-class values. If there are teetotalers in the Community, and some are, it is an individual matter since Anglo-Indian values do not generally prohibit the consumption of alcohol. By comparison, in orthodox Hindu or Islamic cultures drinking or even serving spirituous liquor is generally taboo. Alcohol consumption, however, often exceeds the bounds of conventional social behavior. One of the common complaints of teachers in certain Anglo-Indian schools is that unemployed or destitute fathers often spend for liquor all or most of the money they can obtain, thus depriving their wives and children of the basic necessities of life.

However impoverished or affluent Anglo-Indian families may be, they generally have clean and orderly homes and take pride in maintaining this standard of living. Homes may be scantily furnished because incomes are not sufficient to provide better equipment, but the furnishing and interior usually show evidence of disciplined housekeeping standards. Most middle-class Anglo-Indian families have at least one household servant who, in addition to being a status symbol, can assume part of the responsibility for maintaining the premises, preparing the meals, and serving the food. But household servants are not merely a luxury in many Anglo-Indian homes. Often the wife or mother is gainfully employed and therefore unable to perform the traditional domestic roles. Fortunately for them, the wages of domestic servants are generally low in India.

Of 224 Anglo-Indian students in West Bengal who responded to a questionnaire, 46 per cent reported that their mothers were employed outside the home.[147] This compared with 8 per cent of the Hindu students, and 20 per cent of students from "other" communities included in the survey. The absence of mothers from the home is often associated with problems of child-rearing, especially if there are young children in the home and the family cannot afford to employ domestic servants. Teachers in working-class Anglo-Indian schools report that children are often neglected in the home if the mother is employed or irresponsible. These teachers attribute much of the inferior school work done by such students to this situation.

The principal of an Anglo-Indian school in a low-income district in Bangalore reported the following example of a home environment not conducive to successful achievement in school:

> Mrs. C. is employed at a local hotel with a salary of less than 100 rupees a month. The unemployed father spends for liquor much of the money he can obtain, including some of the earnings of the mother. Often there is insufficient money to buy food for the family, although the mother is sometimes able to bring home food from the hotel where she works. When the school provided uniforms for the children, the father sold them to buy liquor. Since there was little incentive for the children to remain in school, or to do good work when there, they dropped out and drifted into petty delinquency such as running small-time confidence games to "raise funds" for the school.

If personal and social disorganization is fairly common in families that have experienced hardships through unemployment or other forms of adversity, it is by no means a general reality that all low-income families have such a record. The following case is probably representative of families that have experienced serious privations yet have remained stable in the face of adversity.

> Mrs. T., a widow employed as a chambermaid at a Bangalore hotel, has two children, ages 9 and 12. She goes to work about 7 in the morning and returns about 8 in the evening, traveling by bus. Her salary is 90 rupees a month. She lives in a two-room house with ten other persons — her mother, brother, a married sister and family, her own children, and two others. The brother is employed at 45 rupees a month, and the brother-in-law works in a clinic at a low salary. The mother and married sister look after her children while she is away at work, do the cooking, and

---

[147] Survey conducted in West Bengal under the auspices of the Association of Teachers in Anglo-Indian Schools, 1964.

perform other household chores. At the time of the interview her children were not in school because she could not afford the uniforms they were required to wear. She doubts if she will be financially able to send them to high school; she herself has only an eighth grade education. Mrs. T. is a steady worker and there is no visible evidence of personal or family disorganization in the home. Most of their immediate neighbors are Muslims, but members of the family have virtually no intimate contacts with the near-by residents.

The home situation of some working mothers may, however, be favorable for all concerned. This may depend, in considerable measure, on the level of education of the parents, the incomes they receive, and the values they place on occupational success and school achievement. The following cases may be representative of professional or skilled Anglo-Indian families:

Mr. and Mrs. O. are both employed as teachers in a well-known Anglo-Indian school in Calcutta, at salaries reported to be above the average. Both are intelligent and have the reputation of being good teachers. Their home provides a residence for their three children and Mrs. O's mother. It is a well-ordered household with ample facilities and space for comfortable living. A full-time servant prepares the meals and assumes other housekeeping responsibilities. The children have had the advantage of family support and encouragement in their education, all of whom have gone beyond high school. The O's own and operate an automobile, a luxury for most Anglo-Indian families.

Mrs. L., a divorcee, lives in a second-floor flat in a densely populated district of Calcutta. She is an operative in a hair-dressing salon which caters largely to Europeans and Westernized Indians. Her two children of pre-school age are cared for by an Indian servant, who is also responsible for other domestic duties. The living room is fairly spacious and equipped with adequate though not luxurious furniture. The food is prepared by a servant in a "cook shack" near the living quarters but served in one end of the living room. At the time of the interview Mrs. L. was expecting to re-marry, her fiance being a Hindu holding unorthodox views of religion and family life.

Social Clubs

There is a widespread tendency for the peoples of India to identify with their own organized groups or communal associations, and often to exclude from membership or participation those who may represent a different community. The social club is an example. In the large metropolitan centers of India the number of social clubs is large, ranging from those catering to the elite to organizations whose members are drawn mainly from the middle- or lower-classes. These clubs, and other comparable social groups, make for the diversification of Indian society, but they are not always a unifying force.

The early emergence of a community consciousness was manifest in the formation of social clubs which afforded opportunities for Anglo-Indians to meet informally in a spirit of good fellowship. The real *raison d'être* of the early clubs, however, was the defensive psychological armor they afforded against the hostile attitudes and sometimes discriminatory actions of Europeans or Indians. One of the first of these organizations was the East Indian Bengal Club of Calcutta, founded in 1825. The preamble as written by the founder was a frank recognition of the social position of Anglo-Indians: "We are considered, we all know, as a separate class of society. We are deserted by Europeans in this country; and although united with them by the most sacred of bonds of relationships, we are avoided and looked upon as inferiors."[148] The Bengal Club was followed by others in Madras and Bombay. Although these clubs were small and lacking in influence, they were viewed with suspicion by the East India Company on the grounds that they might eventually develop into a system of political power that could challenge the colonial government itself.

But as Goodrich observes, there was growing awareness on the part of Anglo-Indian leaders that if the Community was to have a secure and respected place in Indian society it would be through the medium of organization.[149] As community consciousness crystallized through the remaining decades of the nineteenth century and early years of the twentieth, numerous clubs were formed, most of which had a relatively short span of life. Yet, these groups usually had both expressive and instrumental functions: expressive in that they provided opportunities for Anglo-Indians to share collectively the spirit of good fellowship and informal activities, instrumental in that they afforded an appropriate mechanism for the formulation and promotion of organized programs of welfare, education, and recreation. Today, much of the social life of Anglo-Indians on the middle- and upper-income levels centers in organized clubs.

During the British presence in India social clubs were maintained in various locations for the exclusive benefit of Europeans and a few prestigious Indians or foreigners. Generally Anglo-Indians were denied admission to these elitist social clubs. This exclusionist policy of the "burra" clubs ordinarily applied to other Indians as well. Frank Anthony observes that Anglo-Indian and British men were usually compatible in the clubs, but that the British women viewed with a jaundiced eye female members representing the Anglo-Indian Community. "The British women pursued their social snobbery with a certain feline deadliness," he writes. "Thus not only Anglo-Indian women but British women married to Anglo-Indians who happened to be members of the 'burra' club were usually pointed targets not only of snobbery but of every refinement of feminine vengefulness."[150] These were mainly clubs maintained by the British elite, but there were other clubs in which highly-placed Anglo-Indians and "second class" British officers intermingled freely. Anthony also observes that feminine snobbishness was sometimes exhibited by Anglo-Indian women against other women of their own community who were not in the favor of British or Indian elite or who were educationally or economically deprived.

After Independence the membership policies of some of the European clubs were changed so as to admit Indians and even Anglo-Indians. But this did not

---

[148] Quoted in Dorris L. Goodrich, "The Making of an Ethnic Group: The Eurasian Community in India," Unpublished PhD dissertation, University of California, Berkeley, 1952, p. 141.
[149] *Ibid.*, p. 144.
[150] Frank Anthony, *Britain's Betrayal in India* (New Delhi: Allied Publishers, 1969), pp. 355-357.

apply to all clubs. As late as the 1960's several British clubs in Bombay and Calcutta modified their admission policies only to the extent of accepting certain foreign nationals, but not Indians. In 1963, the Indian government, as well as private groups and individuals, protested this policy on the grounds that admission of other foreigners, but not Indians, was a form of discrimination practiced against Indian citizens in their own country. At the same time the American ambassador issued a formal order prohibiting any American in the foreign service in India from holding membership in such clubs.

Many of the erstwhile exclusionist clubs have now opened their doors to Indian nationals, including Anglo-Indians. The Bengal Club in Calcutta and the Bangalore Club in Bangalore, among others, have adopted such a policy. In fact, non-Anglo-Indians presently represent the majority of members in the Bangalore Club. The Calcutta Football Club was initially a European organization, but numerous Anglo-Indians are now included in the membership. The prestigious Gidney Club in New Delhi, initially organized for the benefit of Anglo-Indians, has adopted an open-membership policy, but non-Anglo-Indians are usually admitted as associate or honorary members.

Functions of the clubs are varied. Probably the central function of most of them is to provide facilities and an appropriate setting for social gatherings and organized or unorganized recreation. Some of the more affluent clubs provide financial and other support for various social services. By far the most influential of the Anglo-Indian organizations is the Rangers Club of Calcutta, founded in 1896. While ostensibly a social and recreational association, the club contributes heavily to charitable and educational programs and to the All-India Anglo-Indian Association.[151] Most of the funds are raised through a lottery system.

Among the social clubs that have long provided recreation and entertainment for Anglo-Indians are the Railway Institutes, established in towns or cities having concentrations of persons engaged in the maintenance and operations of the railways. A contribution of these institutes was the support for all kinds of sports, especially field hockey. Such clubs as the Kharagpur Institute, the Ajmer Institute, the Burt Institute at Lahore, and many others are well known to the Community. Usually these clubs provide facilities for tennis, billiards, swimming, dancing, dramatic performances, musical programs, and such games as "housie" or whist, aside from the opportunities for informal visiting. In or near military establishments the Armed Forces also have similar clubs for service personnel. Through the country there are athletic clubs whose members are predominantly or entirely Anglo-Indians — just as there are sports clubs for other groups.

A sample survey of Anglo-Indians in Calcutta, referred to earlier, resulted in

---

[151] *The Review* 57 : 41 (November-December, 1966) and 60 : 11 (March-April, 1967). In 1959 this club donated some 300,000 rupees to help build the Frank Anthony School in Delhi, and in 1967 contributions to the extent of 50,000 rupees were made to the national defense fund, 40,000 rupees to the Anglo-Indian Association canteen and boys' hostel in Calcutta, and 10,000 rupees to the national drought relief fund. Heavy financial contributions are made to scholarships and education funds and for the support of hospitals and schools through the Calcutta Rangers Educational Fund and the West Bengal Charitable Fund. See also: Frank Anthony, *op. cit.*, chapter 12.

information concerning memberships in social clubs as well as cultural or educational associations.[152] If the information is reasonably accurate, club membership and participation are confined to relatively small portions of the Anglo-Indian population in that city — only nine per cent of the adult males and six per cent of the females reported membership in such organizations. As might be expected, the congested slum district of Entally had the least participation, with only two per cent having club memberships. Slightly higher was Dharamtolla, a low-income area, with about three per cent. Nine per cent of the residents of Park Street, a middle-class district, were members, and 14 per cent of the adults in the "other" districts, also largely middle-class. Members of these clubs presumably represent the higher educational and income levels of the Community.

An even smaller proportion of the Anglo-Indian residents of Calcutta holds memberships in educational or cultural associations. For the entire Anglo-Indian population included in the Calcutta survey, only two per cent were members of such organizations, with the Park Street residents showing a slightly higher percentage of participation than the other districts. The results of the survey probably reflect the distribution of intellectual and cultural interests in the Community.

Of 52 employed adults included in a survey conducted by the senior author in Bangalore, 70 per cent stated that they belonged to a formal organization — club, church, labor union, and the like. About one-fourth (27 per cent) indicated that they held membership in a club. Gaikwad sampled three cities and found an even higher percentage of persons belonging to "any club or institute."[153] From a total of 204 respondents, 70 per cent reported such memberships, but the proportion varied from 90 per cent in Bilaspur, 82 per cent in Jhansi, to 55 per cent in Bangalore.

There are several possible explanations of the marked discrepancies between the results of the three surveys. Sampling methods probably accounted for some of the differences. The Calcutta survey, for example, may have included a larger proportion of low-income respondents than the other two studies. On the other hand, Gist's sample in Bangalore included only employed workers, mostly persons with above-average education and a fairly substantial income. Some of the differences may be the result of interviewing methods and the interpretations the respondents made of the questions which were asked. Finally, it may be that the social and occupational structure of the cities included in the studies are different in certain respects. In the larger cities there may also be more varied social and recreational opportunities than in the smaller ones; hence less tendency to identify with social organizations that have a specific recreational orientation for Anglo-Indians.

Several clubs that originally admitted only Anglo-Indians, or whose members were predominantly Anglo-Indian, have experienced a proportional or even numerical decline in Anglo-Indian membership. Gaikwad found that some of the

---

[152] *Pilot Survey, op. cit.,* pp. 26-27.
[153] E. K. Gaikwad, *The Anglo-Indians* (Bombay: Asia Press, 1967), p. 209.

clubs in Bilaspur and Jhansi experienced a declining membership.[154] He also found that the percentage of Anglo-Indian members in the Bowring Institute of Bangalore declined from 52 to 29 between 1957 and 1960. At the same time there was a corresponding increase in Hindu members, but the proportions of Muslims and Parsees remained about constant. The senior author observed very few Anglo-Indians present at a large social affair held at the Bowring Institute in 1967.

The causes of declining Anglo-Indian memberships in these organizations are not altogether clear, but the heavy selective migration from India of Anglo-Indians have doubtless depleted the ranks of middle-class and upper-class persons who are more likely to join social clubs. Economic pressures on the Community in recent years have also discouraged participation in clubs that are expensive. It is also possible that inter-ethnic relations in some of the clubs have been such as to discourage Anglo-Indian participation in mixed-membership groups. Doubtless some of the clubs catering mainly to persons of a particular religious denomination, such as the Catholic Club in Bangalore or the Grail Club in Calcutta, while not exclusively for Anglo-Indians, provide more satisfying experiences for many participants than clubs having a mixed and often cosmopolitan membership. At any rate, whatever may be the personal preferences of individual Anglo-Indians, the clubs having a mixed membership do afford a setting in which persons representing different communities may interact informally on the basis of presumed equality of status.

Other Forms of Recreation

Common participation in certain forms of organized recreation, or even in unorganized and spontaneous activities, may be viewed as a measure of Anglo-Indian integration into Indian society. But this is certainly not true in all situations. The fact that Anglo-Indians and Indians attend the same movies or racing events does not necessarily indicate intimate association in such activities. It simply means similar interests being manifest in a particular activity.

Competitive sports occupy an important place among the recreational activities of many Anglo-Indians. Indeed, numerous Anglo-Indian athletes have distinguished themselves in intra-mural and extra-mural games and thereby earned the admiration and plaudits of many others, including non-Anglo-Indians. An informant in Kharagpur observed that one point of contact between Anglo-Indians and other Indians is through the medium of organized sports in which teams compete in various kinds of games, including soccer, cricket, and basketball. In most Anglo-Indian schools a "sports day," observed annually, is set aside for competitive games, and awards are publicly made to those individuals who have displayed exceptional athletic prowess and/or to the winning "houses" (school units). Pictures of winning teams or individual athletes are often displayed in *The Review* with laudatory articles about their athletic achievements. Amateur

---

[154] *Ibid.,* p. 151.

sports clubs and athletic teams representing various organizations provide recreation both for participants and interested fans. Many Anglo-Indians are ardent racing fans, finding in horse racing an exciting spectator sport and an opportunity to satisfy their "gambling interest." In this respect they share the interests of other Indians, many of whom attend horse races held during the cool season each year.

Various forms of indoor recreation attract large numbers of participants and onlookers. Friends and relatives often gather in homes or clubs for card games, dancing, and sometimes for amateur dramatic performances. Such games as bridge, whist, billiards, "housie," bingo, and table tennis are popular. In the larger cities night clubs and fashionable restaurants attract youths and older persons who can afford the expenses of food and drinks in such establishments and who may find this kind of activity a pleasant surcease from the routine affairs of work and home life.

Many churches have facilities for the leisure-time pursuits of their members. These situations also provide an opportunity for the Anglo-Indians to associate formally or informally with Indian-Christians or Europeans. The Catholic Churches of New Delhi, for example, provide a variety of recreational activities such as week-end dances, games, ceremonial celebrations of important religious events, musical programs, and so on. The Anglican church, probably the most prestigious Christian institution in India, usually has facilities for extensive recreational and cultural activities by the members. Church-based social activities are, however, provided for Indian-Christians and Europeans as well as Anglo-Indians, who generally are in the minority so far as members are concerned.

The house party is a popular recreational activity, especially for young adults. Because the rules of behavior may be less rigid or formal than in institutionalized settings, or because less expensive activities are involved, dances in homes have a wide appeal. Music for these affairs is usually provided by record players or tape recorders. These parties are usually limited to a small number of intimate friends. In New Delhi, young Anglo-Indians and others often attend a Sunday morning dance session in some of the Western restaurants. From 9 to 1 these restaurants permit young people to dance to "live" music of a band or orchestra without being required to purchase food or drink. These sessions usually attract a capacity crowd.

A prominent Anglo-Indian in Kharagpur observed that many Anglo-Indians are preoccupied with having a "good time," spending lavishly, especially on festive occasions such as Easter, Christmas, or New Year. Such free spending, he said, often works a hardship on the spenders or their families, and efforts of this type even affects adversely the entire community.

The cinema in India has proved popular among all classes and communities; Anglo-Indians are no exception. Their preferences are for motion pictures with Western themes, partly because the language is usually English, their mother tongue. They sometimes attend pictures produced in India, and find that such films may afford an opportunity to learn some of the rudiments of an Indian language.

A survey conducted in Calcutta during 1957 indicated that the cinema is a popular form of recreation.[155] Two-thirds (62 per cent) of the persons interviewed reported that they attended the cinema as a form of recreation, but this participation varied from 54 per cent in Entally, 58 per cent in Dharamtolla, 63 per cent in Park Street, and 76 per cent in "other" areas included in the sample. Much the same pattern was reported for high-frequency attendance, with 11 and 8 per cent in Entally and Dharamtolla, respectively, indicating that they attended the cinema more than three times a month, compared with 18 and 23 per cent in Park Street and "other" districts so indicating. Undoubtedly income level was a factor in these attendance differentials.

The Calcutta survey also indicated that dancing is an important form of leisure-time activity for Anglo-Indians. Almost one-fourth (23 per cent) of the persons interviewed said they were "in the habit" of going to dances.[156] The extent of this activity seems to be influenced by the incomes of members, and perhaps also by age. Only 10 per cent of the persons interviewed in Entally said that they attended dances, but in the other districts the proportions ranged from 17 in Dharamtolla to 28 in the Park Street area.

Intellectual interests play a minor part in the leisure-time of most Anglo-Indians. Social clubs do not usually have extensive library facilities, but there may be displayed popular magazines and possibly a few books of light fiction, especially traditional detective stories. This feature is also found to be a characteristic of Anglo-Indian homes. Since few Anglo-Indians have had the intellectual and cultural experiences of college life it is not surprising that their recreational interests are generally directed toward non-intellectual activities. A cultural activity popular among middle-class Anglo-Indians is the amateur drama or musical show. These are commonly a feature of programs in social clubs which have facilities for such performances.

Group singing of popular and sentimental songs — invariably Western in theme and music — is a favorite form of informal recreation when Anglo-Indians gather in a spirit of good fellowship. Teenagers and young adults usually prefer "rock" and other forms of popular music to the familiar melodies which are favorites of the older adults. One of the most fashionable forms of recreation is the "ball," commonly staged as a ceremonial observance of important religious or cultural dates such as Christmas, New Year, Easter, or the birthdate of a famous Community leader. Another popular event is the ceremonial recognition of the May Day queen, an activity bearing some resemblance to Miss America contests or other rites of status conferred on popular and attractive women or girls.

Many Anglo-Indians do not participate in any type of organized activities, except possibly the church. These non-participants are mainly from the lower income levels of the social structure. Some of them may be unable to afford the costs of participation in organized activities; others may find their recreational or social interests satisfied in other ways, such as informal visiting with kin, neighbors, or friends. Studies in the United States and Great Britain also indicate

---

[155] *Pilot Survey, op. cit.,* p. 28.
[156] *Ibid.,* p. 27.

that organized social activities are primarily a middle- and upper-class phenomenon, that the lower-classes are on the fringe of the mainstream of organized social life. The situation in India is probably no different so far as the Anglo-Indian Community is concerned.

Attire

Dress in Indian society has considerable symbolic significance. Various communal groups in India commonly have distinctive attire which becomes, in a sense, an identifying symbol of the group, or even of India as a whole. The *sari* worn by Indian women, or the *dhoti* worn by men, is a case in point. Consonant with their cultural orientation, Anglo-Indians usually wear Western attire. Almost invariably men and boys adopt Western clothes, although they often wear a "bush" shirt of Indian style, but never a *dhoti*. The women and girls sometimes deviate from the Western-style frock or mini-skirt and wear an Indian *sari,* especially in situations when they are on public display, as in a formal social affair. Occasionally Anglo-Indian women wear a *sari* at the place of employment; in some work roles, such as airline hostess, the *sari* becomes a uniform which is worn mandatorily. Western attire for the Anglo-Indian becomes, therefore, a symbol of Western cultural identity, just as the *sari* and *dhoti* are symbolic of Indian identity.

Within each cultural group or community, attire becomes a unifying symbol, but between the groups it sometimes has a divisive effect. Although many indigenous Indian men themselves have adopted Western attire and are therefore uncritical of Anglo-Indian men who follow the same type of dress, Indian men and women are often critical of Anglo-Indian girls or adult women who, in their judgment, should wear a *sari* as evidence of their identity as Indians.

Hair styling for men and women is also Western in design, but in this instance men's hair styles are usually no different for Anglo-Indians than for most other Indians, at least those of urban middle- or upper-classes. Anglo-Indian women can usually be distinguished from traditional Indian women by their hair styles, although many Indians with cosmopolitan tastes have adopted the Western form of hair dress. In fact, the hair dressing salon in the larger cities usually has considerable numbers of Indian customers. In these establishments the operatives are commonly Anglo-Indian women who, because of their cultural interests, are familiar with prevailing hair styles in Western countries. Male operatives, however, are varied as to community identity.

Speech

Anglo-Indians pride themselves on being the principal repository of the English language in India. In its institutional form this repository is the Anglo-Indian schools (of which there are approximately, in India, 300), employing English as the medium of instruction. Throughout their long history as a minority, Anglo-Indians learned their "father tongue" but were indifferent to their "mother tongue," an indigenous Indian language. Nevertheless, their social experiences and cultural backgrounds did not parallel those of the British; hence it is not surprising that certain linguistic deviations occurred, especially in modes of speech. These deviant forms probably stem from the experiences of the group, i.e., ascription to a low and often undignified position in the social system.

Out of the social and cultural isolation of Anglo-Indians from the mainstream of Western life in India, and partly as a result of limited assimilation of indigenous speech forms, a somewhat distinctive speech developed that tended to set Anglo-Indians apart from either the British or other English-speaking Indians. These speech forms came to be known pejoratively as *chee-chee,* a mincing pronounciation of English words or phrases.[157] The term also became an expression of opprobrium applied by the British (and perhaps Indians as well) to designate categorically the members of the Anglo-Indian Community.[158] The term was comparable to such expressions as "wop" or "kike" as applied to particular minority groups elsewhere.

Frank Anthony, however, views *"chee-chee"* as a grossly exaggerated stereotype, "an ignorant generalization."[159] There are regional and class differences in accent and intonation, he writes, but no "Anglo-Indian" accent as such. Anglo-Indians in the North differ in speech accent from those in the South, for example, and there may be other regional variations. In the Kolar Gold Fields, South India, Anthony observes that many drop the "h's" and "g's", suggestive of early British influence.

A distinction must be made between the language of writing and the language of speech, among Anglo-Indians as among other peoples. Standard written forms are part of the cultural heritage of Anglo-Indians (although a good many are also conversant with Portuguese), and correct usage is a matter of considerable pride. For the Anglo-Indians, English is a living language, not an adopted language. In the language of speech the accent and pronunciation display the influence of Indian vernaculars. Speech forms are replete with idiomatic and colloquial expressions rooted both in Indian and European languages.

Distinctive speech forms appear to have largely disappeared, although Spencer, a trained linguist, observes that the accents or intonations of Anglo-Indians are somewhat different from English as it is spoken by middle- or upper-class Britons, or by English-speaking Indians of other communities.[160] Doubtless this change may be attributable in part to language instruction in Anglo-Indian schools where Anglo-Indian teachers strive to instruct in "pure" English, or at least the English language in its idealized form. At the same time through the socialization of Anglo-Indian children in the family the use of linguistic deviations is discouraged in favor of standard modes of speech in English. Perhaps equally important in this situation is the influence of the radio and phonograph music.

---

[157] John Spencer, "The Anglo-Indians and Their Speech: Socio-Linguistic Essay," *Lingua* 16 : 57-70 (1966).

[158] *Ibid.,* p. 63. The Oxford Dictionary states that the term applied to this linguistic deviation appeared late in the eighteenth century, about the time the British were adopting discriminatory policies concerning Anglo-Indians.

[159] Frank Anthony, *op. cit.,* pp. 373-374.

[160] Spencer, *op. cit.*

CHAPTER TEN

SUMMARY AND CONCLUSION

One major theme has been emphasized in this book: That the Anglo-Indian Community of India has traditionally occupied, and continues to occupy, a marginal position in Indian society. In a synthesis of the contents of the book, each topic will represent a major component developed at length in previous chapters.

The Anglo-Indian Community in History

When viewed in historical perspective it is apparent that the current marginal character, social position, and structural characteristics have a source deeply rooted in past decades of colonial India. Shortly after the Portuguese established a beachhead in India (1498) a racially-hybrid minority appeared. This group was not especially disadvantaged in the Portuguese colony because of its dual racial heritage. Not until the British became a strong colonial power in India, after 1600, did the Anglo-Indians (then known by various names, mainly Eurasian) become a self-conscious unit.

The history of the Anglo-Indian Community in British-controlled India is one of many ups and downs, of vicissitudes and prosperity, of security and insecurity. At times they were protected by the colonial government and at other times rejected. In the early days of the East India Company inter-marriage between British soldiers or civil servants and indigenous women was approved, but later was prohibited or disapproved.

This history of the Anglo-Indian minority may be viewed in four periods. The first period (1498 to 1785) was one during which the minority was treated with consideration and tolerance by the colonial powers, both Portuguese and British, with inter-racial marriages often officially encouraged and sanctioned. These were years of relative prosperity and security for this emergent community.

The second period (1785-1857) was one of repression, rejection, and hardship by the East India Company, which generally represented the power and policy of the British government. Although the Portuguese had been virtually eliminated as a colonial competitor in India, as the British extended the scope of its control, the racial hybrids in Portuguese India did not experience the discrimination encountered in British India. The British during this period imposed many limitations on the Anglo-Indian minority, including exclusion from jobs other than menial tasks. In order to survive, many Anglo-Indians found employment in the regions controlled by native princes. It was during this era that the group emerged as a community having a self-awareness and an embryonic organizational structure.

In 1857 the Sepoy Mutiny (an abortive indigenous revolution) was a turning point in relations between the Anglo-Indian Community and the colonial power.

SUMMARY AND CONCLUSION

Anglo-Indians whose loyalty to the British had previously been suspect demonstrated their loyalty during these times of crisis. Subsequently they were rewarded with jobs and an improved economic life.

The third period dates from the Sepoy Mutiny until a strong Indian Independence movement developed in the 1920's. Following the Mutiny the British relied increasingly on the Anglo-Indians to fill needed job positions; in turn, the Anglo-Indians came to depend on the British for their economic support. This was a period of economic improvement and relative security for the Community.

The fourth period begins with the Independence movement in the 1920's and continues to the present. During the 1920's it became apparent that an independent India was a certainty and that the British would ultimately depart, possibly leaving the Community without its traditional protection. This was a time of widespread anxiety among Anglo-Indians. Many of them migrated from India to seek a better life in England or other Commonwealth countries. Those who remained in India after Independence (1947) began to accept the difficult task of carving a place for themselves in the new order, or otherwise laying plans for departure. Many left the country during this period. When the Community was assured by the new Indian government that Anglo-Indians would be accorded equal rights and privileges with other citizens the flow of out-migrants receded. But a decade later, in the 1960's, the outflow was resumed when England's proposed policy was to limit the number of migrants from the former colony, Anglo-Indians as well as other Indians. That policy went into effect in the 1960's. Since then most of the out-migrants have gone to Canada, Australia, and New Zealand.

Marginality and Identity

The concepts of marginality and identity provide a theoretical framework for the study of minority groups. In this study it affords a conceptual perspective of the Anglo-Indian minority. Marginality refers to inter-group relations when a minority has social, cultural, and/or social-psychological attributes that distinguish it from other groups in the same society and which function to impede or prevent inter-group contacts and cooperative participation in undertakings of mutual interest.

Historically, the Anglo-Indian Community has been, and continues to be, marginal to the various indigenous cultures. It is marginal socially because it is not extensively integrated into the organized social fabric of the larger society. It is marginal culturally because the basic culture of the Community — religion, family organization, language, styles of life — separates Anglo-Indians from the majority of other Indians. It is marginal psychologically because the attitudes and images, often reflecting social and cultural differences, are such as to create and maintain social distances between the Anglo-Indians and others. Taken together these attributes — social, cultural, psychological — represent barriers which have had the effect of limiting or obstructing social interaction and cultural exchange between the people of the sub-continent.

SUMMARY AND CONCLUSION

Attitudes and Images

Attitudes held by Anglo-Indians have often been positive toward the British and other peoples of European heritage, and negative toward Indian people having a different culture and way of life. During the colonial period of India's history the Anglo-Indians generally identified with the British and expressed their admiration of British character and culture. The British, on the other hand, generally refused to accept the Anglo-Indians socially, viewing them collectively as a "half-caste" whose members were morally and intellectually inferior to the sons and daughters of Britain, although they were useful as tools in the hands of the empire-builders. Many of the prejudices of the British toward the Indian people of dark complexion were acquired by the Anglo-Indians. Though smarting under British social snobbery, the Anglo-Indians often rejected other Indians as inferior to the peoples of the West. The reactions of the Indians, as might be expected, was essentially negative. They, too, developed stereotypical images of the Anglo-Indians who were commonly regarded as British lackeys whose conduct often violated traditional values of Indian society. The Anglo-Indians were especially suspect as anti-Indian.

Rejection of the Anglo-Indians both by the British and other Indian communities created an identity problem for the members of the Community. The British frequently viewed them stereotypically as Indians with some European blood; the Indians often considered them Europeans with some Indian blood. In the early days of colonial rule it was difficult for the Anglo-Indians to answer with certainty the question, "Who am I?" As a genuine community consciousness developed this identity dilemma lessened, but it was never firmly resolved by those members of the Community whose sentimental ties were with the British, or at least with Great Britain as a prospective social and cultural homeland.

As the symbolic shores of Britain became dimly perceived with the passing of time, and as the opportunities for a resolution of the identity conflict through migration faded, a new identity orientation was necessary. The new self-image, at least as outwardly displayed, was that of an Indian national with all the rights, privileges, and responsibilities of Indian citizenship. Many Anglo-Indians have been unable or unwilling to make such a turn-about of identity. Those who achieve this shift have attempted to display an image of themselves as loyal citizens and patriots; others, feeling insecure without the protective imperial umbrella, have opted to leave the country.

Anglo-Indian and Indian leaders alike have urged that attitudes of mutual resentment and hostility be discarded and that manifestations of loyalty to the country and inter-group harmony become the guidelines of the future. To achieve such reciprocity has not been easy, either for Anglo-Indians or other Indians, but considerable progress has been made.

The Anglo-Indian World of Work

The Anglo-Indian world of work can best be understood in light of the historical, though changing, position of the Community. Generally, Anglo-Indians

SUMMARY AND CONCLUSION

resided within proximity of overseas European settlements in cities. Except during periods of complete rejection the colonial establishment allocated certain jobs within the system to members of the Community. These jobs were usually on the lower levels of the bureaucracy, but nevertheless vital to colonial expansion and control (police and military forces, customs, railroads, telegraphic communication). Eventually Anglo-Indians became dependent on the British for continued job guarantees; the British in turn became dependent upon the Anglo-Indians for continued service in these fields. Yet seldom did an Anglo-Indian rise to the top of the occupational power structure in colonial India, although a few soldiers did ascend to the higher ranks.

Within this context the coming of Independence changed the job structure. More and more the system of employment was modified as other Indians entered jobs traditionally the domain of Anglo-Indians. The virtual monopoly of certain jobs by Anglo-Indians undoubtedly led to resentment on the part of other Indians. When the labor market became increasingly competitive, Anglo-Indians and other Indian peoples viewed each other as a threat to their own security and welfare. There were also fears among Anglo-Indians that an independent government would reject the former occupational protection as other Indians demanded and received a larger share of the economic pie. Yet, when Independence finally came to India, these fears were found to be exaggerated. The new government granted constitutional guarantees that allowed Anglo-Indians to continue working for a decade in certain protected jobs. A formula was adapted in which all occupations would eventually become openly competitive. The Anglo-Indians like all others would have to swim with the current or sink. Many "sank."

Today Anglo-Indian males are still found in the occupations traditionally reserved for them. But the job structure has undergone changes as Anglo-Indians, and others, find employment in occupations created by a developing economy and technology. Women have entered the labor force in increasing numbers, mainly in nursing, teaching, and secretarial work, but also in such work roles as that of airline hostess or receptionist in hotels and public offices. An Anglo-Indian woman, because of her familiarity with the English language, can often find employment as a secretary, especially in European firms based in India. Actually, a woman generally finds it easier to obtain work than does an Anglo-Indian male. Often she becomes the principal breadwinner of the family. Unemployment is high among the males, often as much as 40 per cent of the potential labor force in the complete Community.

Social Structure and Social Relations

India is a highly stratified society containing a hierarchy of groups arranged in a status system. The emergent Anglo-Indian Community became another group located within the complex stratification system involving caste, religion, language, wealth, and occupation. But even this system is continually undergoing change. Groups rise and fall, individuals experience vertical mobility, upward or downward. This is true of Anglo-Indians as well as other Indians. Yet there is considerable evidence that the dominant mobility trend since Independence has been downward for the majority of adults.

One indicator of social change in inter-group relations is that of inter-group marriages. Although marriage is usually consummated within the Anglo-Indian Community, there appears to be an increase in out-marriage, especially for females. Some Anglo-Indian women state that they would prefer to marry outside the Community than force themselves into a lifetime of work as the major breadwinner if they married an Anglo-Indian man.

Another indicator of change in social relations is the extensive intermingling of children and youth from various religious or ethnic communities. Still another is the opendoor policies adopted by many organizations, especially social clubs, making possible informal interaction between members representing different communities.

Social Organization and Community Life.

The heterogeneous nature of Indian society creates a situation wherein various peoples maintain a degree of mutual exclusiveness through organized groups. These groups often erect barriers confining membership and participation to individuals of particular identifiable characteristics. The Anglo-Indian Community of India is such a group. Through social organization this minority is able to maintain its distinctive character — a Western style of life, a British-oriented system of education, universal use of English as a household language and medium of instruction in schools, and Christian churches (shared with Indian-Christians and Europeans).

A basic component essential to community life in a complex society is a set of formal and informal organizations whose functions are to satisfy certain needs and desires of its members in the various affairs of social life. These organizations, essentially to the extent that they involve numbers of persons, make it possible for a people to think of themselves as a distinct collectivity whose members share a common or similar set of interests, values, and cultural elements. As the Anglo-Indian community evolved, various social organizations were needed to provide the formal structure for a viable social life. Since Anglo-Indians were commonly excluded, in the past, from the organized life of other Indians and overseas British, or they themselves preferred not to participate in organizations dominated by Europeans or Indians, it was necessary for them to develop their own organizations.

Through the years many organizations came into existence, but only a few have survived. The organization which in recent times has provided the structure and leadership essential for a viable community is the All-India Anglo-Indian Association, with some seventy chapters or branches in cities over the country. This association functions as the major focus of Anglo-Indian power, mainly through its president, who is also a member of Parliament. It also extends beyond the political sphere into educational, social, welfare, and recreational activities, and provides a major channel of communication among Anglo-Indians and between a major portion of the Community and other Indians in positions of power and influence. A unique organization is the Calcutta Rangers Club which not only sponsors social activities for its members but also makes large contributions to welfare and educational programs.

Education

Anglo-Indians rely heavily on English-medium schools as the major instrumentality for insuring the continuation of the Community. Fundamental to the existence of the Community is a Western cultural heritage and the English language. The preservation of these features of Anglo-Indian society involves both socialization of the child in the home and formal instruction in the schools.

In the colonial period there were numerous European-style schools located throughout India. Here the overseas British and Anglo-Indian youth could learn what was needed for the continuation of Western culture in India. But with the rise of Indian nationalism leading to an Independent India the modified educational policy was to support schools that would foster the "great tradition" of India and employ Indian languages as a medium of instruction. But English-medium schools also continued to increase, serving the educational needs of Anglo-Indians as well as many other Indians. Today there are nearly three hundred so-called Anglo-Indian schools in the country.

Although most of the Anglo-Indian schools are supported by private organizations such as churches or missionary societies, they generally receive financial assistance from the government, provided that students other than Anglo-Indians are admitted. Many of the elite Anglo-Indian schools have such high tuition costs that most Anglo-Indian children cannot afford to attend, unless they are supported by scholarships or given free board and lodging. A program to construct twenty large schools has been launched by the All-India Anglo-Indian Association, and three of these schools (known as the Frank Anthony Public Schools) are already in operation. But even in these elitist schools, and in many others of similar character, only a small minority of the students are Anglo-Indian.

Styles of Life

Life styles followed by members of the Anglo-Indian Community represents a blending of diverse cultures, but mainly the Community represents a European cultural heritage. Housing arrangements, home life, food habits, social clubs, attire, speech, religion, and other patterns bear the heavy imprint of Western influence, but with components of indigenous culture according to need or preference. In certain respects the Indian cultural patterns are in sharp contrast to the traditional way of life followed by most Anglo-Indians.

Cultural contrasts are apparent in dietary habits. Food, modes of cooking and serving, and eating techniques separate the Anglo-Indians from Indians following traditional cultural practices. Whereas most Indians use only their hands in eating, this practice is seldom if ever followed by Anglo-Indians, for whom the procedure is often offensive or at least ill-mannered. Yet many Indian cultural practices or traits are acceptable to the Anglo-Indians. Anglo-Indian women, for example, may wear the Indian *sari*, both on social occasions and in the work situation, although Western styles are usually preferred.

Prospects

One can never map precisely the future of any group, especially an ethnic or cultural minority whose destiny depends on the course of events in the entire society of which it is a part. Certainly this is true of the Anglo-Indians in India. Nevertheless, it may be instructive to observe what has occurred in other countries of Asia where there are also peoples whose origin was similar to that of the Anglo-Indian Community.

With the emergence of numerous colonial empires in Asia there appeared various peoples of dual or multiple racial heritage and which were commonly designated as Eurasians, persons of mixed European and indigenous parentage. Eurasian minorities were found in Burma, Pakistan (both Burma and Pakistan were originally administered as part of colonial India), Ceylon, Singapore, Malaysia, Hongkong, Netherlands Indies (now Indonesia), Indo-China, and Thailand (although Thailand was never a part of the colonial system).

Each of these groups were in certain respects similar to the Anglo-Indian peoples of India. Often they were accorded vocational preference and were generally treated by the administering colonial agency and local population as discrete entities. Yet the life-history of these racially-mixed minorities varied from one society to another and did not necessarily parallel the evolution and position of the Anglo-Indian peoples of India. The values and structures that have deterred the Anglo-Indians from being culturally assimilated and socially integrated into the larger society have not always been present in the other countries. As a result many of the Eurasian peoples have been at least partly assimilated into indigenous culture, integrated extensively into the social fabric, and often amalgamated through inter-marriage. Furthermore, they have not usually been objects of discrimination and hostility as experienced by the Anglo-Indians in India. Eurasians in other Asian countries did not develop an extensive communal apparatus such as the All-India Anglo-Indian Association (and other less influential or long-lasting organizations) which has provided a useful structure for maintaining *esprit de corps* and providing guidelines for social action.

The ethnocentric character of the Community, and especially its pro-British stance during the colonial period and even afterward, understandably produced negative reactions by many Indians, who often considered the Anglo-Indians outside the mainstream of Indian society, or even alien misfits who would not likely accept the role and responsibilities of Indian citizenship. As long as the memory of the British colonial period remains and the Anglo-Indian Community continues to be symbolic of the British, the minority will be alienated from those Indians who are strongly nationalistic in their sentiments.

SUMMARY AND CONCLUSION

Yet there is abundant evidence that estrangement is being reduced as many Anglo-Indians and other Indians alike strive to work out a *modus vivendi* satisfactory for all parties concerned. Above all, many Anglo-Indians who want and expect to remain in India have seriously demonstrated their loyalty to the country. Those who cannot make this accommodation will either sink into the mire of hopelessness and frustration or else migrate to other lands. But even migration has become increasingly difficult, especially for the masses of impoverished Anglo-Indians who have neither the money necessary to migrate nor the occupational skills to gain them admittance to another country.

Certain other minorities in India have fared better economically and socially than the Anglo-Indians. One of these is the Parsee Community, whose religion and traditions are as alien to India as the Christian faith and style of life of the Anglo-Indians. Yet the Parsees have been eminently successful in almost every sphere of Indian life—economic, educational, political, and cultural. Strongly motivated toward educational achievement and success in the business world, they have furnished many notable leaders and thereby earned the gratitude of the Indian people for contributions to the common good of all. The Jews and Armenians also represent Western-oriented minorities in India which have become integrated into the economic system and have furnished effective leadership in various aspects of Indian society. They, like the Parsees, found higher education and technical training to offer an avenue to achievement in business and the professions. But the Armenians and Jews have migrated to other countries in proportionally greater numbers than have the Anglo-Indians.

In the meantime the outward flow of Anglo-Indians to other lands continues. Whether the volume will increase or decline in the days ahead depends on developments in various areas of Indian society. Out-migrations in the immediate post-war period reflected widespread apprehensions concerning future political policies of the Indian government. When their anxieties turned out to be unfounded the outward flow subsided. By the middle 1960's and the early 1970's the volume of migrations again increased, not because of political repression but mainly because of domestic economic and political instability which threatened the middle-class way of life and values which the Anglo-Indians cherished.

As a well-informed member of the Community, who now lives in a western country, has interpreted the situation, "This wave of migration in recent years has been motivated essentially by what was viewed as a real threat to a middle class sense of values—security, discipline, order in public life, and communist subversion—rather than by any discrimination or lack of loyalty to the country." In other words, they have gravitated to those countries which have apparently offered a greater degree of economic and political security and an opportunity to enjoy a satisfactory standard of living. Their destinations have, for the most part, been England, Canada, Australia, and New Zealand.

There is reason to believe that the Anglo-Indians will continue indefinitely to be a part of the human map of India. Their survival as an organized community will, however, depend on the ability to maintain functional political and cultural organizations and to preserve the English language and Anglo-Indian school system. But economic and political developments in the larger society will inevitably be instrumental in shaping the course of Anglo-India in the future. How effectively Anglo-Indian leadership can direct the future evolution of the Community as a microcosm in a vast macrocosm remains to be seen.

INDEX

Acculturation, 134-135
All-India Anglo-Indian Association, 24, 87, 89, 100-102, 105, 109, 110, 114, 118, 119, 121, 128, 150
   criticisms of, 103-105
   membership in, 101-102
   political function of, 110-111
   publisher of *The Review*, 102-103
   structure and functions, 100-101
   support of scholarships, 118, 122
   support of schools, 131
Anglo-Indians,
   definition of, 2, 18, 58
   early discrimination against, 11-15
   future prospects, 156-158
   income, 90
   name changes, 86
   numbers, 3, 20
   political activities, 109-111
   recreation, 145-148
   religion, 89, 111-112
   speech, 148-149
Anglo-Indian Community, 1-3
   community consciousness, 34-35
   in historical perspective, 7-20, 150-151
   infiltration and seepage, 85-88
   inter-marriage, 78-81, 154
   psychological and organizational components, 96
   representation in legislative bodies, 20
Anthony, Frank, 5, 7, 16, 19, 20, 48-49, 56, 91, 98, 100, 111, 117, 128, 133, 142, 143, 149
Attire, 148
Attitudes, 37-56, 152
   how Anglo-Indians imagine others see them, 47-49
   in historical perspective, 16-17, 37-39
   of Anglo-Indians toward other Indians, 39, 49-51
   of Anglo-Indians toward the British, 39, 51
   of British toward Anglo-Indians, 12-13, 37-39
   of Indian students toward Anglo-Indians, 39-43
   of Indian students toward the British, 40-43
   of others concerning Anglo-Indians, 44-47
   self-images, 52-54
   toward inter-marriage, 78-81
   toward the work situation, 60-68

Barrow, A. E. T., 6, 20, 117
Britasian League, 99-100
British, in India, 2-3, 8, 10-11, 13-19

Charter Act of 1833, 14, 58
Chaudhuri, Nirad C., 45
Chee-chee, as form of speech, 149
Churches, 108
   as sponsors of social organizations, 113
   and social welfare, 108
Clubs, social, 15, 141-145
Coloureds, in South Africa, 29, 32
Community, components of, 96
Constitution of India,
   and Anglo-Indian schools, 116
   and definition of Anglo-Indians, 2
   and employment of Anglo-Indians, 61-62
   protective provisions for Anglo-Indians, 19-20
Cooperatives, Anglo-Indian, 108-109
Council for Indian school Certificate, 117-118, 131

Derozio, Henry, 56, 105
Dickie-Clark, H. F., 25, 28, 29, 31-32
Domiciled Europeans, 17, 19, 78
Dover, Cedric, 46, 56, 102
Dr. Graham's Homes, 121
D'Souza, Austin, 115
Dutch, in India, 9

East India Charitable Trust, 95, 107-108
East India Company, 10-14, 15, 17, 38, 57, 58, 114
Education of Anglo-Indians, 113-133, 155
   contemporary trends, 116-117
   costs to students, 120-121
   Council for Indian School Certificate, 117-118, 131
   disadvantaged students, 120-122
   handicaps in job market, 128-129
   in 18th and 19th centuries, 113-115
   levels of attained schooling, 130
   report of Barnes Commission, 117
   scholarships, 118-119
   student interests, 125-128
   See also, Schools
Employment, *see* Work
English language, *see* Language
Eurasians, 1, 7, 156

Family, *see* Marriage and family
Food habits of Anglo-Indians, 139
Francis, Dudley, 6, 51, 125
French, in India, 9-10

Gaikwad, E. K., 62, 98, 130, 144-145

Gandhi, Mahatma, 61, 136
Gidney, Henry, 18, 19, 98, 100
Gidney Club, 89
Goodrich, Dorris L., 8, 11, 14, 15, 23, 37, 38, 57, 78, 87, 96, 114, 142
Government of India Act of 1919, 18, 59

Hindus, educational interests of, 125-127
Homes, Dr. Graham's, 121
Housing and home life, 136-138, 139-141

Identity, problem of dual or multiple, 33-35, 55-56, 77, 87-88
Incomes of Anglo-Indians in Calcutta, 90
Indian-Christians, 89, 95
Indian Independence Movement, 8, 20
Infiltration into Anglo-Indian Community, 85-87
Inter-group relations,
  attitudes toward, 81-83
  differentials of, 83-85
  infiltration and seepage, 85-88
  language as barrier to, 85
  marriage, 78-81, 154

Jews, 40, 157
Johnson, Charles S., 29

Kaplan, S. J., 28
Kerckhoff, A. C., 31
Kolaja, J., 28
Kraus, Irving, 21-22

Language,
  as medium of instruction, 118, 131-133
  in inter-group relations, 85
  See also, Speech

Maher, R. J. N., 6, 52, 88
MacRae, John, 16, 17
Marginal situations, 31-33
Marginality, 21-36, 151
  ambiguities of status and role, 33-35
  and status differentials, 31-33
  as focus of study, 3-4
  cultural, 25-27, 135
  identity and, 33-36, 77, 151
  personality syndromes and, 35-36
  psychological dimension of, 29-30
  social, 27-28
  social barriers and, 22-25
  social organization and mobility, 30-31
Marriage and family, 10-11, 78-81, 106-107
  See also, Inter-group relations
McCormick, Thomas C., 31
McCluskie, E. T., 99

McCluskiegunj, 99
Migration of Anglo-Indians, 157
Muslims, 32
Myrdal, Gunnar, 27

Names of Anglo-Indians, 7, 86, 116
Nehru, Jawaharlal, 61, 136

Occupations, see Work
Organizations of Anglo-Indians, 95-112, 154-155
  All-India Anglo-Indian Association, 100-102, 103-105
  Anglo-Indian and Domiciled European Association of South India, 98
  Britasian League, 99-100
  cooperatives, 108-109
  early developments, 15, 97-99
  participation in, 105-106
  political, 109-111
  religion, 111-112
  social clubs, 105, 141-145
  social welfare, 107-108
  Union of Anglo-Indian Associations, 98

Park, Robert E., 35
Parsees, 40, 43, 157
Political organization and activities, 109-111
Portuguese, in India, 9
Prospects, future, 156-158

Rangers Club, 89, 143, 155
Recreation, 141-148
  See also, Styles of life
Religion, 89, 111-112
Reuter, E. B., 45-46
Review, The, 102-105
  contents of, 102-103, 145
  criticisms of, 103-104
Ricketts, John, 14, 15, 97

Scholarships, 118-119, 122
Schools of Anglo-Indians,
  changing functions, 117-118
  contemporary trends, 116-117
  disadvantaged students, 120-122
  Frank Anthony Public Schools, 116
  inadequacy of facilities, 121-122
  institutional stratification, 119-120
  language instruction, 131-133
  philanthropic and church support, 121
  regulation, 130-131
  scholarships, 118-119
  See also, Education,
Sepoy Mutiny, 7, 8, 15-16, 43, 58-59, 150-151
Seepage from Anglo-Indian community, 87-88

INDEX

Social mobility of Anglo-Indians, 30, 91-94
   See also, Stratification
Social Welfare, 107-108
Speech, 148-149
Spencer, John, 149
Sports and games, 145-146
Stark, Herbert A., 10-11, 13, 14, 15, 16, 50, 56, 59, 114
Stereotypes, *see* Attitudes
Stonequist, Everett V., 35
Stratification of Anglo-Indian Community, 88-91, 92-96
   See also, Social mobility
Styles of life, 134-149, 155-156
   acculturation and, 134-135
   attire, 148
   food habits and preferences, 139
   housing and home life, 136-138
   other forms of recreation, 146-148
   social clubs, 141-145
   sports and games, 145-146
   See also, Organizations

Unemployment in Calcutta, 92

Valentia, Viscount George, 13

Wardwell, Walter I, 22
Weston, C. N., 53
Wittermans, Tamme, 21-22
Work of Anglo-Indians, 57-75, 152-153
   Anglo-Indian and British reciprocity, 58-60
   Anglo-Indian men, 62-64
   Anglo-Indian women, 65-66
   business and the professions, 64
   competition with Indian workers, 60-61
   educational handicaps in employment, 128-129
   employment of mothers, 140-141
   job satisfaction and dissatisfaction, 69-71
   occupational discrimination, 57-58, 68
   prospects for future, 71-72
   protective legislation after Independence, 61-62
   selective employment, 66-68
   student occupational aspirations, 72-76